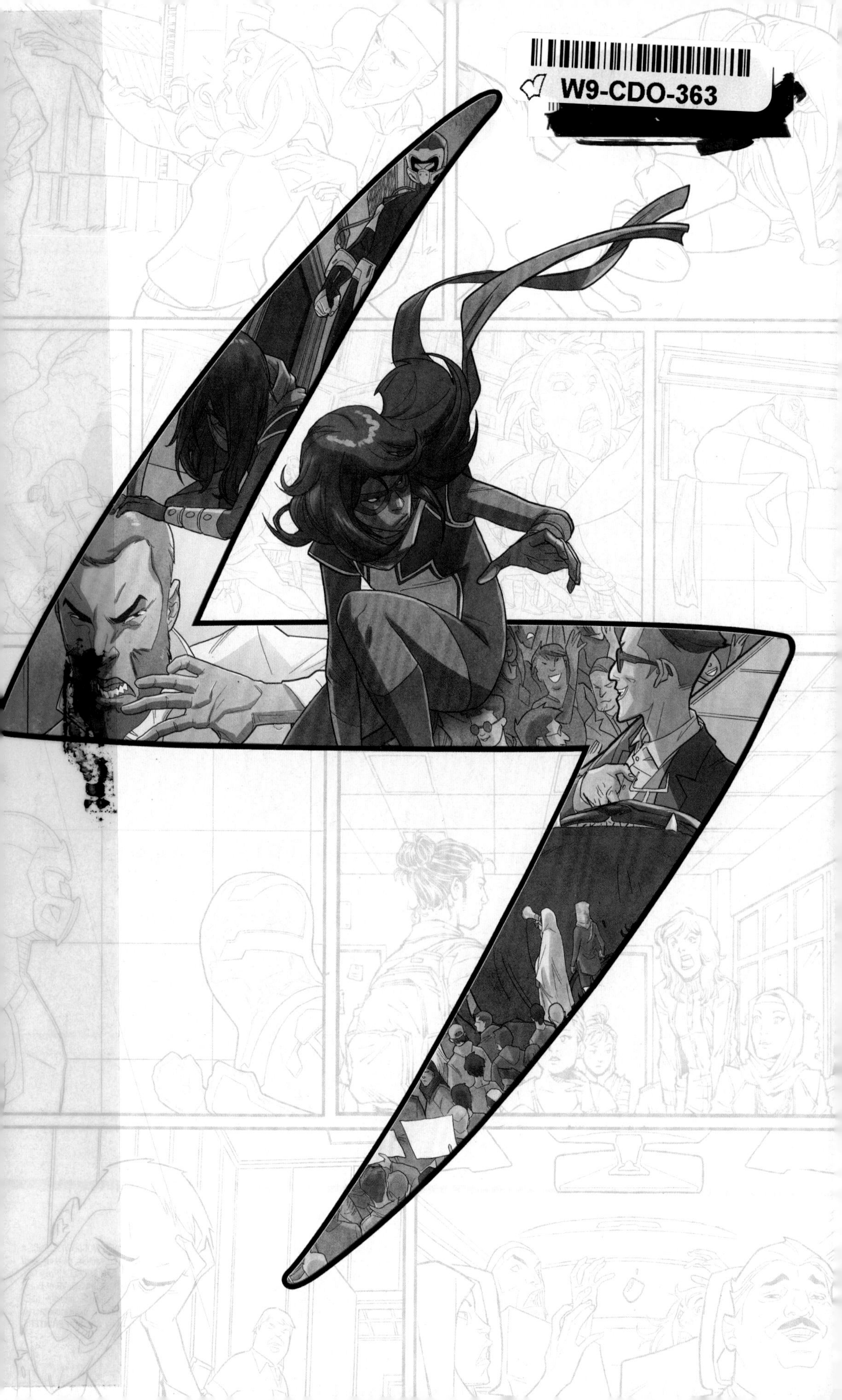

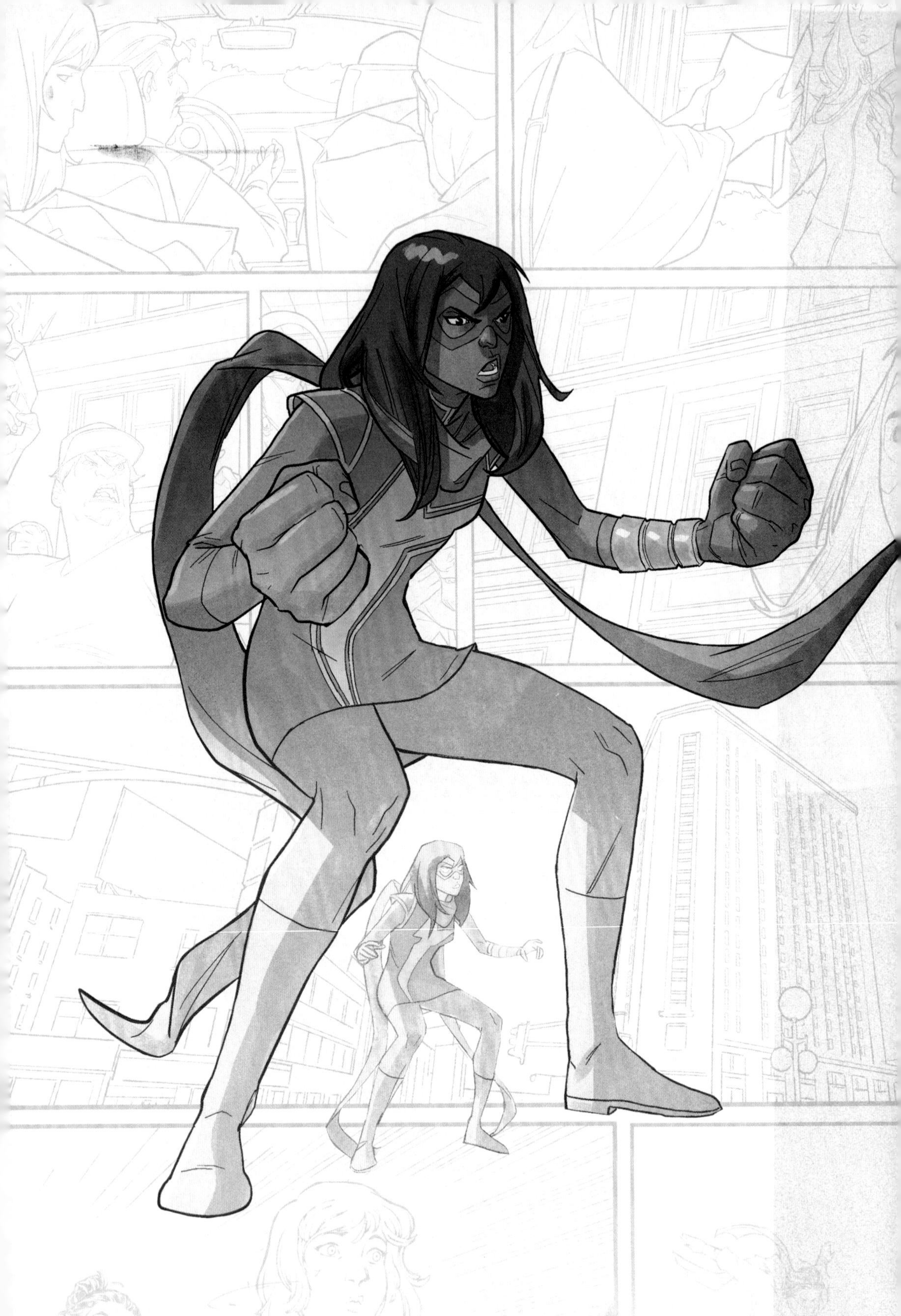

MS. MARVEL VOL. 8: MECCA. Contains material originally published in magazine form as MS. MARVEL #19-24. First printing 2017. ISBN# 978-1-302-90608-5. Published by MARVEL WORLDWIDE, INC., a subsidiary of MARVEL ENTERTAINMENT, LLC. OFFICE OF PUBLICATION: 135 West 50th Street, New York, NY 10020. Copyright © 2017 MARVEL No similarity between any of the names, characters, persons, and/or institutions in this magazine with those of any living or dead person or institution is intended, and any such similarity which may exist is purely coincidental. **Printed in Canada.** DAN BUCKLEY, President, Marvel Entertainment; JOE QUESADA, Chief Creative Officer; TOM BREVOORT, SVP of Publishing; DAVID BOGART, SVP of Business Affairs & Operations, Publishing & Partnership; C.B. CEBULSKI, VP of Brand Management & Development, Asia; DAVID GABRIEL, SVP of Sales & Marketing, Publishing; JEFF YOUNGQUIST, VP of Production & Special Projects; DAN CARR, Executive Director of Publishing Technology; ALEX MORALES, Director of Publishing Operations; SUSAN CRESPI, Production Manager; STAN LEE, Chairman Emeritus. For information regarding advertising in Marvel Comics or on Marvel.com, please contact Vit DeBellis, Integrated Sales Manager, at vdebellis@marvel.com. For Marvel subscription inquiries, please call 888-511-5480. **Manufactured between 10/20/2017 and 11/21/2017 by SOLISCO PRINTERS, SCOTT, QC, CANADA.**

10 9 8 7 6 5 4 3 2 1

MS. MARVEL

writer
G. WILLOW WILSON

artists
MARCO FAILLA (#19-22) & **DIEGO OLORTEGUI** (#23-24)

color artist
IAN HERRING

letterers
VC's JOE CARAMAGNA (#19, #21-24) & **TRAVIS LANHAM** (#20)

cover art
NELSON BLAKE II & RACHELLE ROSENBERG (#19)
AND **VALERIO SCHITI & RACHELLE ROSENBERG** (#20-24)

assistant editor
CHARLES BEACHAM

associate editor
MARK BASSO

editor
SANA AMANAT

collection editor
JENNIFER GRÜNWALD

assistant editor
CAITLIN O'CONNELL

associate managing editor
KATERI WOODY

editor, special projects
MARK D. BEAZLEY

vp production & special projects
JEFF YOUNGQUIST

svp print, sales & marketing
DAVID GABRIEL

editor in chief
AXEL ALONSO

chief creative officer
JOE QUESADA

president
DAN BUCKLEY

executive producer
ALAN FINE

PREVIOUSLY

WHEN A STRANGE TERRIGEN MIST DESCENDED UPON JERSEY CITY, KAMALA KHAN WAS IMBUED WITH POLYMORPH POWERS. USING HER NEW ABILITIES TO FIGHT EVIL AND PROTECT JERSEY CITY, SHE BECAME THE ALL-NEW

MS.MARVEL

HER LIFE WAS CHANGED FOREVER... AND SO WERE THE LIVES OF HER FAMILY AND FRIENDS.

MONTHS AGO, MS. MARVEL'S IMAGE WAS PLASTERED ACROSS JERSEY CITY IN A CAMPAIGN THAT MADE HER THE POSTER CHILD FOR GENTRIFICATION — WITHOUT HER CONSENT.

AS IT TURNS OUT, THE CULPRIT WAS ONE CHUCK WORTHY, AN AGENT OF HYDRA WHO WAS TRYING TO USE THE MAYORAL RACE TO TAKE OVER JERSEY CITY. THOUGH KAMALA DEFEATED CHUCK, THE DAMAGE TO HER REPUTATION WAS ALREADY DONE. AND NOW, IT'S THOSE SHE LOVES MOST WHO WILL SUFFER...

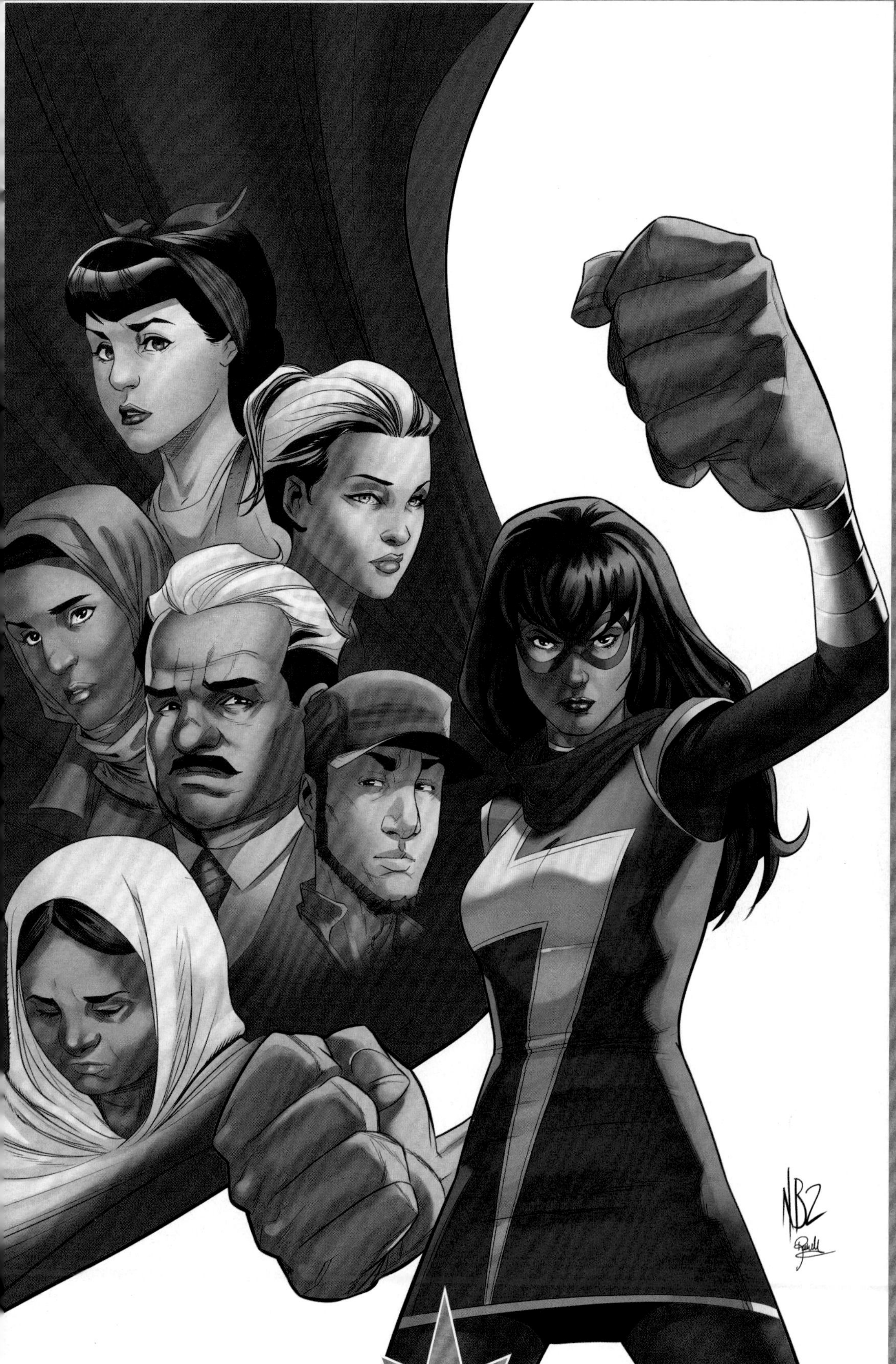
19

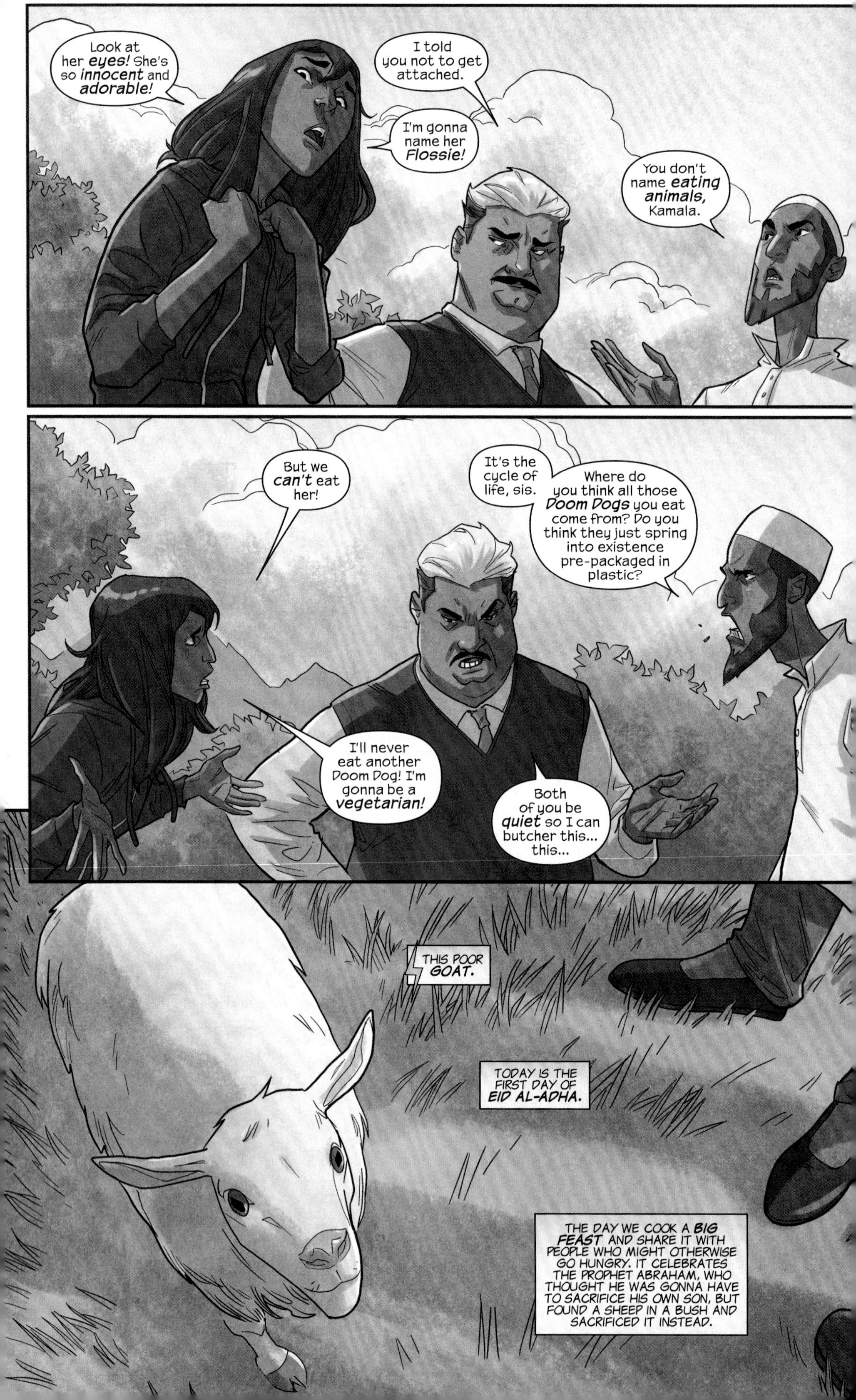

Look at her eyes! She's so innocent and adorable!
I told you not to get attached.
I'm gonna name her Flossie!
You don't name eating animals, Kamala.
But we can't eat her!
It's the cycle of life, sis.
Where do you think all those Doom Dogs you eat come from? Do you think they just spring into existence pre-packaged in plastic?
I'll never eat another Doom Dog! I'm gonna be a vegetarian!
Both of you be quiet so I can butcher this... this...
THIS POOR GOAT.
TODAY IS THE FIRST DAY OF EID AL-ADHA.
THE DAY WE COOK A BIG FEAST AND SHARE IT WITH PEOPLE WHO MIGHT OTHERWISE GO HUNGRY. IT CELEBRATES THE PROPHET ABRAHAM, WHO THOUGHT HE WAS GONNA HAVE TO SACRIFICE HIS OWN SON, BUT FOUND A SHEEP IN A BUSH AND SACRIFICED IT INSTEAD.

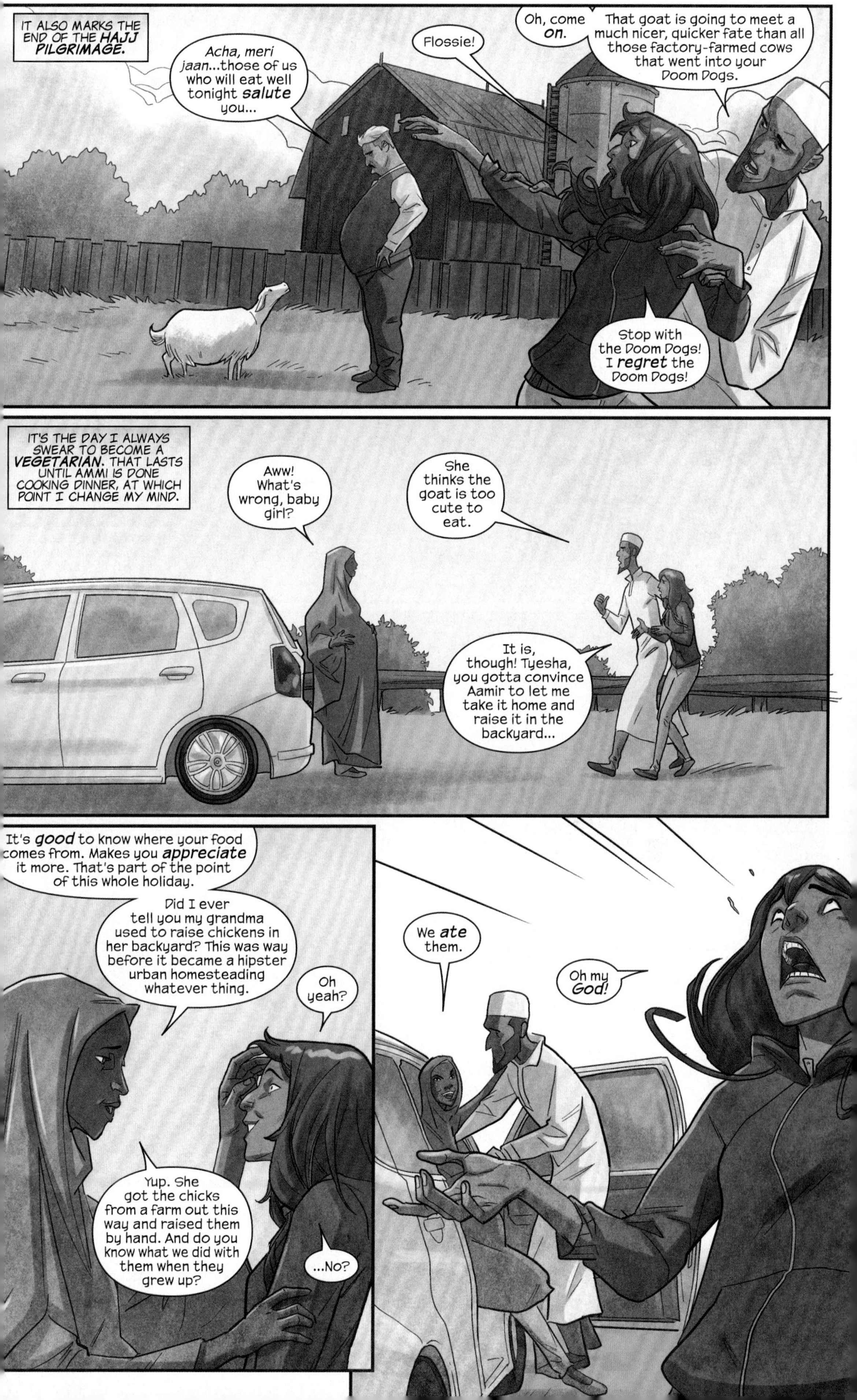
IT ALSO MARKS THE END OF THE HAJJ PILGRIMAGE.
Acha, meri jaan...those of us who will eat well tonight salute you...
Flossie!
Oh, come on.
That goat is going to meet a much nicer, quicker fate than all those factory-farmed cows that went into your Doom Dogs.
Stop with the Doom Dogs! I regret the Doom Dogs!
IT'S THE DAY I ALWAYS SWEAR TO BECOME A VEGETARIAN. THAT LASTS UNTIL AMMI IS DONE COOKING DINNER, AT WHICH POINT I CHANGE MY MIND.
Aww! What's wrong, baby girl?
She thinks the goat is too cute to eat.
It is, though! Tyesha, you gotta convince Aamir to let me take it home and raise it in the backyard...
It's good to know where your food comes from. Makes you appreciate it more. That's part of the point of this whole holiday.
Did I ever tell you my grandma used to raise chickens in her backyard? This was way before it became a hipster urban homesteading whatever thing.
Oh yeah?
Yup. She got the chicks from a farm out this way and raised them by hand. And do you know what we did with them when they grew up?
...No?
We ate them.
Oh my God!

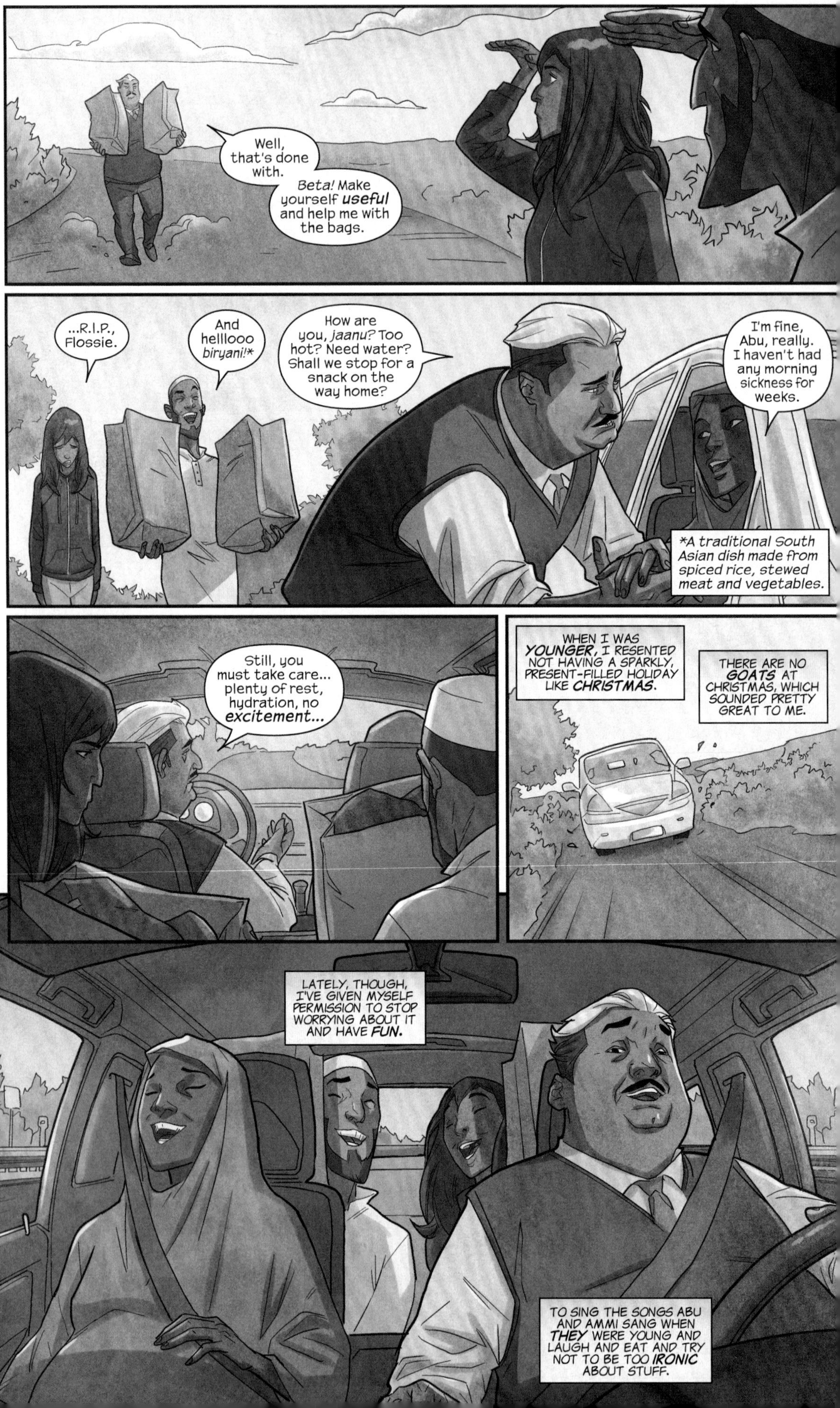
Well, that's done with.
Beta! Make yourself useful and help me with the bags.
...R.I.P., Flossie.
And hellllooo biryani!*
How are you, jaanu? Too hot? Need water? Shall we stop for a snack on the way home?
I'm fine, Abu, really. I haven't had any morning sickness for weeks.
*A traditional South Asian dish made from spiced rice, stewed meat and vegetables.
Still, you must take care... plenty of rest, hydration, no excitement...
WHEN I WAS YOUNGER, I RESENTED NOT HAVING A SPARKLY, PRESENT-FILLED HOLIDAY LIKE CHRISTMAS.
THERE ARE NO GOATS AT CHRISTMAS, WHICH SOUNDED PRETTY GREAT TO ME.
LATELY, THOUGH, I'VE GIVEN MYSELF PERMISSION TO STOP WORRYING ABOUT IT AND HAVE FUN.
TO SING THE SONGS ABU AND AMMI SANG WHEN THEY WERE YOUNG AND LAUGH AND EAT AND TRY NOT TO BE TOO IRONIC ABOUT STUFF.

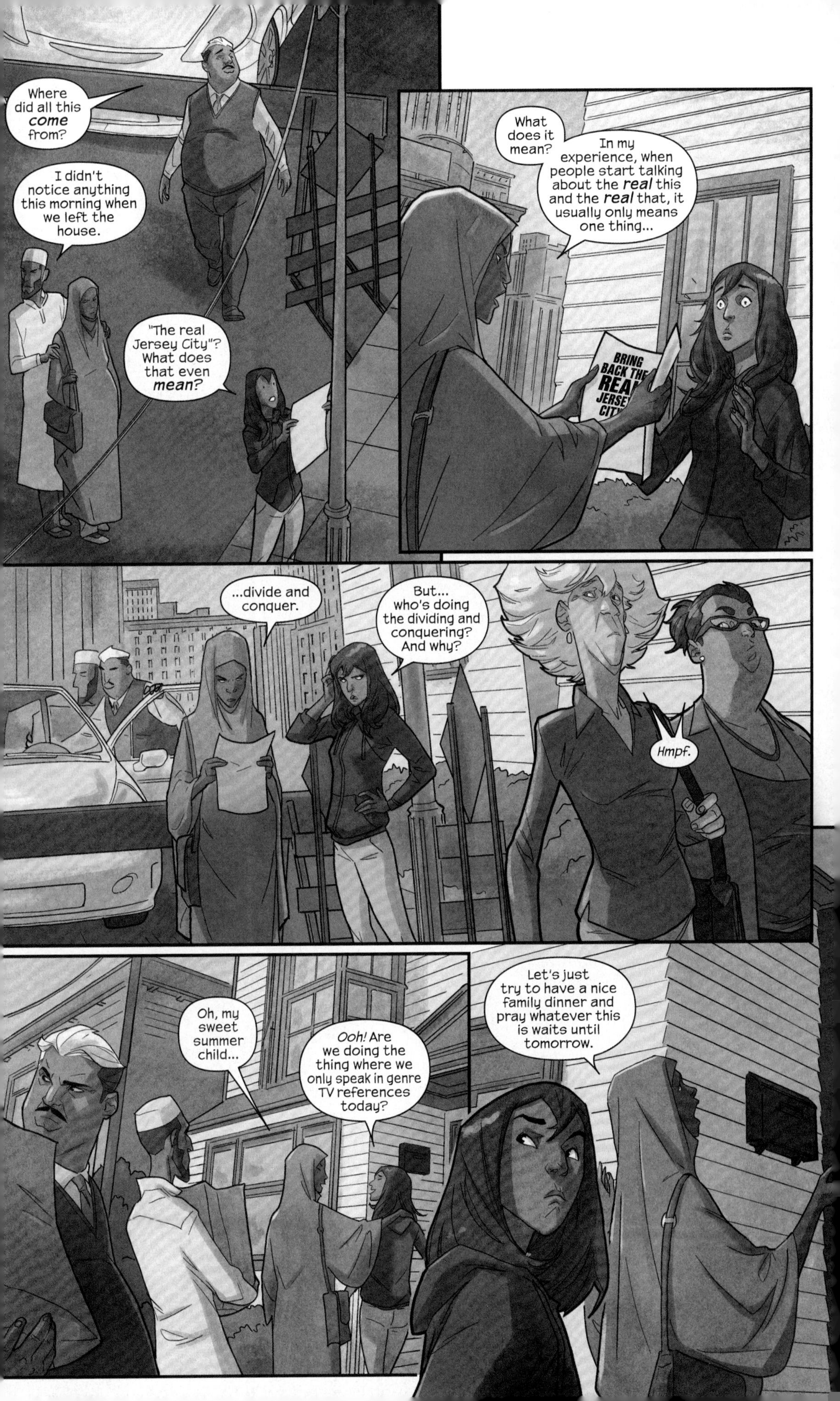

Where did all this *come* from?
I didn't notice anything this morning when we left the house.
"The real Jersey City"? What does that even *mean*?
What does it mean?
In my experience, when people start talking about the *real* this and the *real* that, it usually only means one thing...
BRING BACK THE REA JERSE CIT
...divide and conquer.
But... who's doing the dividing and conquering? And why?
Hmpf.
Oh, my sweet summer child...
Ooh! Are we doing the thing where we only speak in genre TV references today?
Let's just try to have a nice family dinner and pray whatever this is waits until tomorrow.

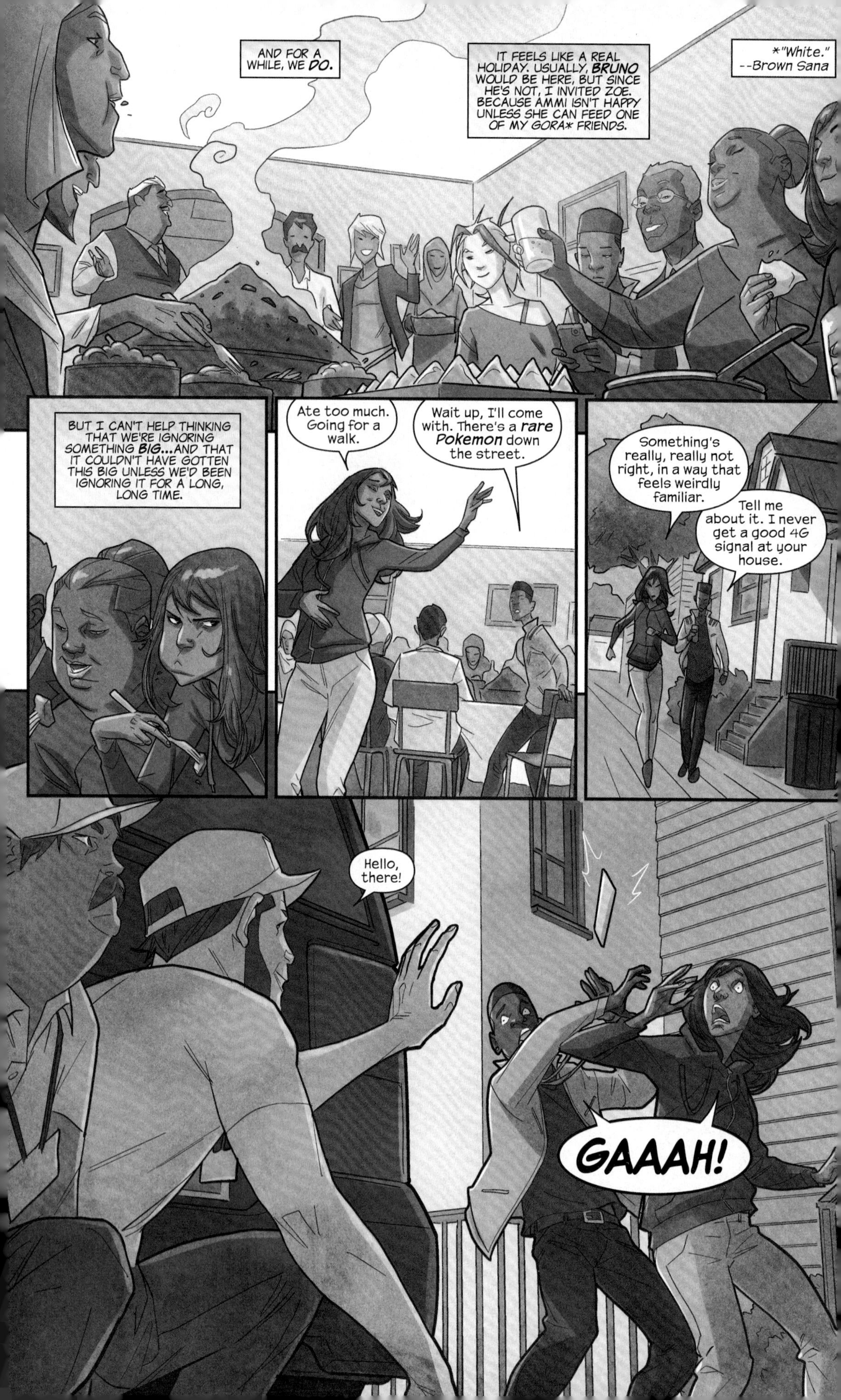

AND FOR A WHILE, WE DO.
IT FEELS LIKE A REAL HOLIDAY. USUALLY, BRUNO WOULD BE HERE, BUT SINCE HE'S NOT, I INVITED ZOE. BECAUSE AMMI ISN'T HAPPY UNLESS SHE CAN FEED ONE OF MY GORA* FRIENDS.
*"White." --Brown Sana
BUT I CAN'T HELP THINKING THAT WE'RE IGNORING SOMETHING BIG...AND THAT IT COULDN'T HAVE GOTTEN THIS BIG UNLESS WE'D BEEN IGNORING IT FOR A LONG, LONG TIME.
Ate too much. Going for a walk.
Wait up, I'll come with. There's a rare Pokemon down the street.
Something's really, really not right, in a way that feels weirdly familiar.
Tell me about it. I never get a good 4G signal at your house.
Hello, there!
GAAAH!

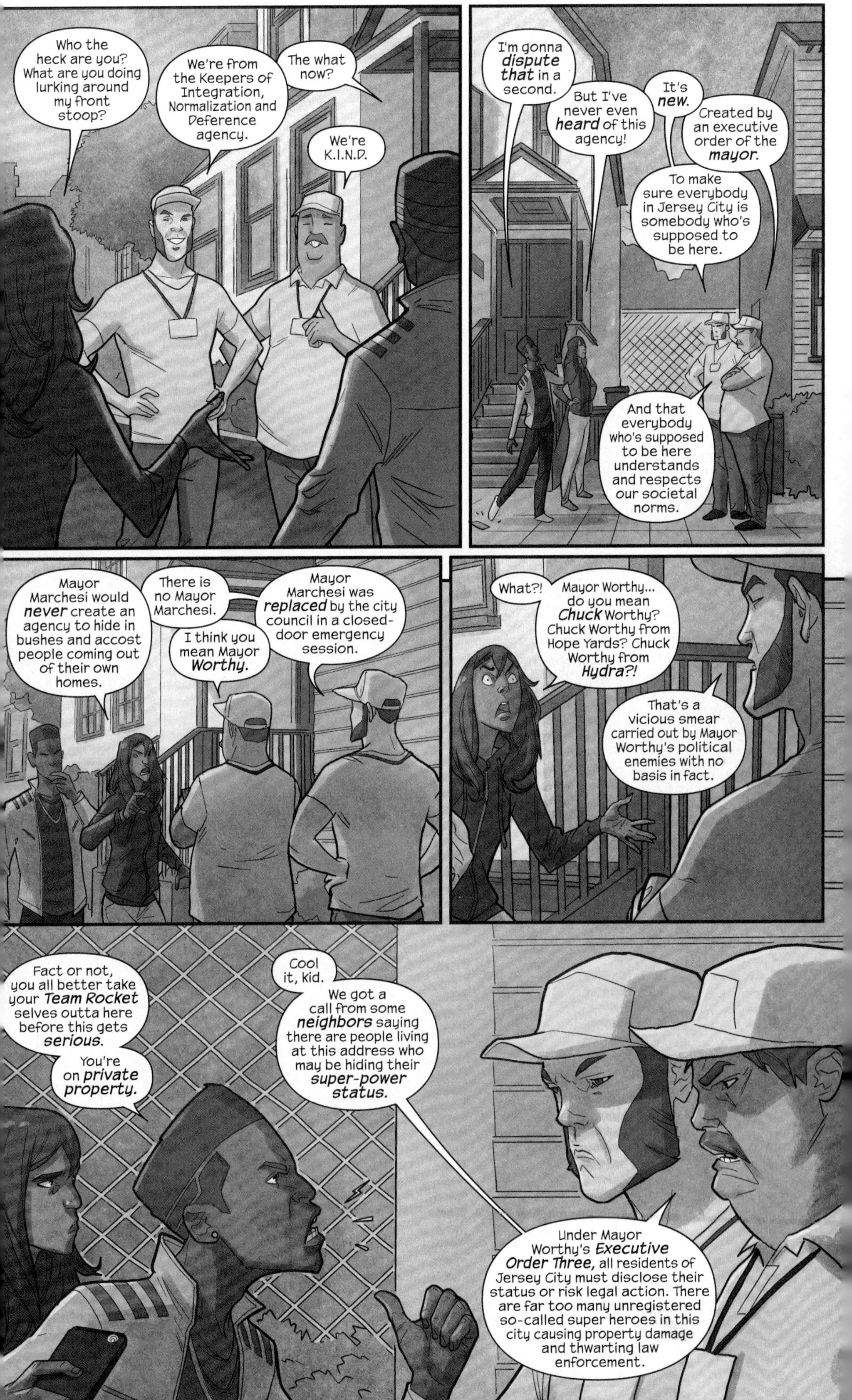

Who the heck are you? What are you doing lurking around my front stoop?
We're from the Keepers of Integration, Normalization and Deference agency.
The what now?
We're K.I.N.D.
I'm gonna *dispute that* in a second.
But I've never even *heard* of this agency!
It's *new*.
Created by an executive order of the *mayor*.
To make sure everybody in Jersey City is somebody who's supposed to be here.
And that everybody who's supposed to be here understands and respects our societal norms.
Mayor Marchesi would *never* create an agency to hide in bushes and accost people coming out of their own homes.
There is no Mayor Marchesi.
I think you mean Mayor *Worthy*.
Mayor Marchesi was *replaced* by the city council in a closed-door emergency session.
What?!
Mayor Worthy... do you mean *Chuck* Worthy? Chuck Worthy from Hope Yards? Chuck Worthy from *Hydra?!*
That's a vicious smear carried out by Mayor Worthy's political enemies with no basis in fact.
Fact or not, you all better take your *Team Rocket* selves outta here before this gets *serious*.
You're on *private property*.
Cool it, kid.
We got a call from some *neighbors* saying there are people living at this address who may be hiding their *super-power status*.
Under Mayor Worthy's *Executive Order Three*, all residents of Jersey City must disclose their status or risk legal action. There are far too many unregistered so-called super heroes in this city causing property damage and thwarting law enforcement.

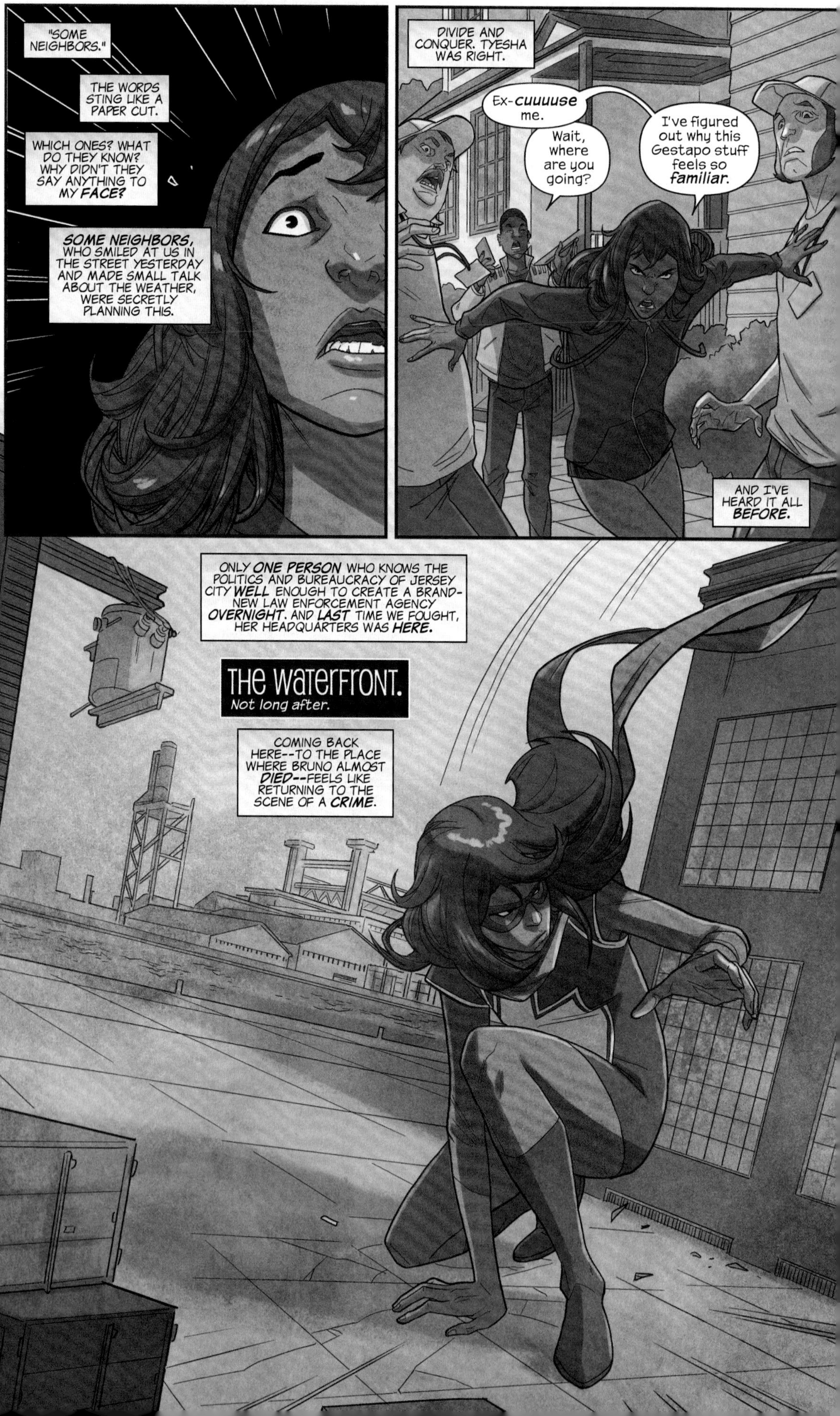
"SOME NEIGHBORS."
THE WORDS STING LIKE A PAPER CUT.
WHICH ONES? WHAT DO THEY KNOW? WHY DIDN'T THEY SAY ANYTHING TO MY FACE?
SOME NEIGHBORS, WHO SMILED AT US IN THE STREET YESTERDAY AND MADE SMALL TALK ABOUT THE WEATHER, WERE SECRETLY PLANNING THIS.
DIVIDE AND CONQUER. TYESHA WAS RIGHT.
Ex-cuuuuse me.
Wait, where are you going?
I've figured out why this Gestapo stuff feels so familiar.
AND I'VE HEARD IT ALL BEFORE.
ONLY ONE PERSON WHO KNOWS THE POLITICS AND BUREAUCRACY OF JERSEY CITY WELL ENOUGH TO CREATE A BRAND-NEW LAW ENFORCEMENT AGENCY OVERNIGHT. AND LAST TIME WE FOUGHT, HER HEADQUARTERS WAS HERE.
THE WATERFRONT.
Not long after.
COMING BACK HERE--TO THE PLACE WHERE BRUNO ALMOST DIED--FEELS LIKE RETURNING TO THE SCENE OF A CRIME.

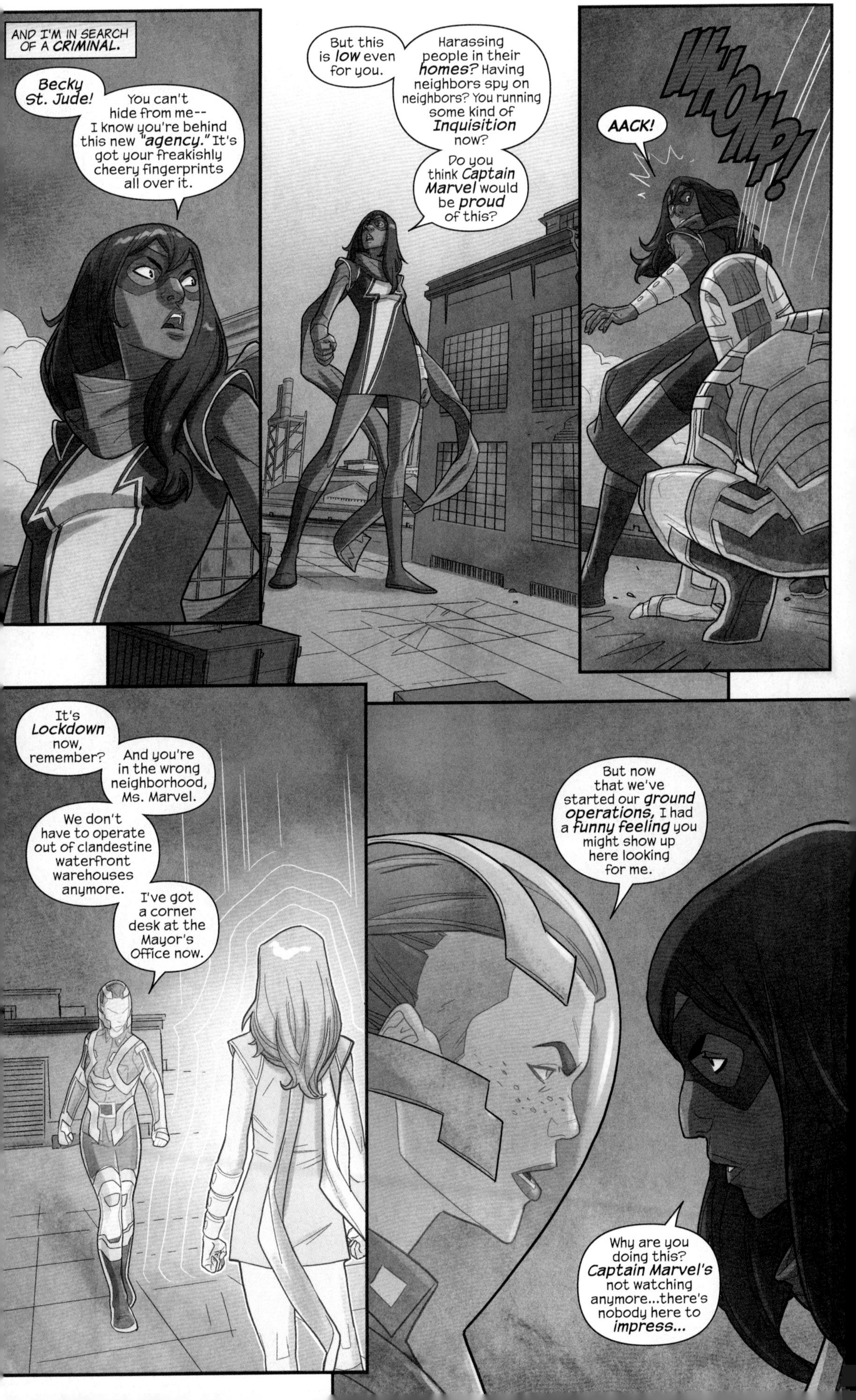

AND I'M IN SEARCH OF A CRIMINAL.
Becky St. Jude!
You can't hide from me-- I know you're behind this new "agency." It's got your freakishly cheery fingerprints all over it.
But this is low even for you.
Harassing people in their homes? Having neighbors spy on neighbors? You running some kind of Inquisition now?
Do you think Captain Marvel would be proud of this?
WHOMP!
AACK!
It's Lockdown now, remember?
And you're in the wrong neighborhood, Ms. Marvel.
We don't have to operate out of clandestine waterfront warehouses anymore.
I've got a corner desk at the Mayor's Office now.
But now that we've started our ground operations, I had a funny feeling you might show up here looking for me.
Why are you doing this? Captain Marvel's not watching anymore...there's nobody here to impress...

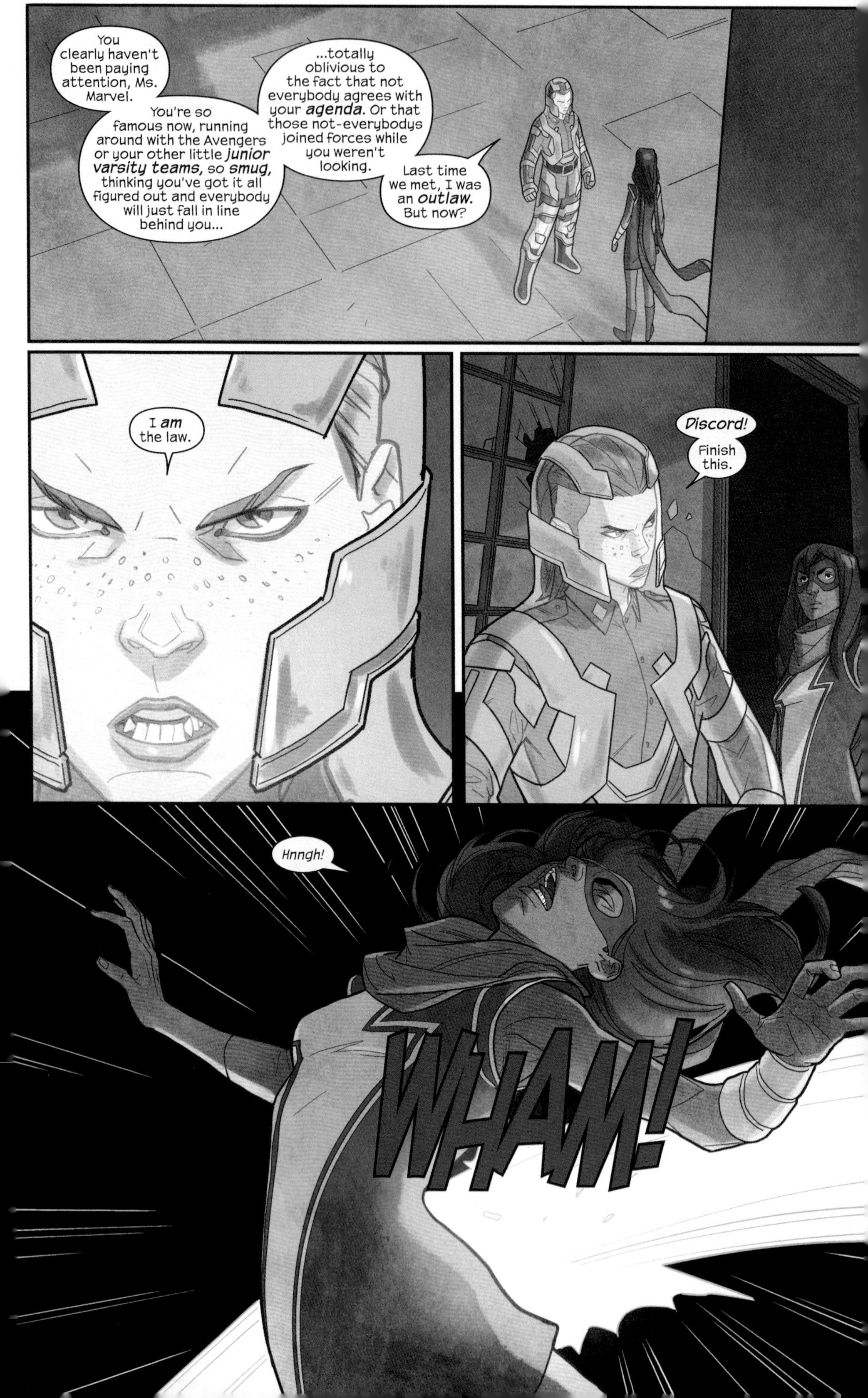
You clearly haven't been paying attention, Ms. Marvel.
You're so famous now, running around with the Avengers or your other little *junior varsity teams,* so *smug,* thinking you've got it all figured out and everybody will just fall in line behind you...
...totally oblivious to the fact that not everybody agrees with your *agenda.* Or that those not-everybodys joined forces while you weren't looking.
Last time we met, I was an *outlaw.* But now?
I *am* the law.
Discord!
Finish this.
Hnngh!
WHAM!

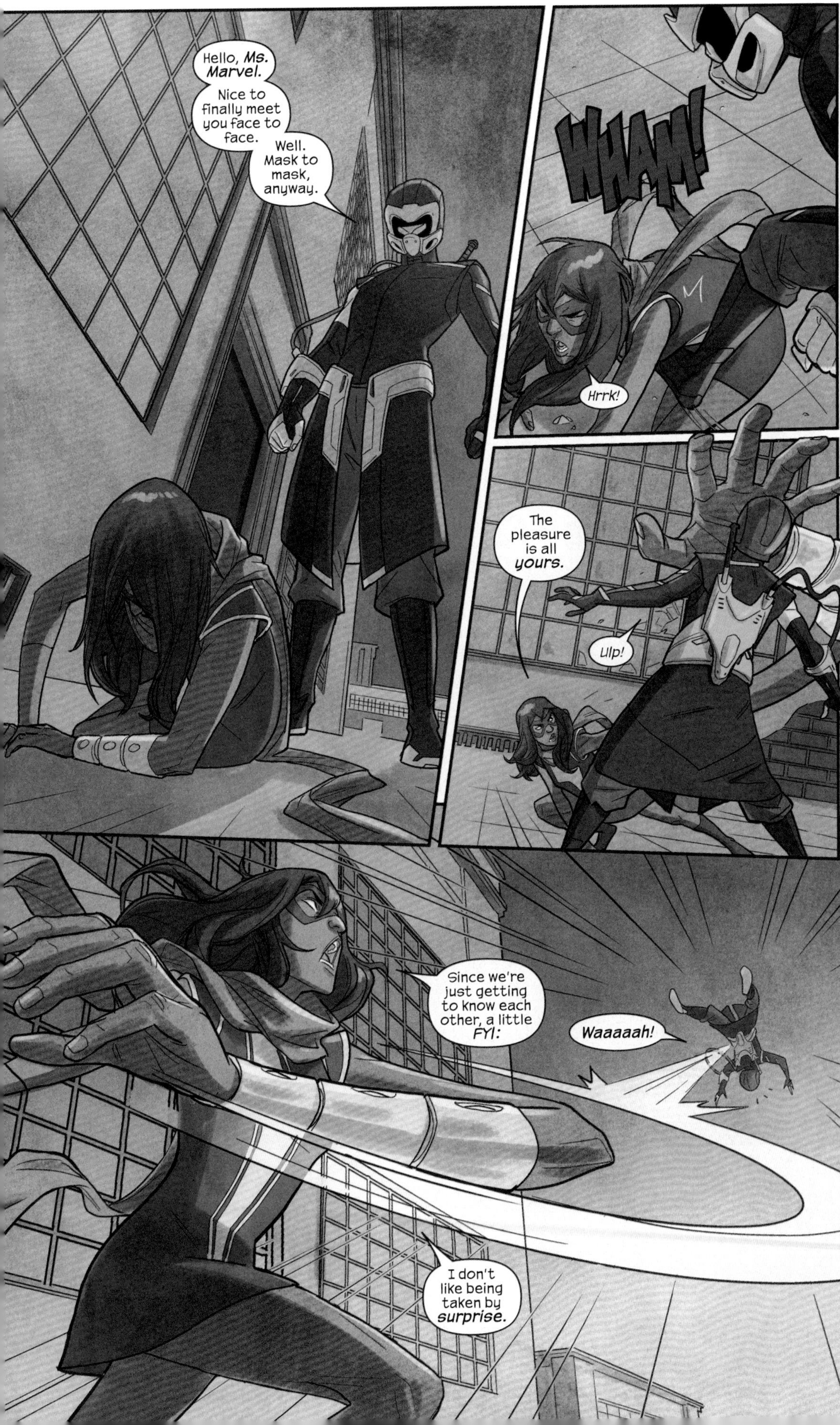

Hello, Ms. Marvel.
Nice to finally meet you face to face.
Well. Mask to mask, anyway.
WHAM!
Hrrk!
The pleasure is all yours.
Ulp!
Since we're just getting to know each other, a little FYI:
Waaaaah!
I don't like being taken by surprise.

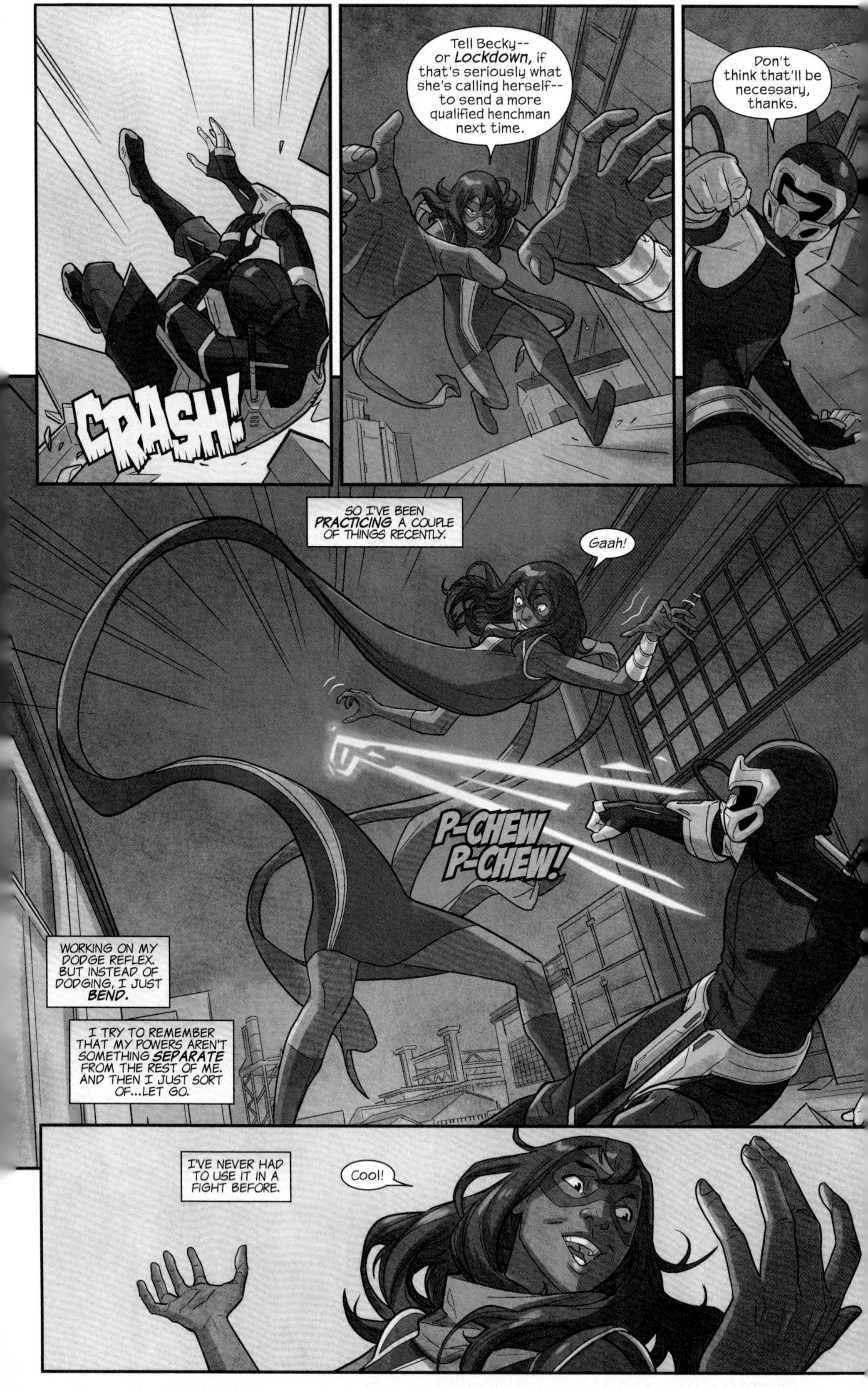
CRASH!
Tell Becky-- or Lockdown, if that's seriously what she's calling herself-- to send a more qualified henchman next time.
Don't think that'll be necessary, thanks.
SO I'VE BEEN PRACTICING A COUPLE OF THINGS RECENTLY.
Gaah!
P-CHEW P-CHEW!
WORKING ON MY DODGE REFLEX. BUT INSTEAD OF DODGING, I JUST BEND.
I TRY TO REMEMBER THAT MY POWERS AREN'T SOMETHING SEPARATE FROM THE REST OF ME. AND THEN I JUST SORT OF...LET GO.
I'VE NEVER HAD TO USE IT IN A FIGHT BEFORE.
Cool!

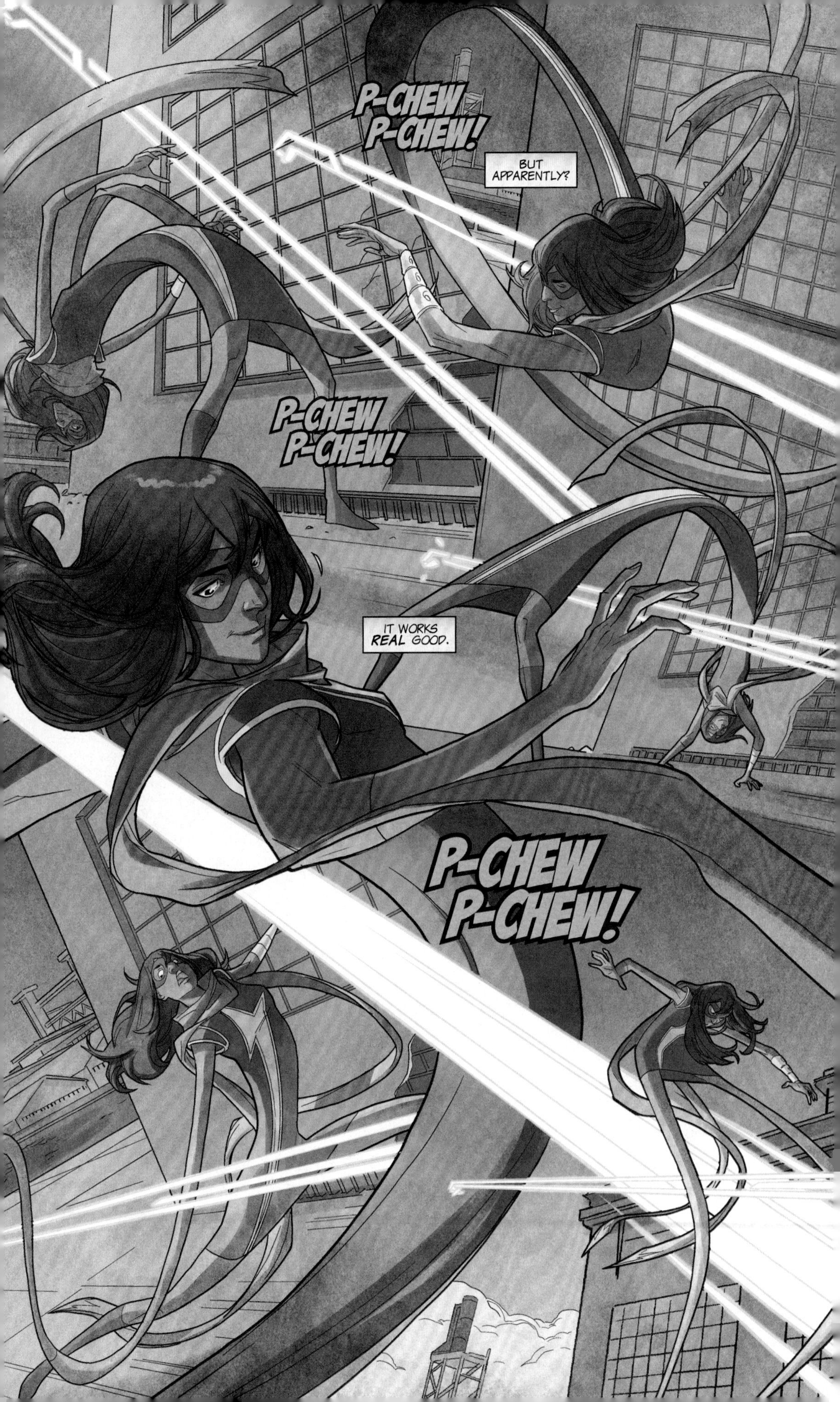
P-CHEW P-CHEW!
BUT APPARENTLY?
P-CHEW P-CHEW!
IT WORKS REAL GOOD.
P-CHEW P-CHEW!

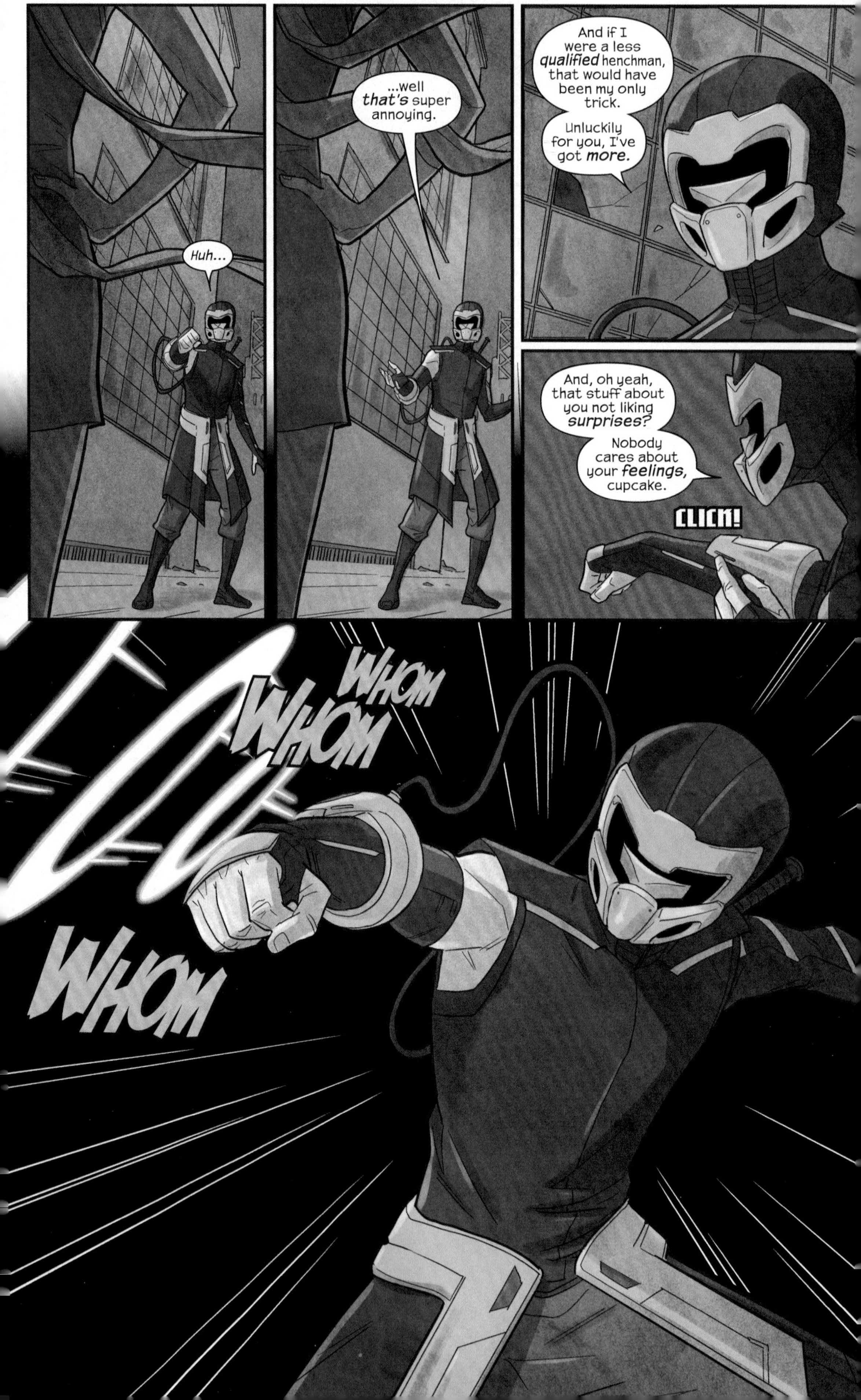
Huh...
...well *that's* super annoying.
And if I were a less *qualified* henchman, that would have been my only trick.
Unluckily for you, I've got *more.*
And, oh yeah, that stuff about you not liking *surprises?*
Nobody cares about your *feelings,* cupcake.
CLICK!
WHOM
WHOM
WHOM

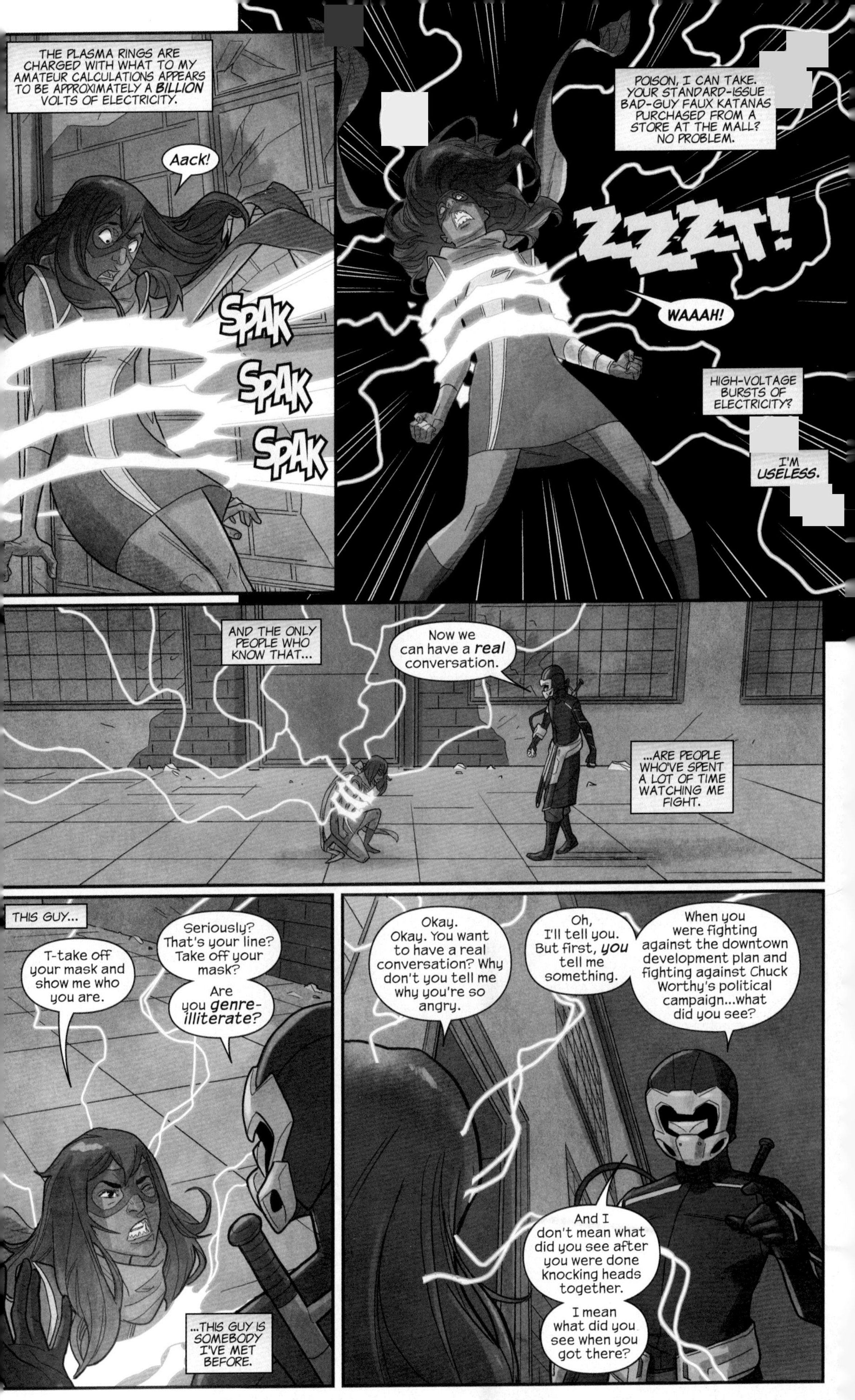
THE PLASMA RINGS ARE CHARGED WITH WHAT TO MY AMATEUR CALCULATIONS APPEARS TO BE APPROXIMATELY A BILLION VOLTS OF ELECTRICITY.
Aack!
SPAK
SPAK
SPAK
POISON, I CAN TAKE. YOUR STANDARD-ISSUE BAD-GUY FAUX KATANAS PURCHASED FROM A STORE AT THE MALL? NO PROBLEM.
ZZZT!
WAAAH!
HIGH-VOLTAGE BURSTS OF ELECTRICITY?
I'M USELESS.
AND THE ONLY PEOPLE WHO KNOW THAT...
Now we can have a real conversation.
...ARE PEOPLE WHO'VE SPENT A LOT OF TIME WATCHING ME FIGHT.
THIS GUY...
T-take off your mask and show me who you are.
Seriously? That's your line? Take off your mask?
Are you genre-illiterate?
...THIS GUY IS SOMEBODY I'VE MET BEFORE.
Okay. Okay. You want to have a real conversation? Why don't you tell me why you're so angry.
Oh, I'll tell you. But first, you tell me something.
When you were fighting against the downtown development plan and fighting against Chuck Worthy's political campaign...what did you see?
And I don't mean what did you see after you were done knocking heads together.
I mean what did you see when you got there?

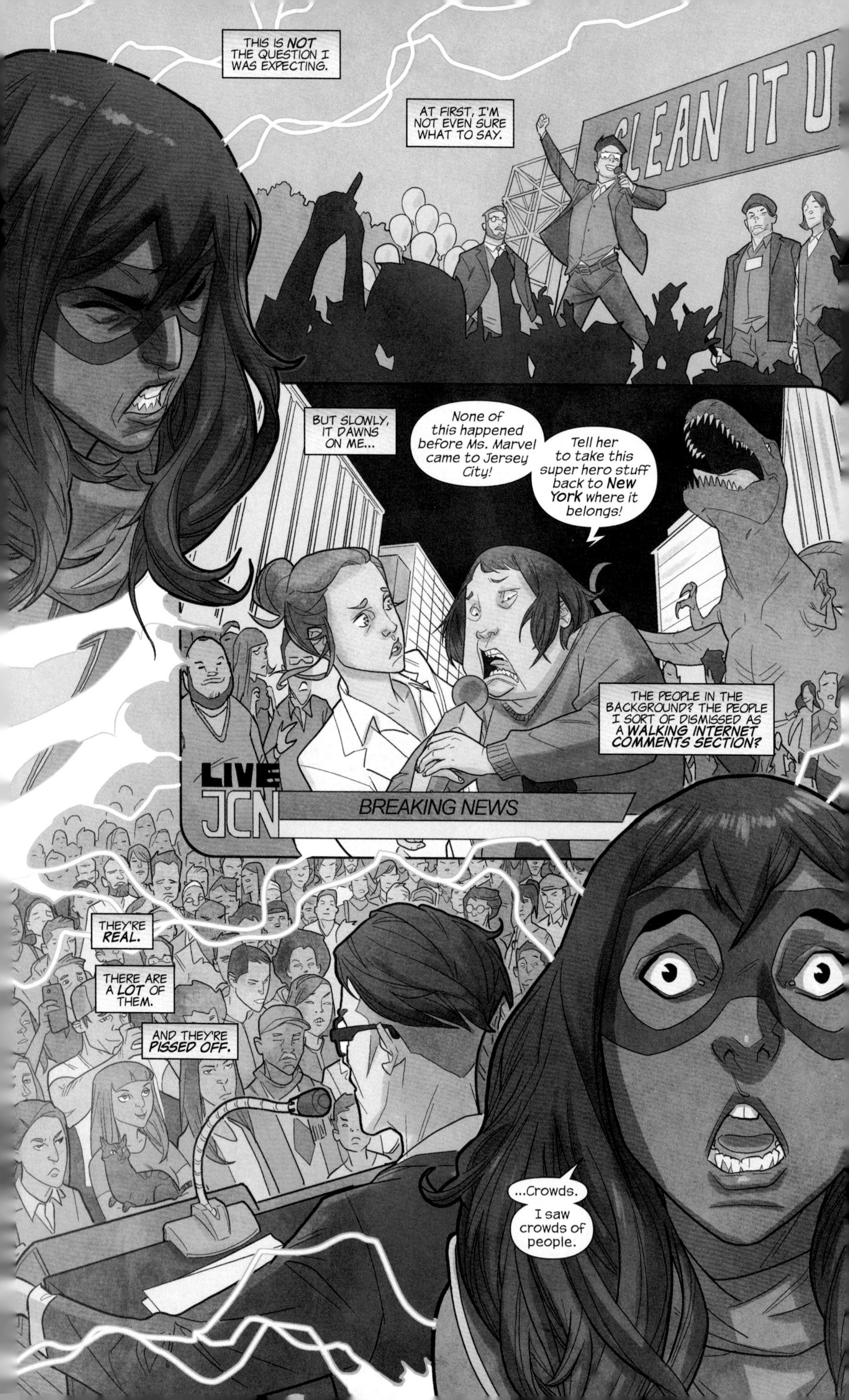

THIS IS NOT THE QUESTION I WAS EXPECTING.
AT FIRST, I'M NOT EVEN SURE WHAT TO SAY.
CLEAN IT U
BUT SLOWLY, IT DAWNS ON ME...
None of this happened before Ms. Marvel came to Jersey City!
Tell her to take this super hero stuff back to New York where it belongs!
THE PEOPLE IN THE BACKGROUND? THE PEOPLE I SORT OF DISMISSED AS A WALKING INTERNET COMMENTS SECTION?
LIVE
JCN
BREAKING NEWS
THEY'RE REAL.
THERE ARE A LOT OF THEM.
AND THEY'RE PISSED OFF.
...Crowds.
I saw crowds of people.

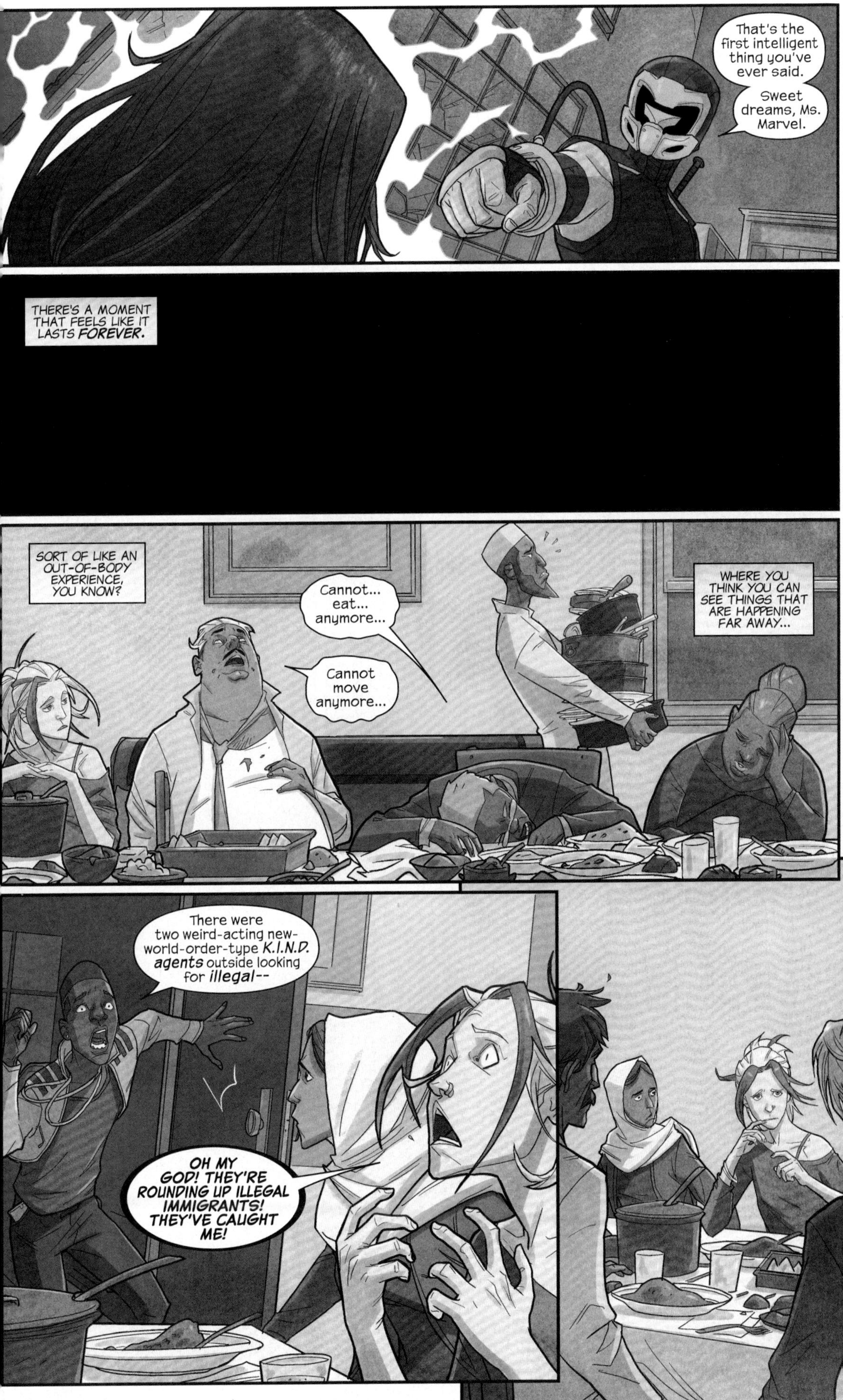
That's the first intelligent thing you've ever said.
Sweet dreams, Ms. Marvel.
THERE'S A MOMENT THAT FEELS LIKE IT LASTS FOREVER.
SORT OF LIKE AN OUT-OF-BODY EXPERIENCE, YOU KNOW?
Cannot... eat... anymore...
Cannot move anymore...
WHERE YOU THINK YOU CAN SEE THINGS THAT ARE HAPPENING FAR AWAY...
There were two weird-acting new-world-order-type K.I.N.D. agents outside looking for illegal--
OH MY GOD! THEY'RE ROUNDING UP ILLEGAL IMMIGRANTS! THEY'VE CAUGHT ME!

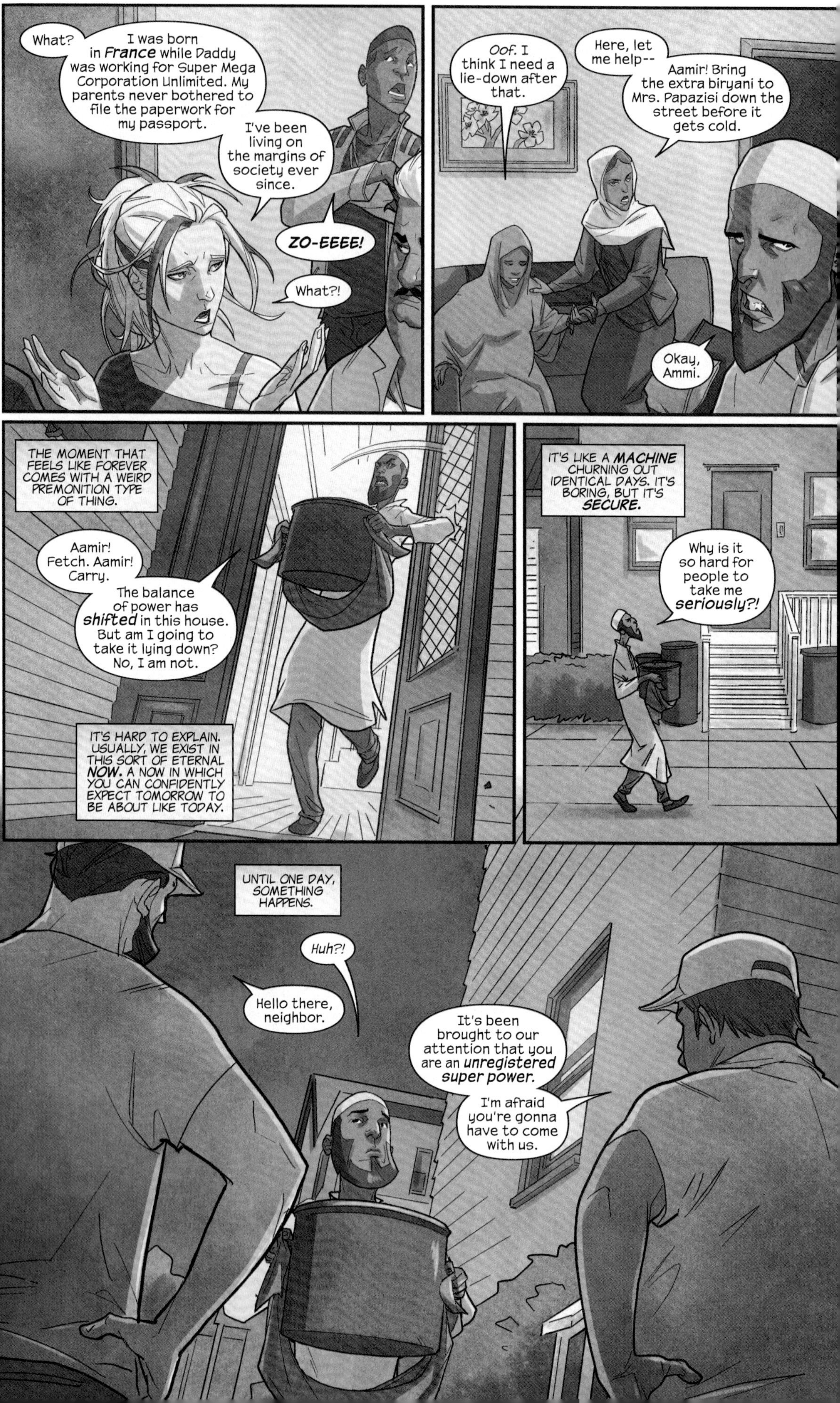
What?
I was born in *France* while Daddy was working for Super Mega Corporation Unlimited. My parents never bothered to file the paperwork for my passport.
I've been living on the margins of society ever since.
ZO-EEEE!
What?!
Oof. I think I need a lie-down after that.
Here, let me help--
Aamir! Bring the extra biryani to Mrs. Papazisi down the street before it gets cold.
Okay, Ammi.
THE MOMENT THAT FEELS LIKE FOREVER COMES WITH A WEIRD PREMONITION TYPE OF THING.
Aamir! Fetch. Aamir! Carry.
The balance of power has *shifted* in this house. But am I going to take it lying down? No, I am not.
IT'S HARD TO EXPLAIN. USUALLY, WE EXIST IN THIS SORT OF ETERNAL **NOW**. A NOW IN WHICH YOU CAN CONFIDENTLY EXPECT TOMORROW TO BE ABOUT LIKE TODAY.
IT'S LIKE A **MACHINE** CHURNING OUT IDENTICAL DAYS. IT'S BORING, BUT IT'S **SECURE.**
Why is it so hard for people to take me ***seriously?!***
UNTIL ONE DAY, SOMETHING HAPPENS.
Huh?!
Hello there, neighbor.
It's been brought to our attention that you are an ***unregistered super power.***
I'm afraid you're gonna have to come with us.

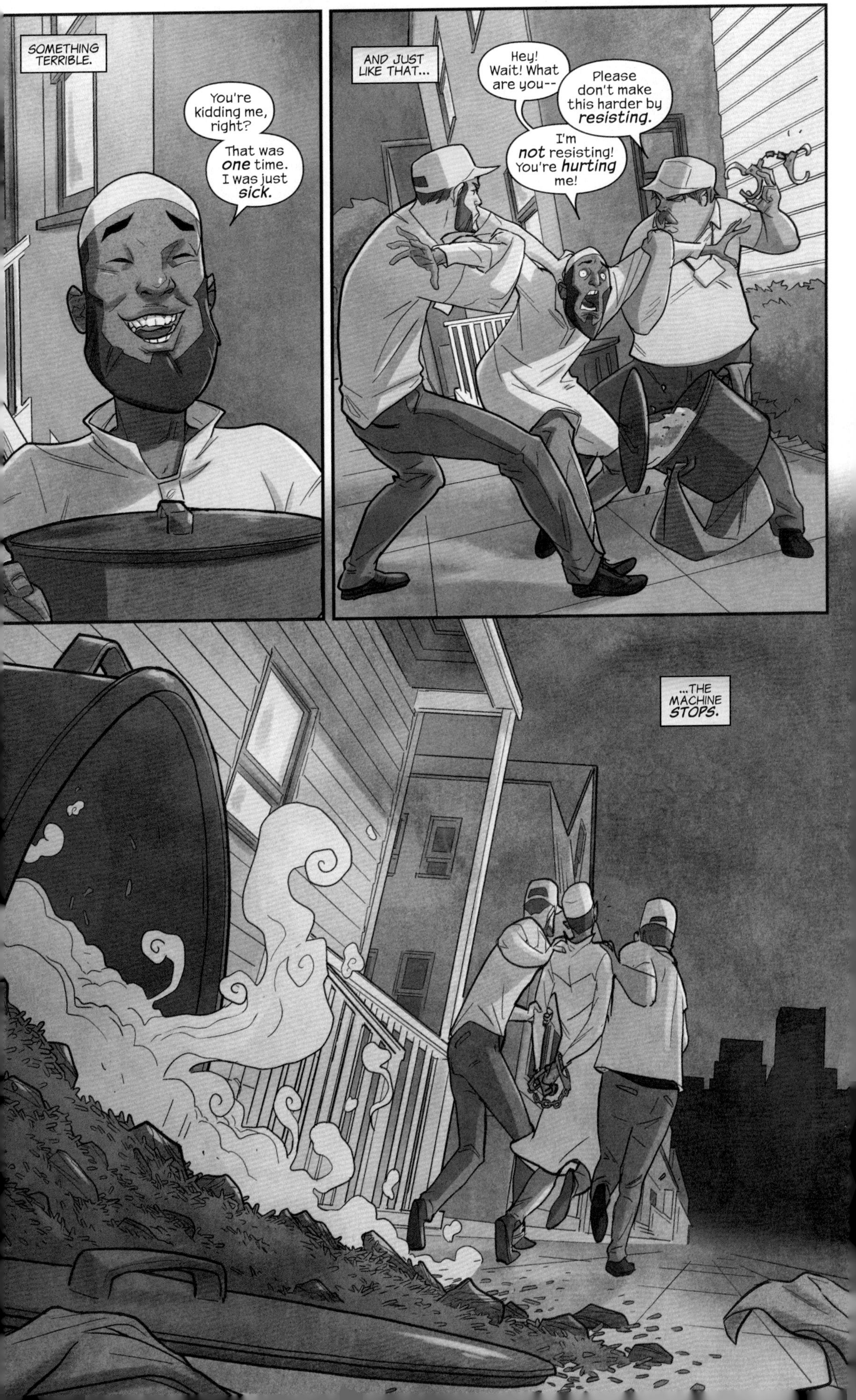
SOMETHING TERRIBLE.
You're kidding me, right?
That was *one* time. I was just *sick.*
AND JUST LIKE THAT...
Hey! Wait! What are you--
Please don't make this harder by *resisting.*
I'm *not* resisting! You're *hurting* me!
...THE MACHINE *STOPS.*

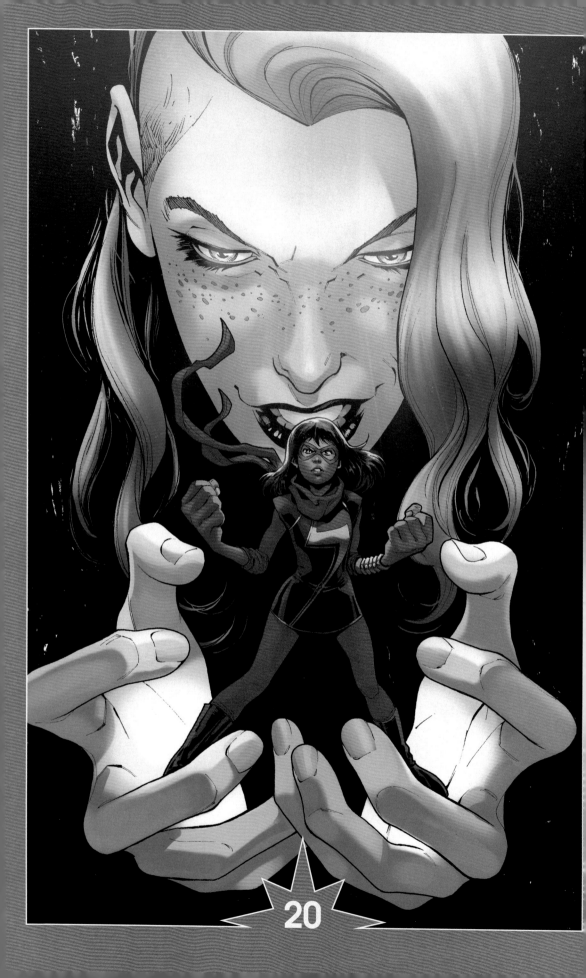

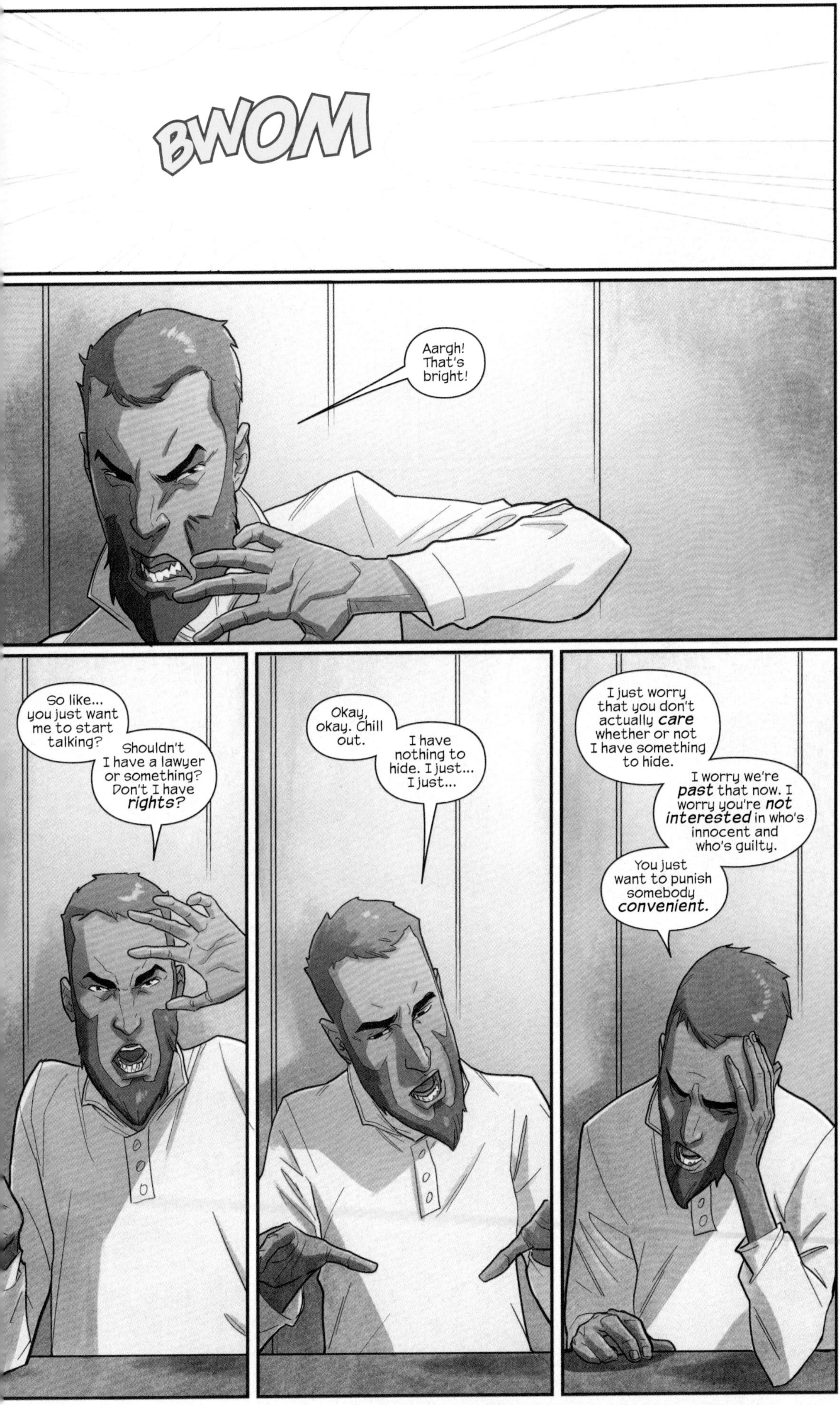
BWOM
Aargh! That's bright!
So like... you just want me to start talking?
Shouldn't I have a lawyer or something? Don't I have *rights?*
Okay, okay. Chill out.
I have nothing to hide. I just... I just...
I just worry that you don't actually *care* whether or not I have something to hide.
I worry we're *past* that now. I worry you're *not interested* in who's innocent and who's guilty.
You just want to punish somebody *convenient.*

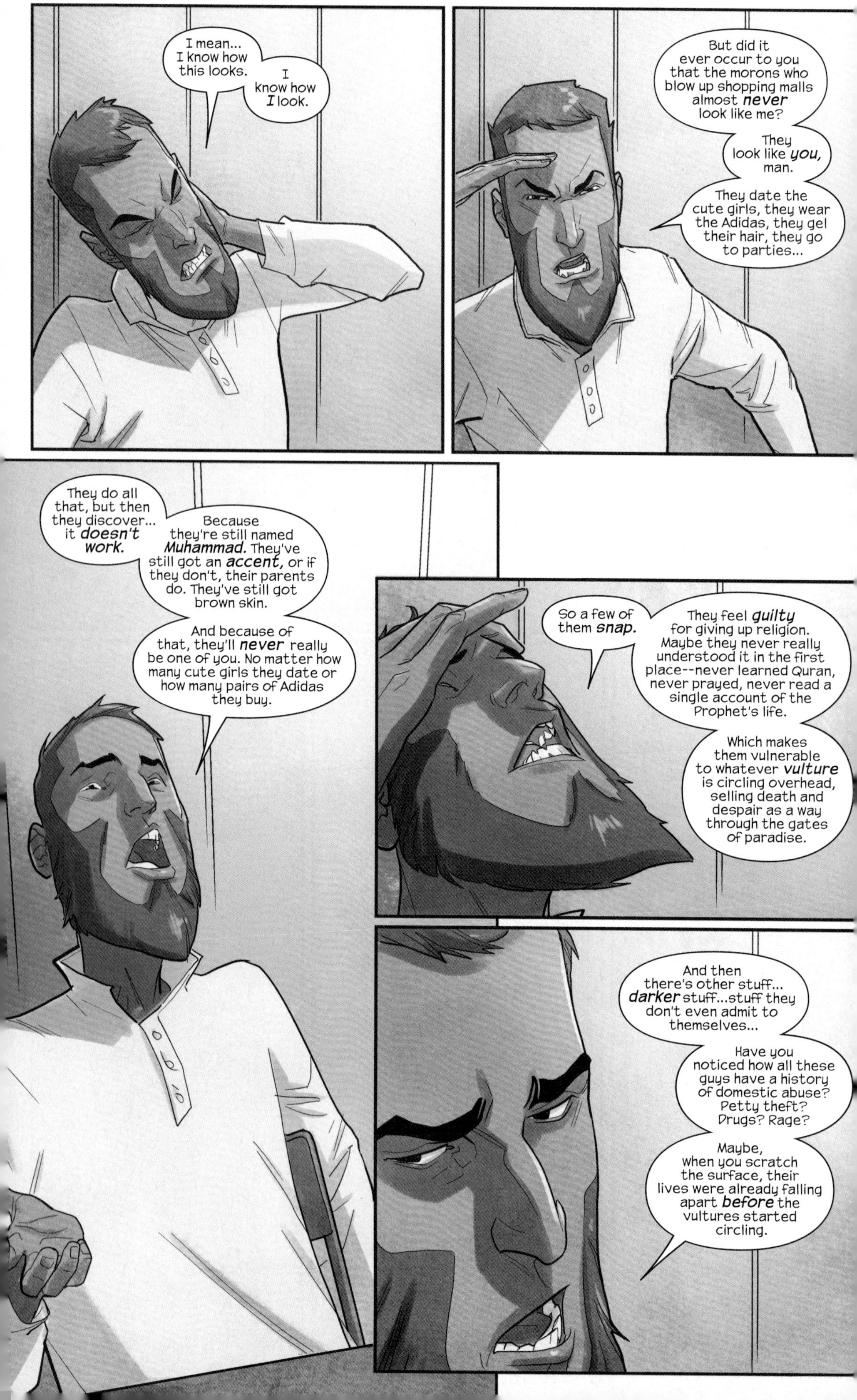

I mean... I know how this looks.
I know how I look.
But did it ever occur to you that the morons who blow up shopping malls almost never look like me?
They look like you, man.
They date the cute girls, they wear the Adidas, they gel their hair, they go to parties...
They do all that, but then they discover... it doesn't work.
Because they're still named Muhammad. They've still got an accent, or if they don't, their parents do. They've still got brown skin.
And because of that, they'll never really be one of you. No matter how many cute girls they date or how many pairs of Adidas they buy.
So a few of them snap.
They feel guilty for giving up religion. Maybe they never really understood it in the first place--never learned Quran, never prayed, never read a single account of the Prophet's life.
Which makes them vulnerable to whatever vulture is circling overhead, selling death and despair as a way through the gates of paradise.
And then there's other stuff... darker stuff...stuff they don't even admit to themselves...
Have you noticed how all these guys have a history of domestic abuse? Petty theft? Drugs? Rage?
Maybe, when you scratch the surface, their lives were already falling apart before the vultures started circling.

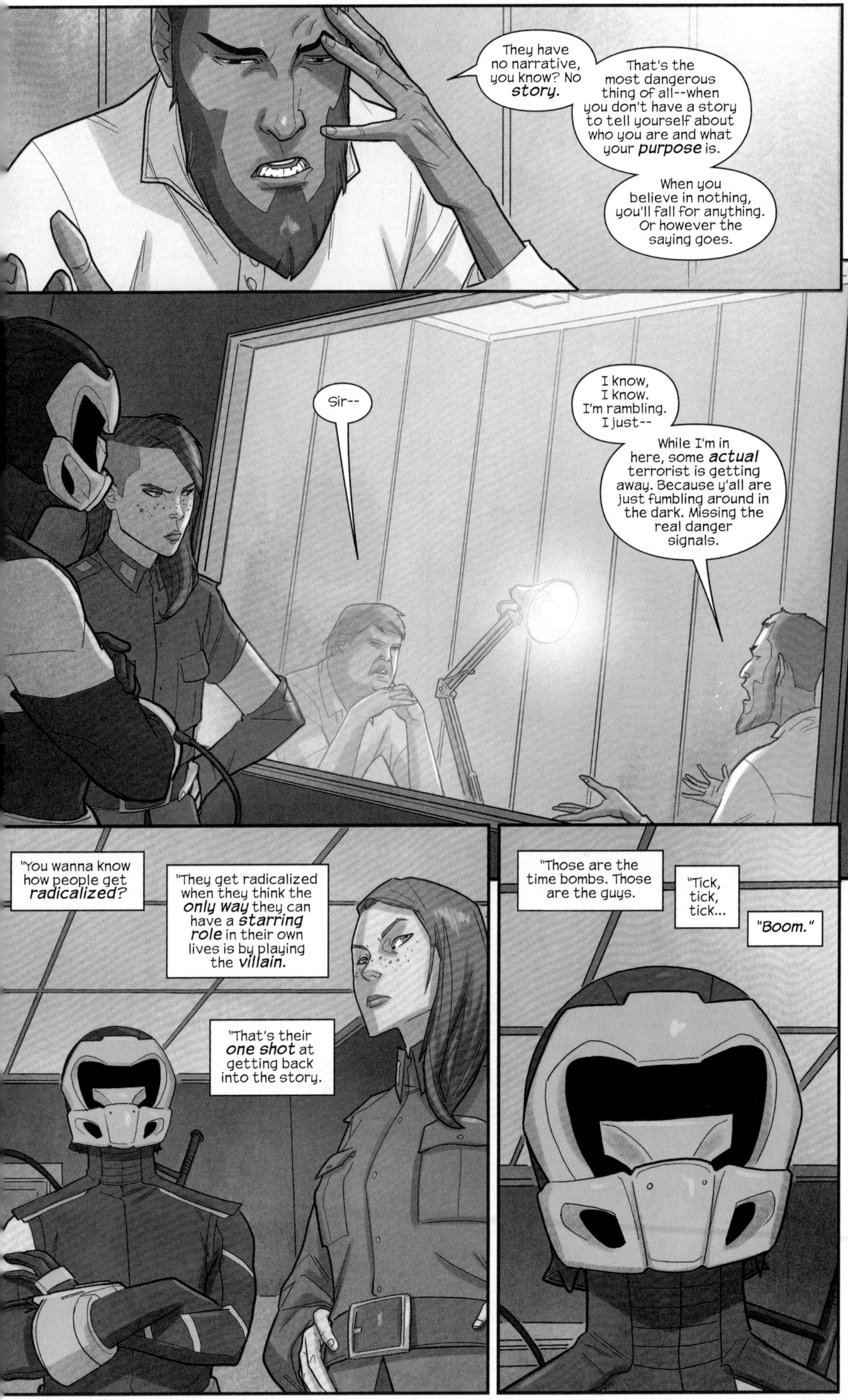
They have no narrative, you know? No *story.*
That's the most dangerous thing of all--when you don't have a story to tell yourself about who you are and what your *purpose* is.
When you believe in nothing, you'll fall for anything. Or however the saying goes.
Sir--
I know, I know. I'm rambling. I just--
While I'm in here, some *actual* terrorist is getting away. Because y'all are just fumbling around in the dark. Missing the real danger signals.
"You wanna know how people get *radicalized?*
"They get radicalized when they think the *only way* they can have a *starring role* in their own lives is by playing the *villain.*
"That's their *one shot* at getting back into the story.
"Those are the time bombs. Those are the guys.
"Tick, tick, tick...
"Boom."

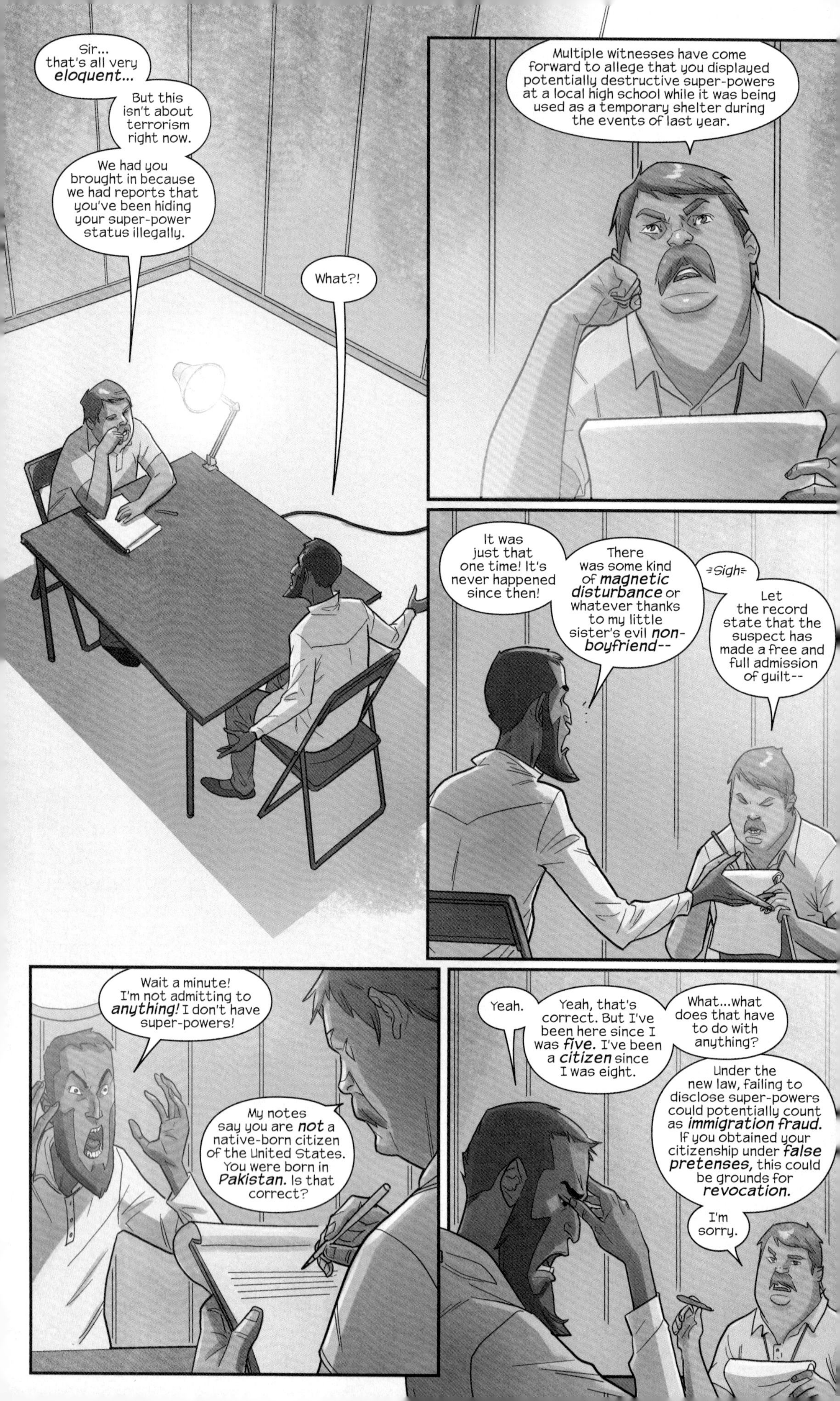
Sir... that's all very *eloquent*...
But this isn't about terrorism right now.
We had you brought in because we had reports that you've been hiding your super-power status illegally.
What?!
Multiple witnesses have come forward to allege that you displayed potentially destructive super-powers at a local high school while it was being used as a temporary shelter during the events of last year.
It was just that one time! It's never happened since then!
There was some kind of *magnetic disturbance* or whatever thanks to my little sister's evil *non-boyfriend*--
=Sigh=
Let the record state that the suspect has made a free and full admission of guilt--
Wait a minute! I'm not admitting to *anything!* I don't have super-powers!
My notes say you are *not* a native-born citizen of the United States. You were born in *Pakistan.* Is that correct?
Yeah.
Yeah, that's correct. But I've been here since I was *five.* I've been a *citizen* since I was eight.
What...what does that have to do with anything?
Under the new law, failing to disclose super-powers could potentially count as *immigration fraud.* If you obtained your citizenship under *false pretenses,* this could be grounds for *revocation.*
I'm sorry.

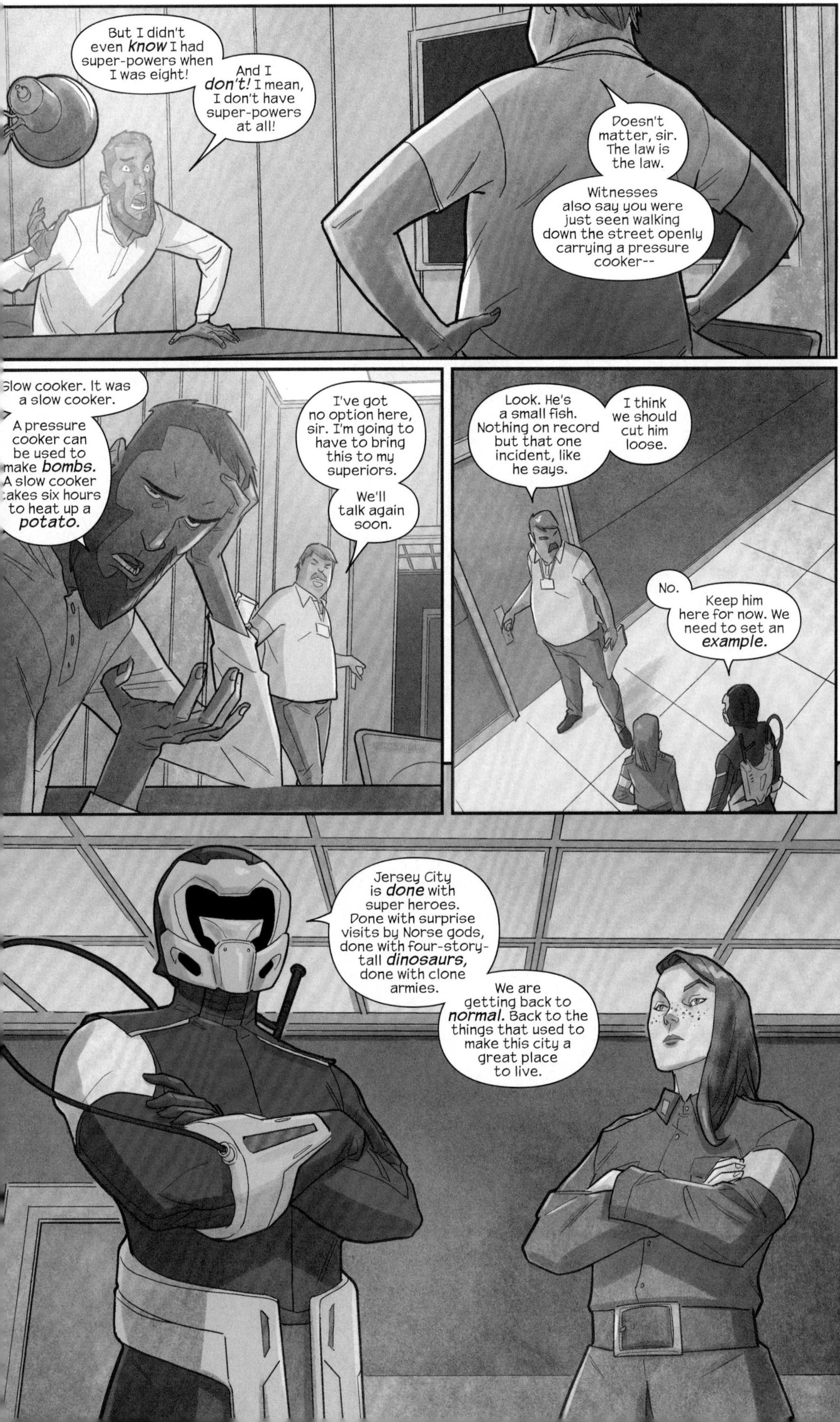
But I didn't even *know* I had super-powers when I was eight!
And I *don't!* I mean, I don't have super-powers at all!
Doesn't matter, sir. The law is the law.
Witnesses also say you were just seen walking down the street openly carrying a pressure cooker--
Slow cooker. It was a slow cooker.
A pressure cooker can be used to make **bombs.** A slow cooker takes six hours to heat up a *potato.*
I've got no option here, sir. I'm going to have to bring this to my superiors.
We'll talk again soon.
Look. He's a small fish. Nothing on record but that one incident, like he says.
I think we should cut him loose.
No.
Keep him here for now. We need to set an *example.*
Jersey City is *done* with super heroes. Done with surprise visits by Norse gods, done with four-story-tall *dinosaurs,* done with clone armies.
We are getting back to *normal.* Back to the things that used to make this city a great place to live.

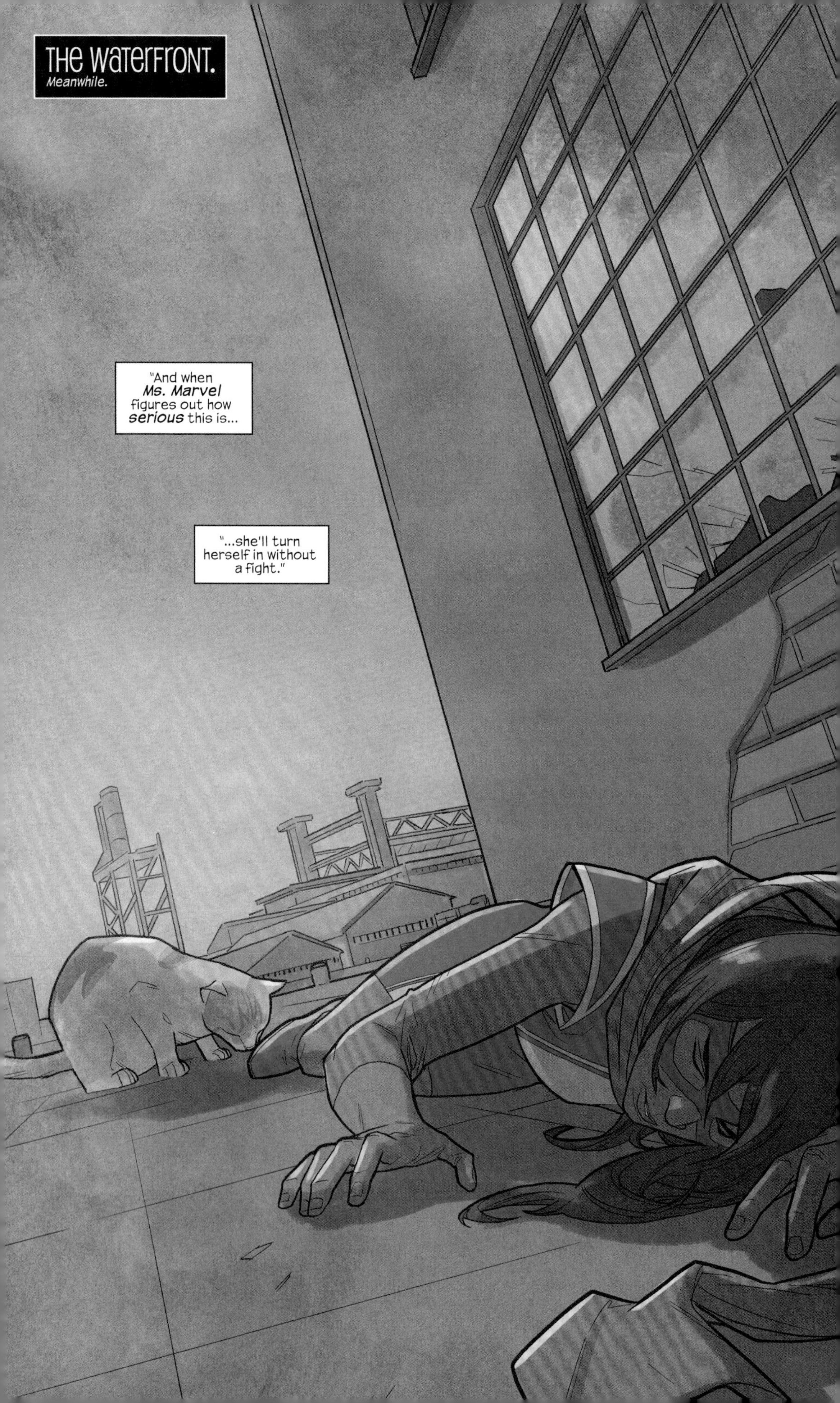
THE WATERFRONT.
Meanwhile.
"And when *Ms. Marvel* figures out how *serious* this is...
"...she'll turn herself in without a fight."

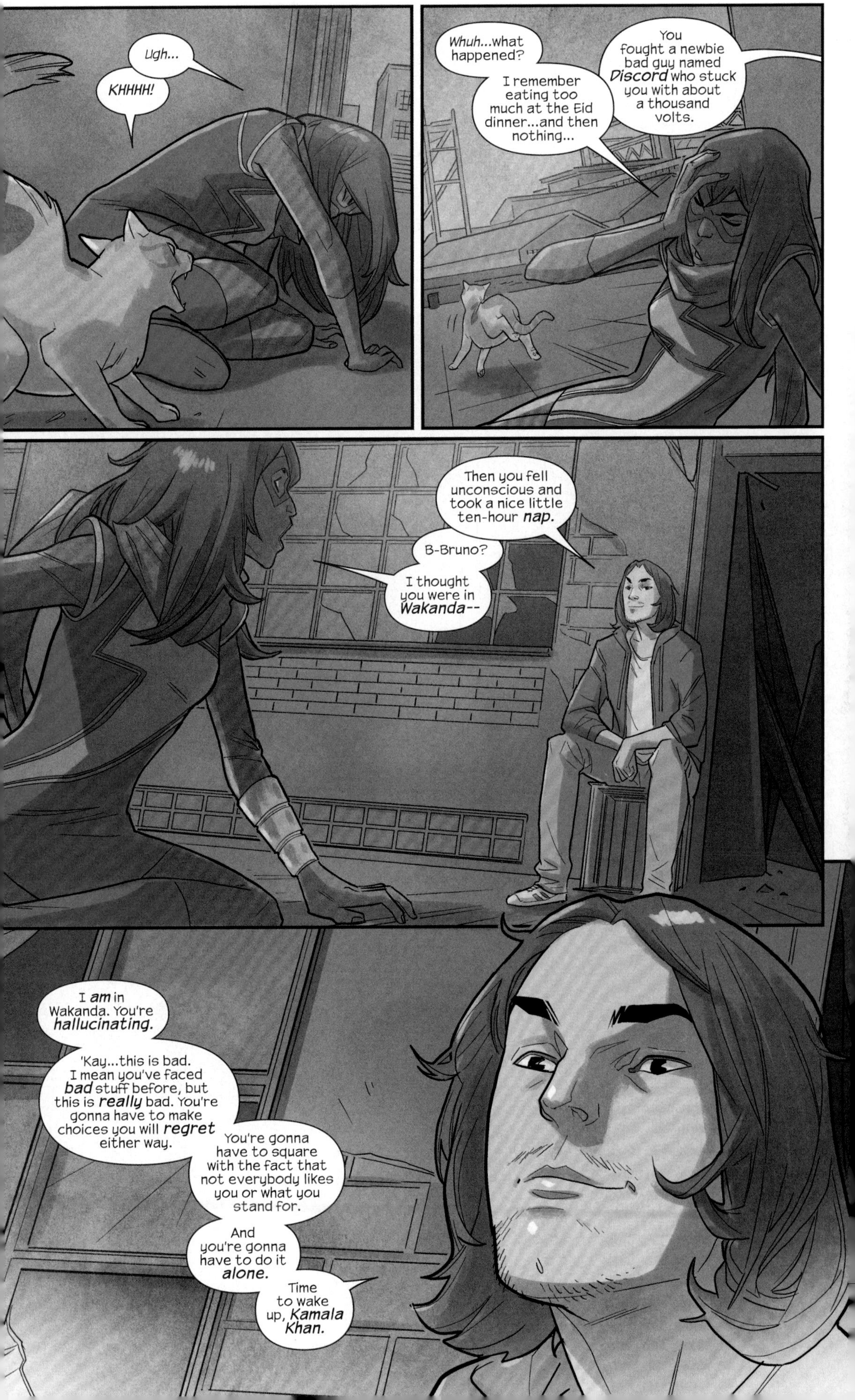
Ugh...
KHHHH!
Whuh...what happened?
I remember eating too much at the Eid dinner...and then nothing...
You fought a newbie bad guy named Discord who stuck you with about a thousand volts.
Then you fell unconscious and took a nice little ten-hour nap.
B-Bruno?
I thought you were in Wakanda--
I am in Wakanda. You're hallucinating.
'Kay...this is bad. I mean you've faced bad stuff before, but this is really bad. You're gonna have to make choices you will regret either way.
You're gonna have to square with the fact that not everybody likes you or what you stand for.
And you're gonna have to do it alone.
Time to wake up, Kamala Khan.

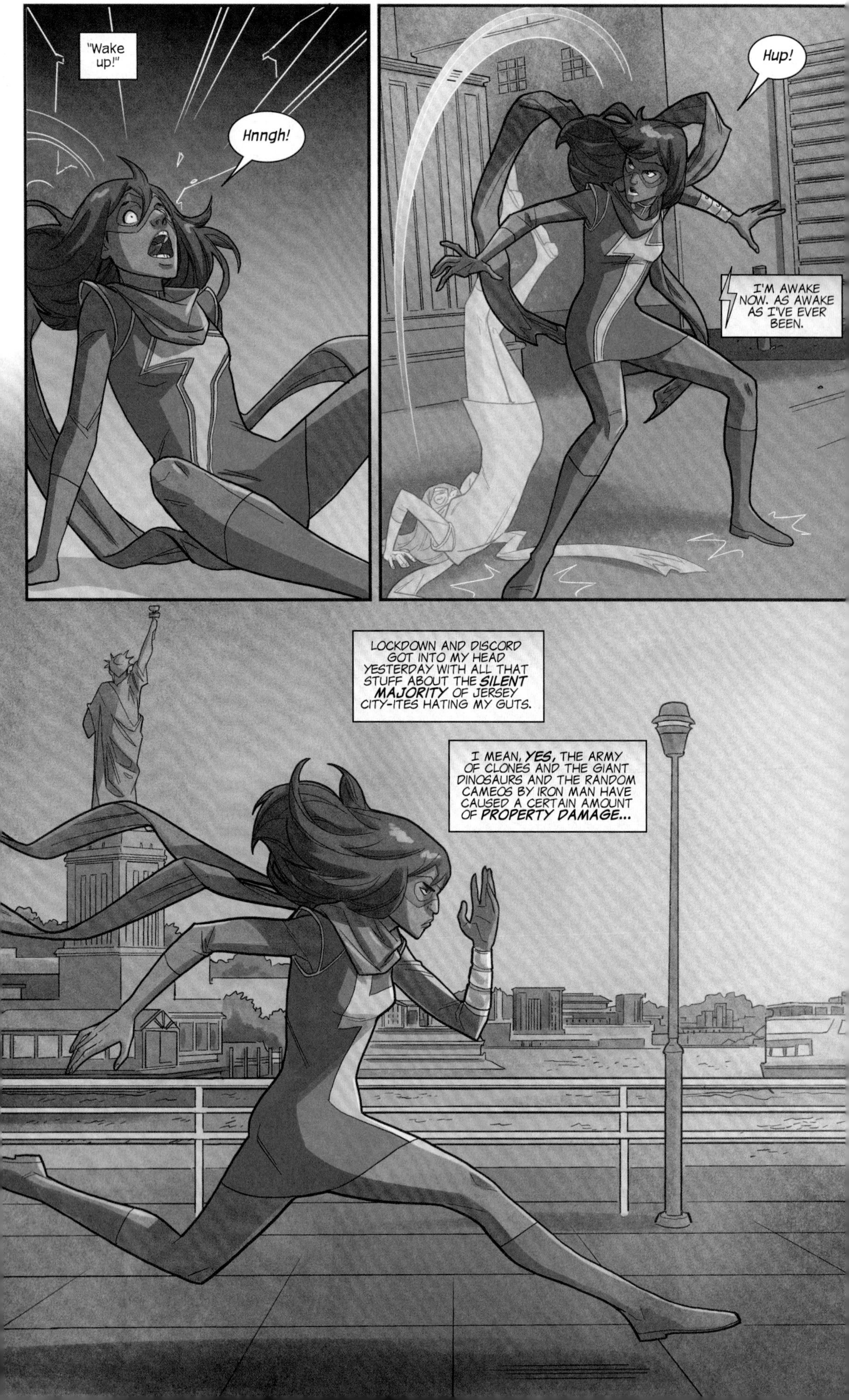
"Wake up!"
Hnngh!
Hup!
I'M AWAKE NOW. AS AWAKE AS I'VE EVER BEEN.
LOCKDOWN AND DISCORD GOT INTO MY HEAD YESTERDAY WITH ALL THAT STUFF ABOUT THE SILENT MAJORITY OF JERSEY CITY-ITES HATING MY GUTS.
I MEAN, YES, THE ARMY OF CLONES AND THE GIANT DINOSAURS AND THE RANDOM CAMEOS BY IRON MAN HAVE CAUSED A CERTAIN AMOUNT OF PROPERTY DAMAGE...

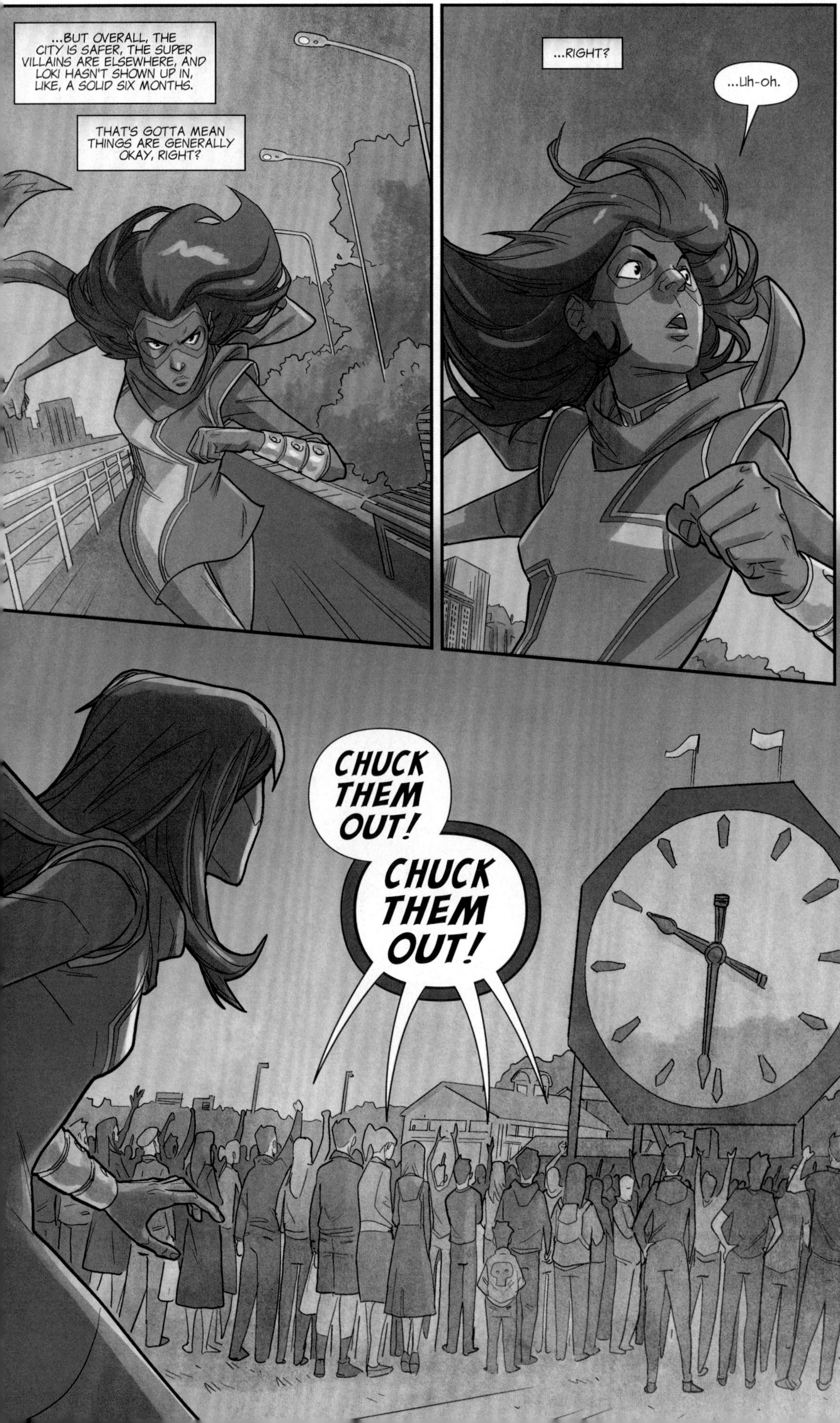
...BUT OVERALL, THE CITY IS SAFER, THE SUPER VILLAINS ARE ELSEWHERE, AND LOKI HASN'T SHOWN UP IN, LIKE, A SOLID SIX MONTHS.
THAT'S GOTTA MEAN THINGS ARE GENERALLY OKAY, RIGHT?
...RIGHT?
...Uh-oh.
CHUCK THEM OUT!
CHUCK THEM OUT!

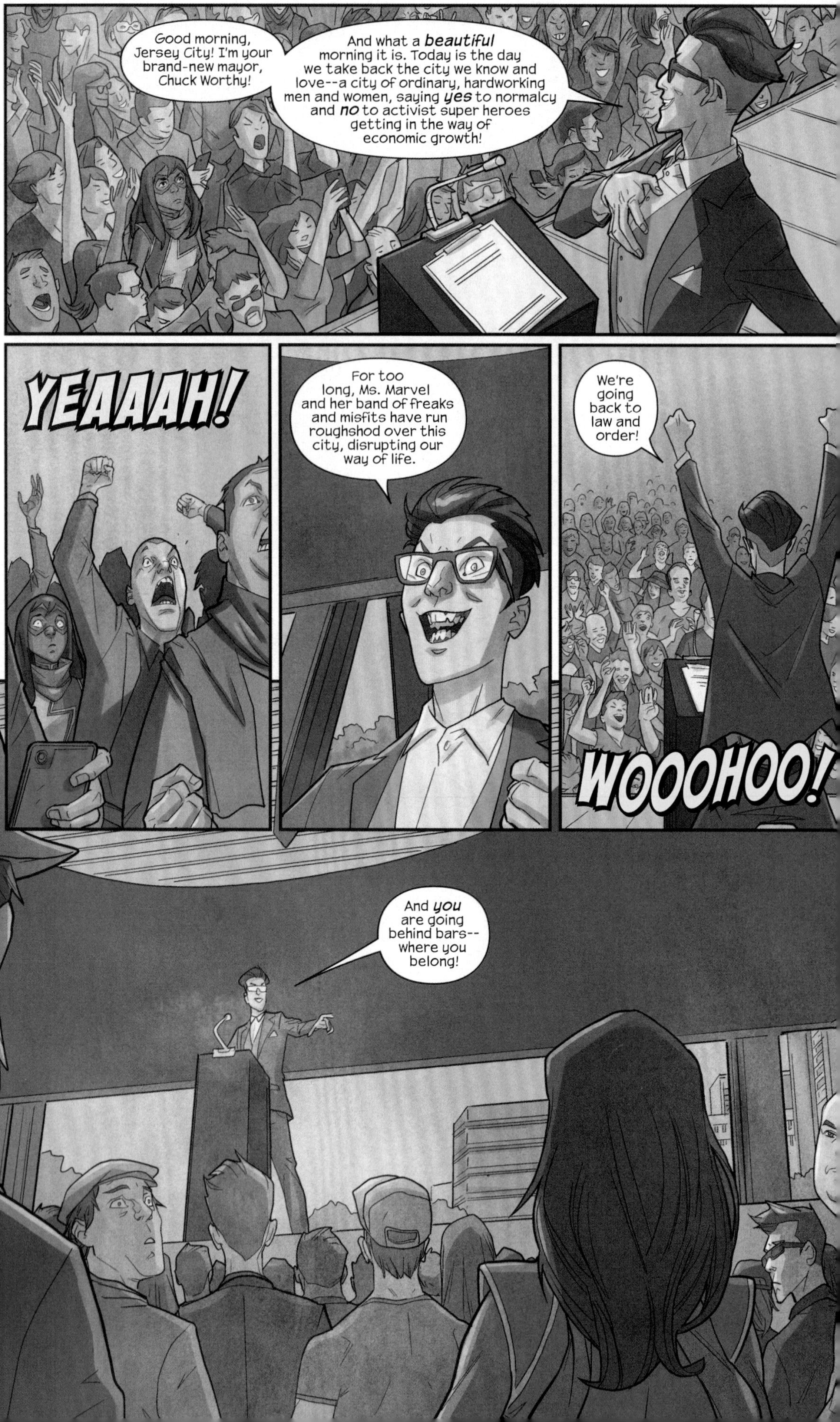
Good morning, Jersey City! I'm your brand-new mayor, Chuck Worthy!
And what a *beautiful* morning it is. Today is the day we take back the city we know and love--a city of ordinary, hardworking men and women, saying *yes* to normalcy and *no* to activist super heroes getting in the way of economic growth!
YEAAAH!
For too long, Ms. Marvel and her band of freaks and misfits have run roughshod over this city, disrupting our way of life.
We're going back to law and order!
WOOOHOO!
And *you* are going behind bars--where you belong!

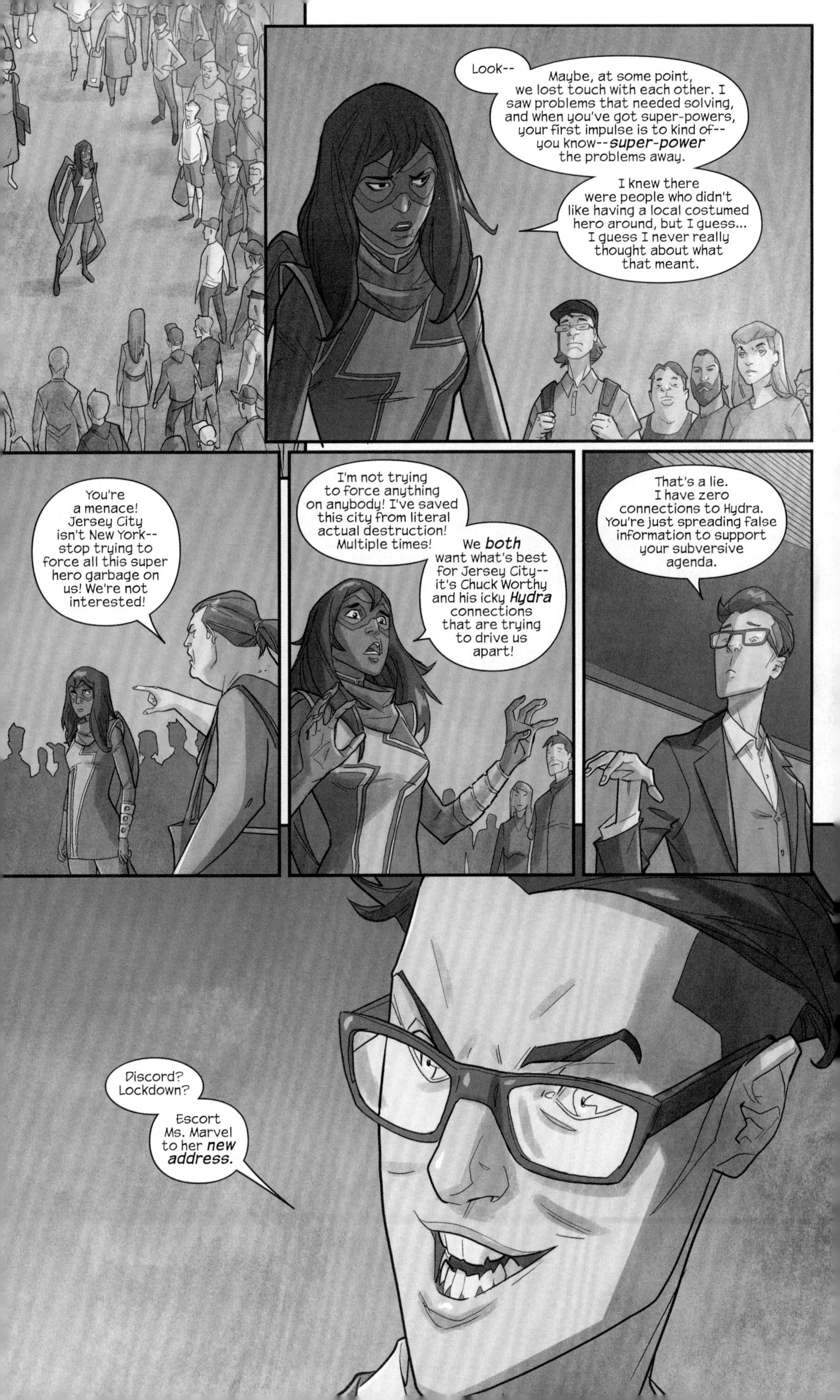
Look--
Maybe, at some point, we lost touch with each other. I saw problems that needed solving, and when you've got super-powers, your first impulse is to kind of-- you know--*super-power* the problems away.
I knew there were people who didn't like having a local costumed hero around, but I guess... I guess I never really thought about what that meant.
You're a menace! Jersey City isn't New York--stop trying to force all this super hero garbage on us! We're not interested!
I'm not trying to force anything on anybody! I've saved this city from literal actual destruction! Multiple times!
We *both* want what's best for Jersey City--it's Chuck Worthy and his icky *Hydra* connections that are trying to drive us apart!
That's a lie. I have zero connections to Hydra. You're just spreading false information to support your subversive agenda.
Discord? Lockdown?
Escort Ms. Marvel to her *new address.*

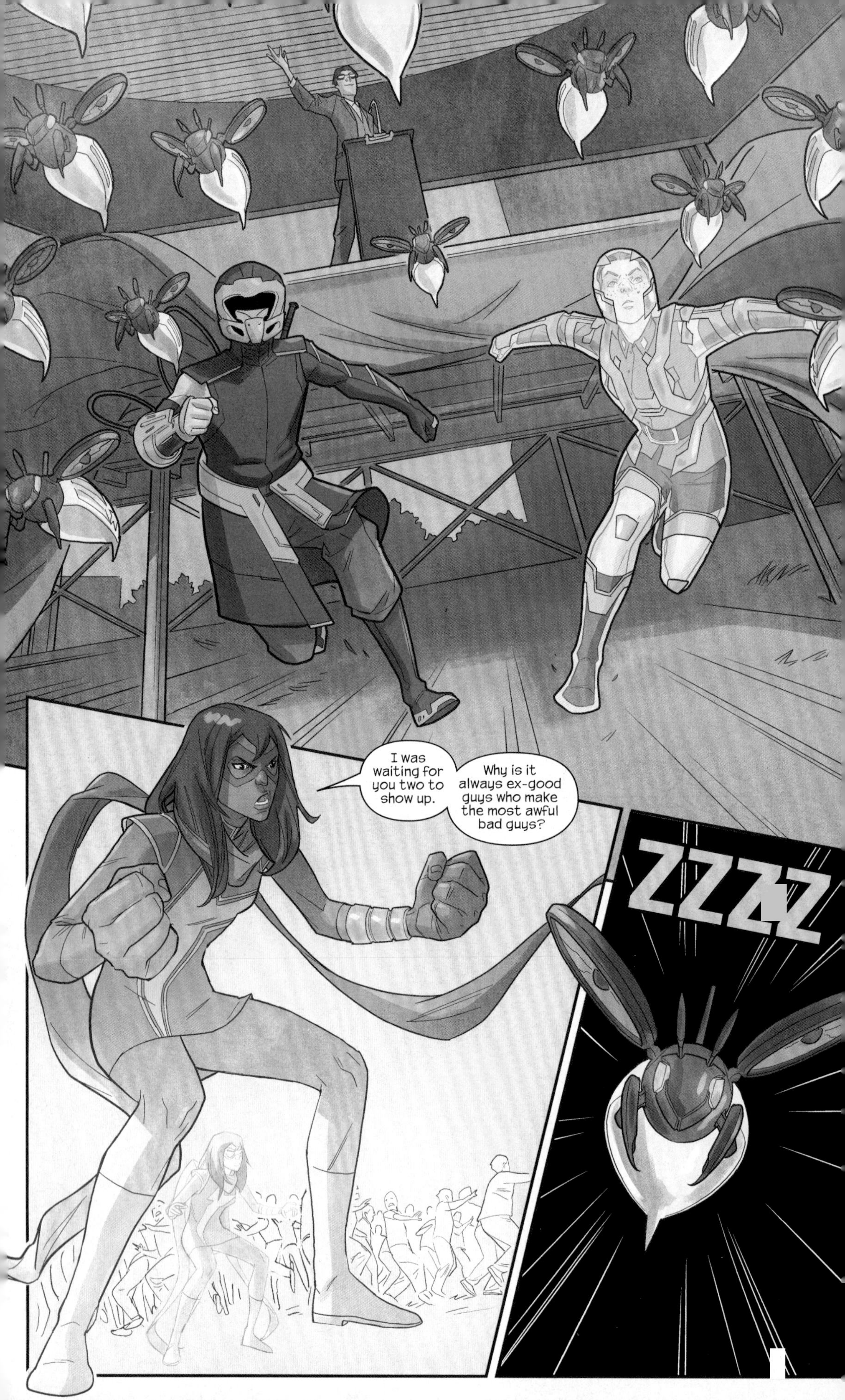
I was waiting for you two to show up.
Why is it always ex-good guys who make the most awful bad guys?
ZZZZ

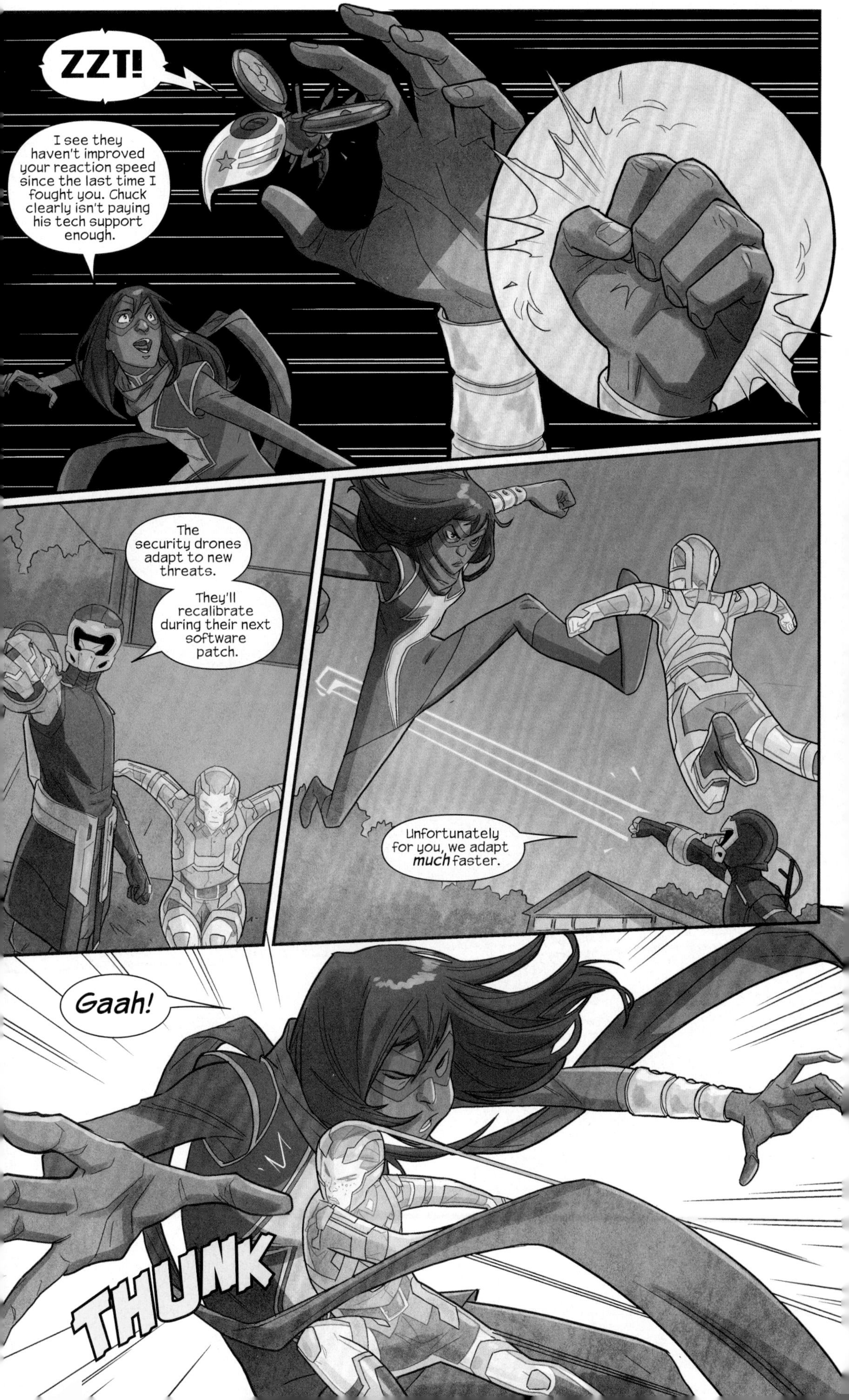
ZZT!
I see they haven't improved your reaction speed since the last time I fought you. Chuck clearly isn't paying his tech support enough.
The security drones adapt to new threats.
They'll recalibrate during their next software patch.
Unfortunately for you, we adapt *much* faster.
Gaah!
THUNK

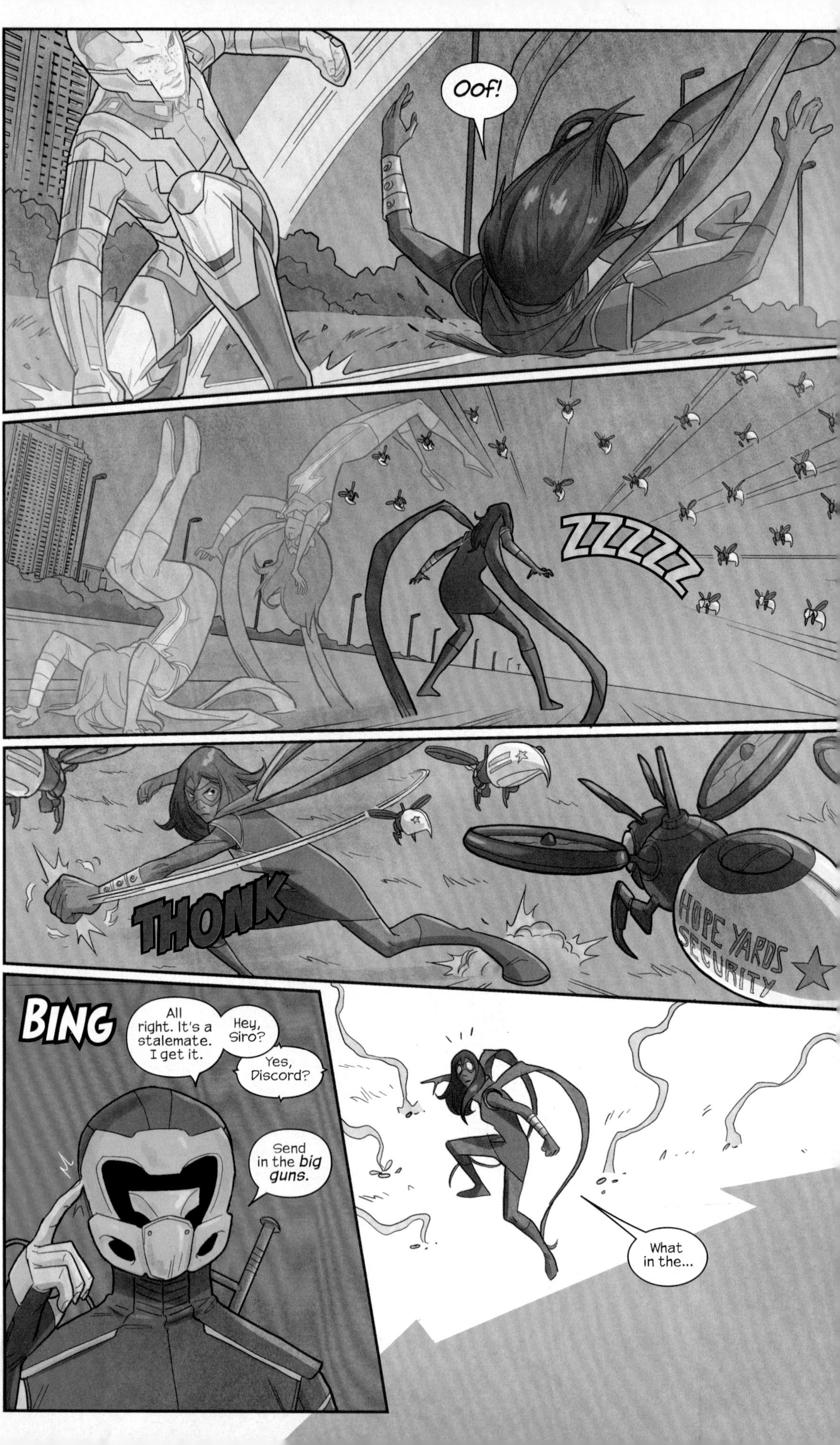
Oof!
ZZZZZZ
THONK
HOPE YARDS SECURITY
BING
All right. It's a stalemate. I get it.
Hey, Siro?
Yes, Discord?
Send in the *big guns.*
What in the...

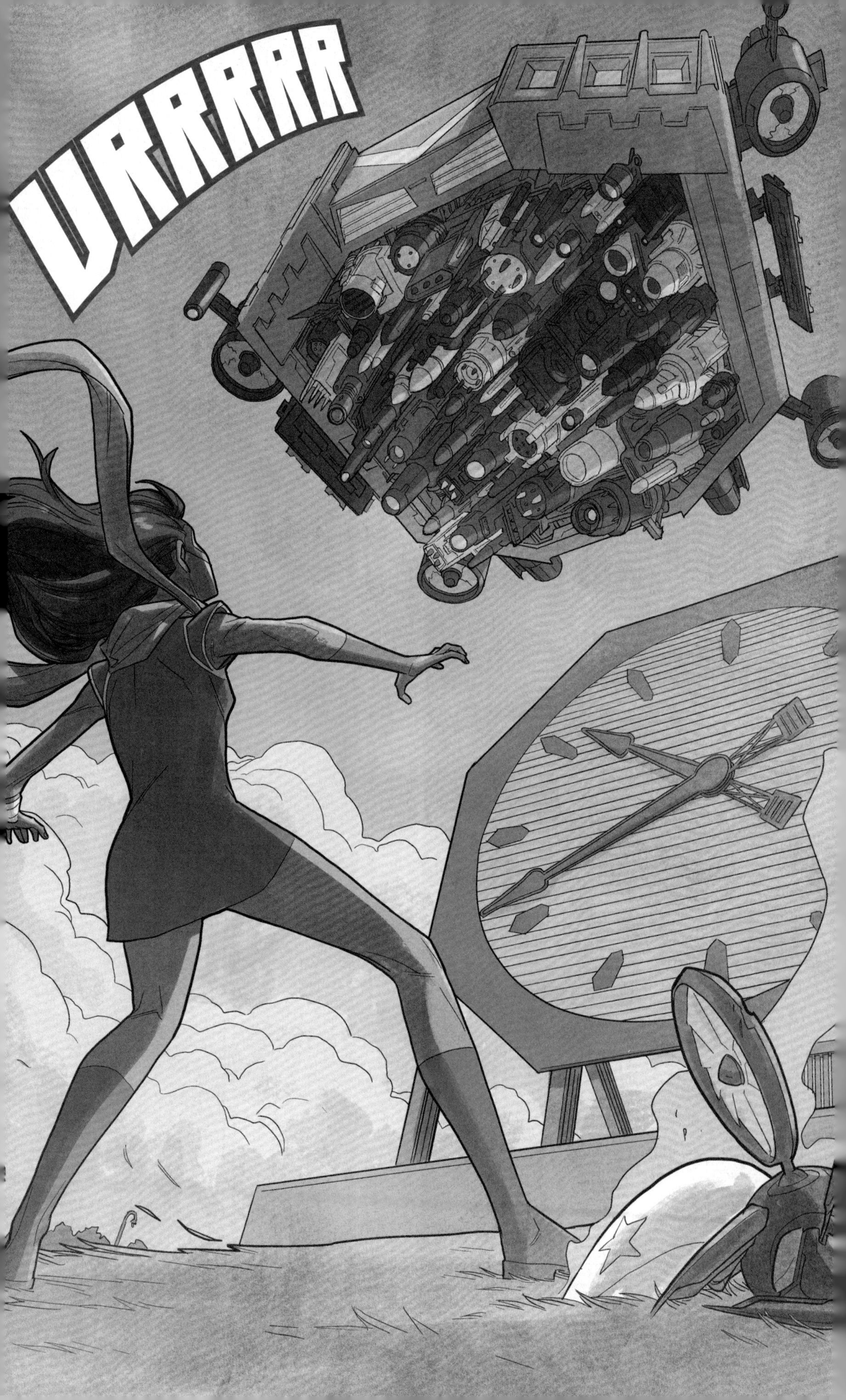
URRRRR

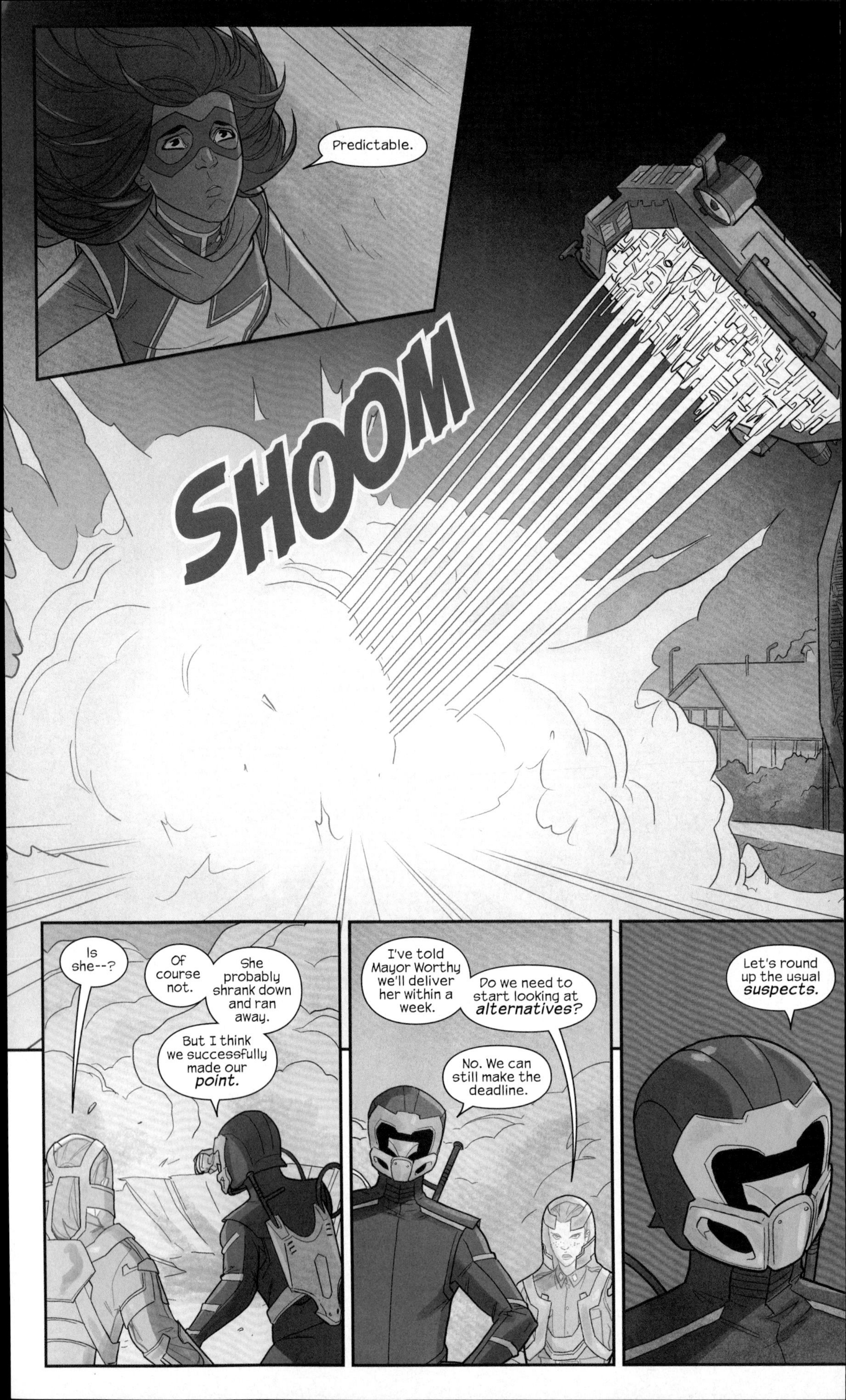
Predictable.
SHOOM
Is she--?
Of course not.
She probably shrank down and ran away.
But I think we successfully made our *point.*
I've told Mayor Worthy we'll deliver her within a week.
Do we need to start looking at *alternatives?*
No. We can still make the deadline.
Let's round up the usual *suspects.*

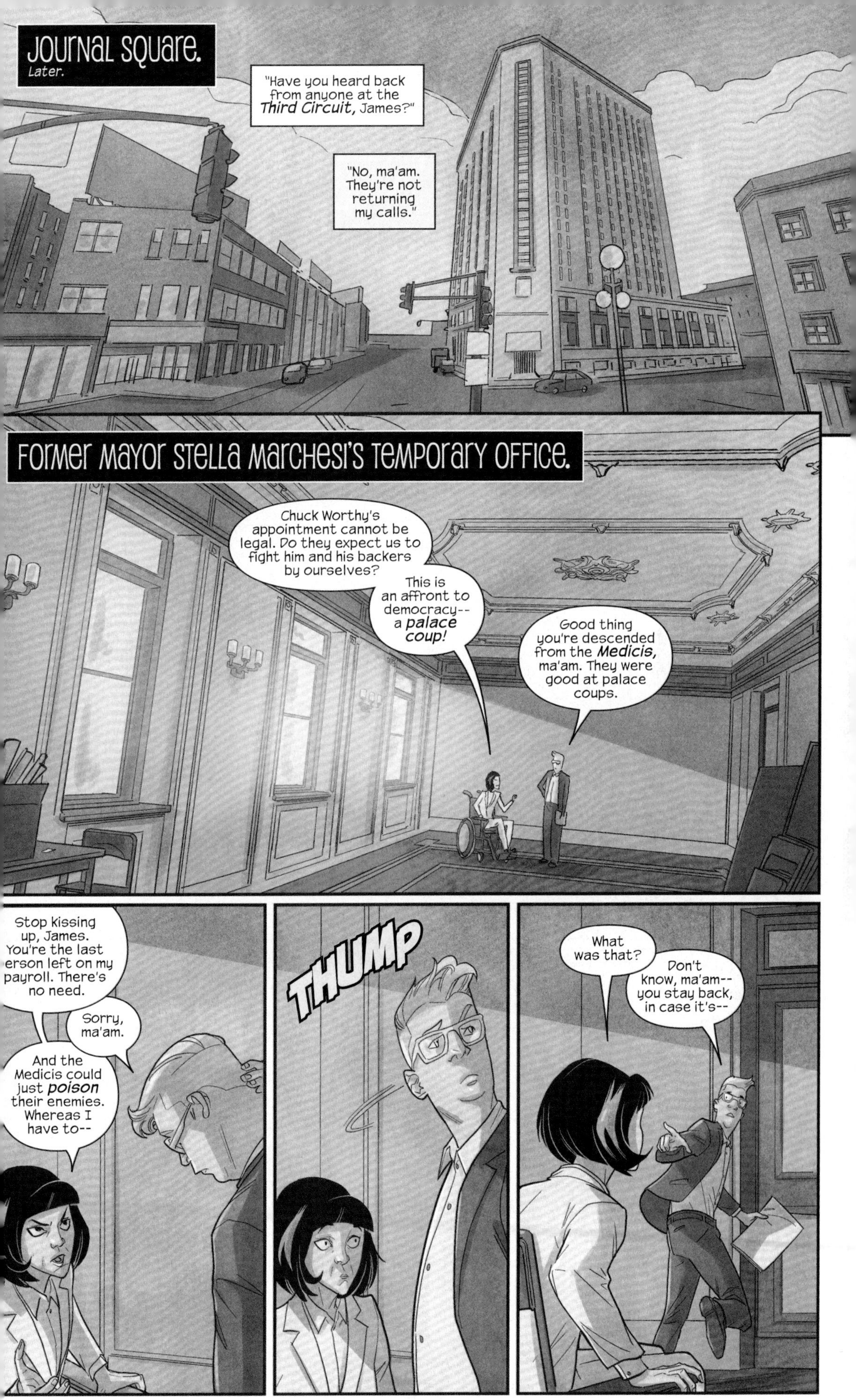
JOURNAL SQUARE.
Later.
"Have you heard back from anyone at the Third Circuit, James?"
"No, ma'am. They're not returning my calls."
FORMER MAYOR STELLA MARCHESI'S TEMPORARY OFFICE.
Chuck Worthy's appointment cannot be legal. Do they expect us to fight him and his backers by ourselves?
This is an affront to democracy-- a palace coup!
Good thing you're descended from the Medicis, ma'am. They were good at palace coups.
Stop kissing up, James. You're the last erson left on my payroll. There's no need.
Sorry, ma'am.
And the Medicis could just poison their enemies. Whereas I have to--
THUMP
What was that?
Don't know, ma'am-- you stay back, in case it's--

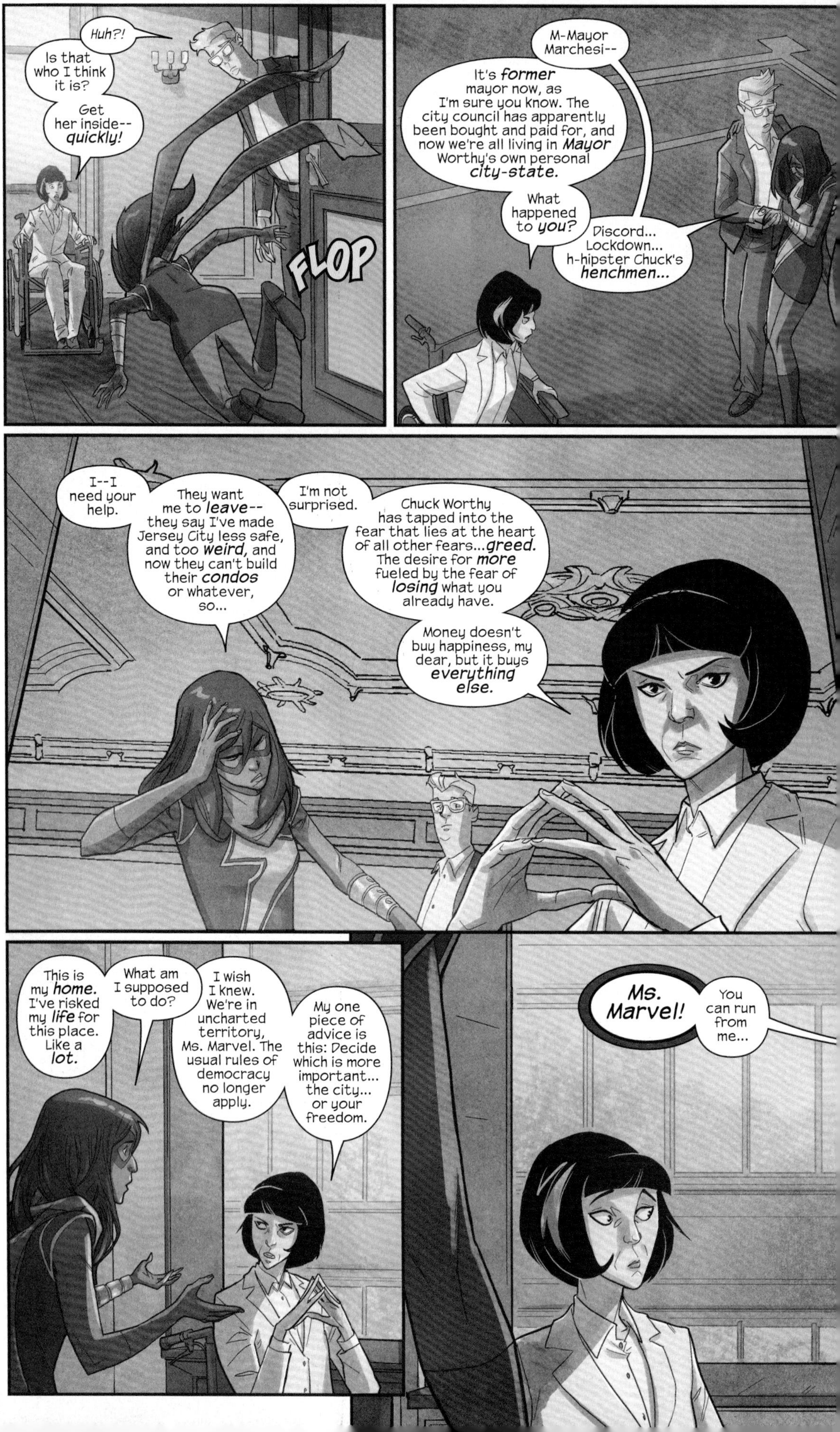
Huh?!
Is that who I think it is?
Get her inside-- quickly!
FLOP
M-Mayor Marchesi--
It's former mayor now, as I'm sure you know. The city council has apparently been bought and paid for, and now we're all living in Mayor Worthy's own personal city-state.
What happened to you?
Discord... Lockdown... h-hipster Chuck's henchmen...
I--I need your help.
They want me to leave-- they say I've made Jersey City less safe, and too weird, and now they can't build their condos or whatever, so...
I'm not surprised.
Chuck Worthy has tapped into the fear that lies at the heart of all other fears...greed. The desire for more fueled by the fear of losing what you already have.
Money doesn't buy happiness, my dear, but it buys everything else.
This is my home. I've risked my life for this place. Like a lot.
What am I supposed to do?
I wish I knew. We're in uncharted territory, Ms. Marvel. The usual rules of democracy no longer apply.
My one piece of advice is this: Decide which is more important... the city... or your freedom.
Ms. Marvel!
You can run from me...

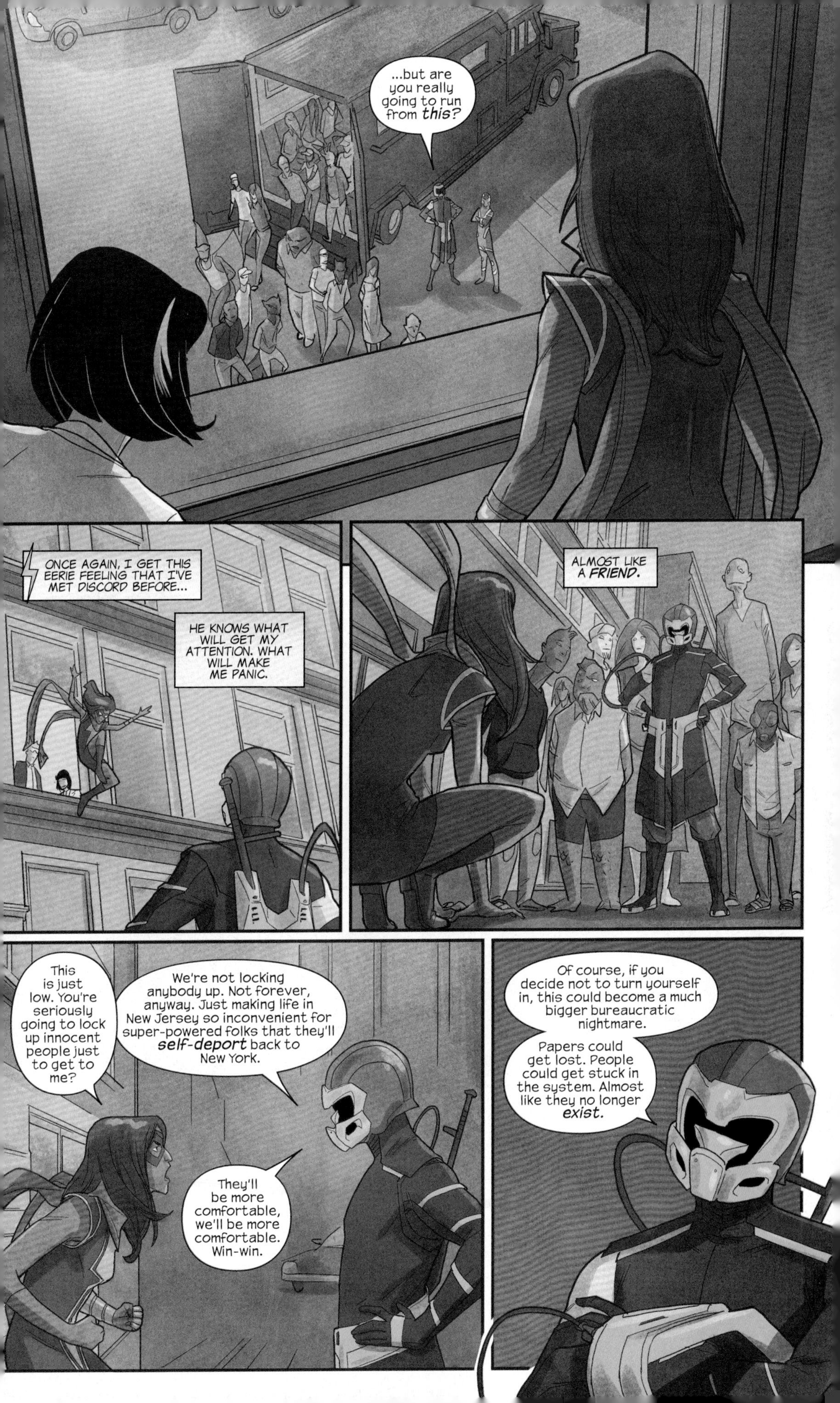

...but are you really going to run from *this?*
ONCE AGAIN, I GET THIS EERIE FEELING THAT I'VE MET DISCORD BEFORE...
HE KNOWS WHAT WILL GET MY ATTENTION. WHAT WILL MAKE ME PANIC.
ALMOST LIKE A *FRIEND.*
This is just low. You're seriously going to lock up innocent people just to get to me?
We're not locking anybody up. Not forever, anyway. Just making life in New Jersey so inconvenient for super-powered folks that they'll *self-deport* back to New York.
They'll be more comfortable, we'll be more comfortable. Win-win.
Of course, if you decide not to turn yourself in, this could become a much bigger bureaucratic nightmare.
Papers could get lost. People could get stuck in the system. Almost like they no longer *exist.*

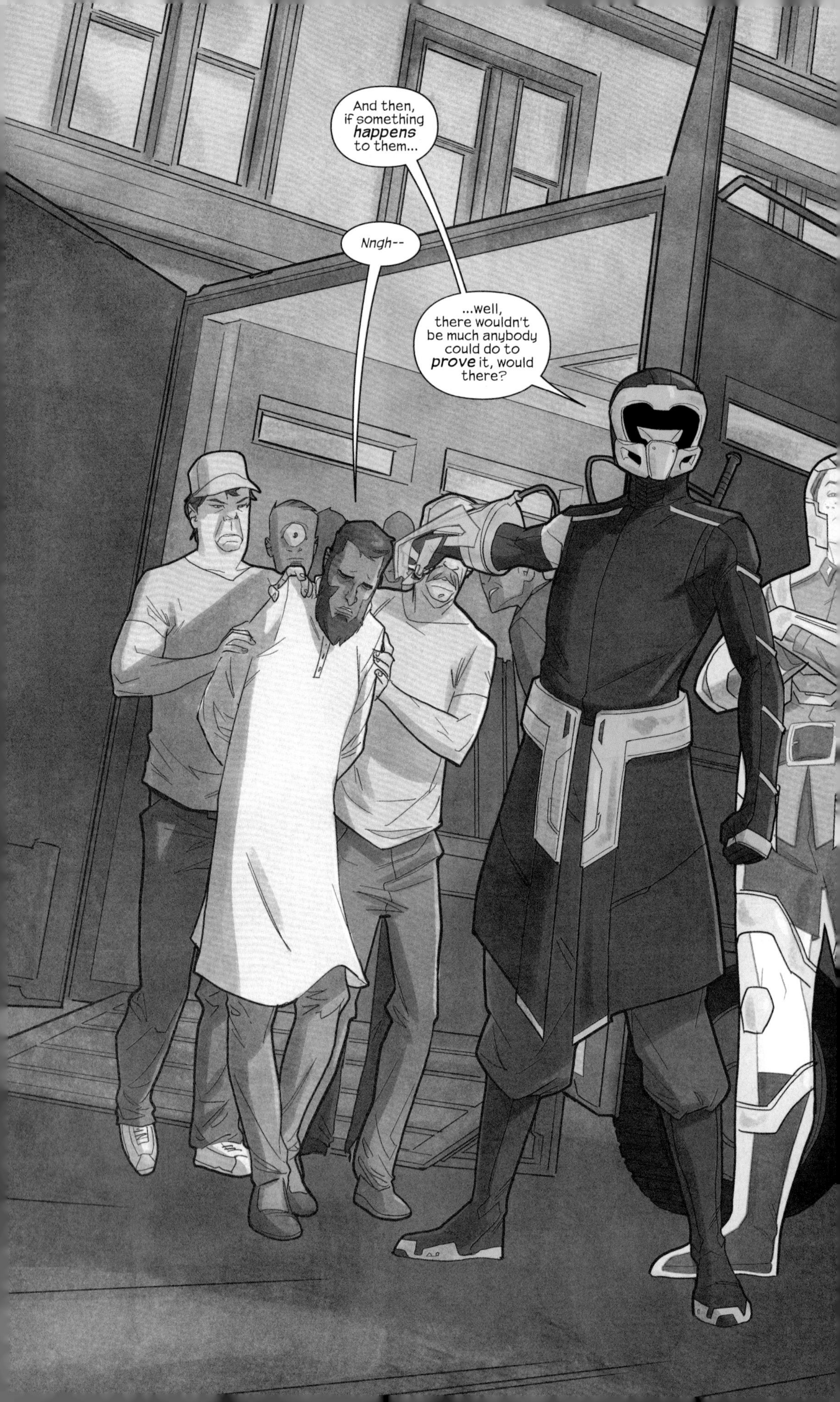
And then, if something happens to them...
Nngh--
...well, there wouldn't be much anybody could do to prove it, would there?

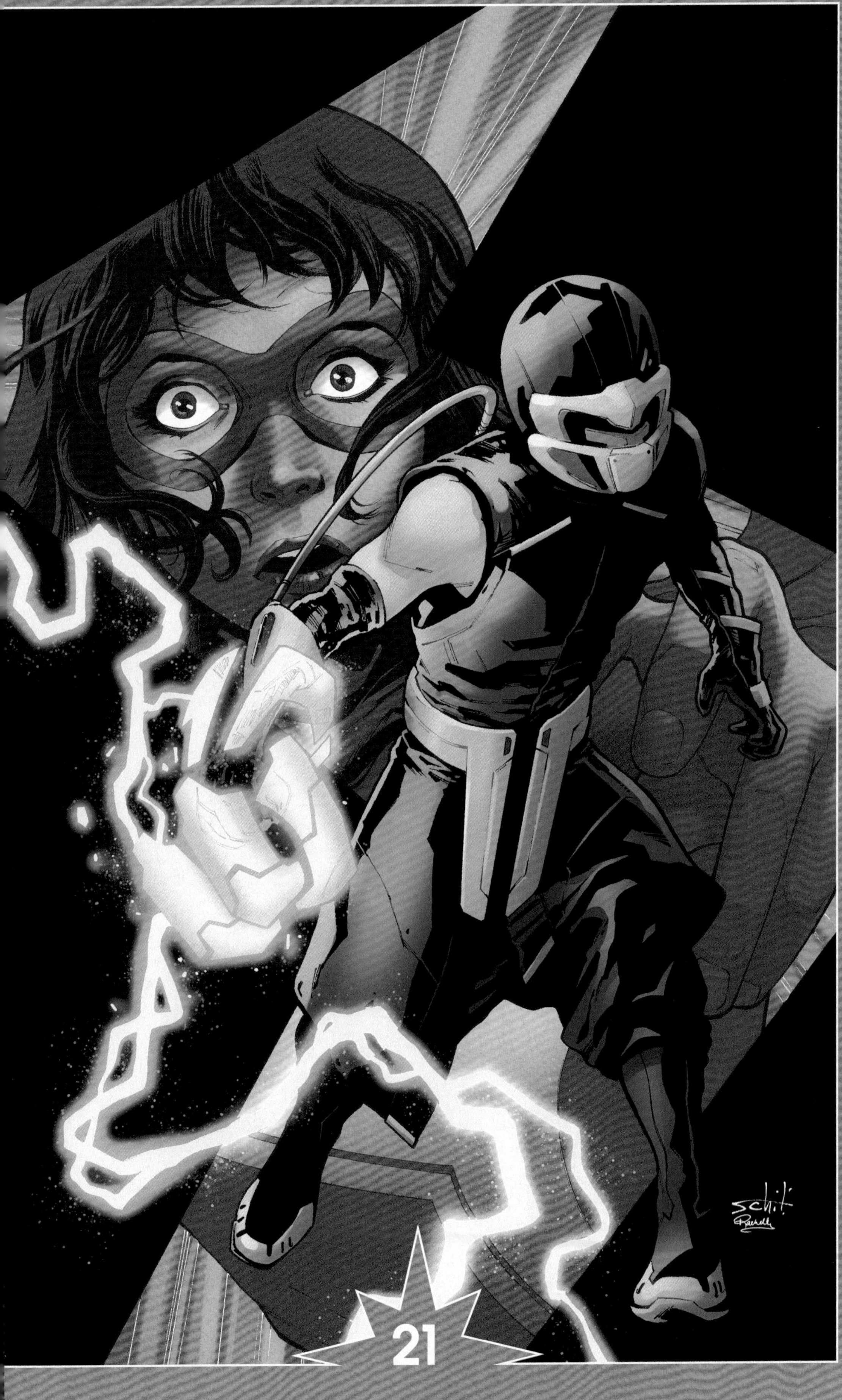
21

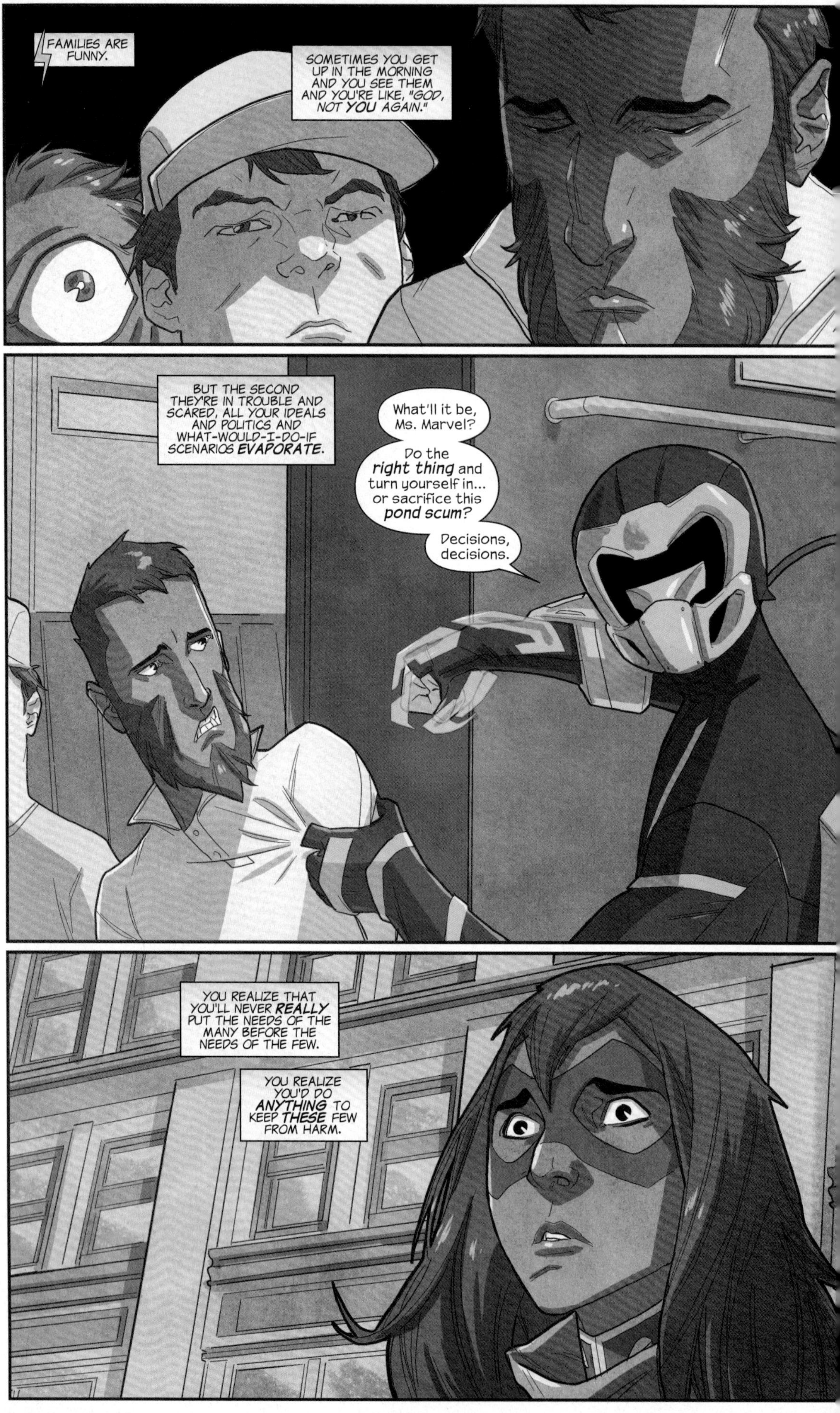
FAMILIES ARE FUNNY.
SOMETIMES YOU GET UP IN THE MORNING AND YOU SEE THEM AND YOU'RE LIKE, "GOD, NOT YOU AGAIN."
BUT THE SECOND THEY'RE IN TROUBLE AND SCARED, ALL YOUR IDEALS AND POLITICS AND WHAT-WOULD-I-DO-IF SCENARIOS EVAPORATE.
What'll it be, Ms. Marvel?
Do the right thing and turn yourself in... or sacrifice this pond scum?
Decisions, decisions.
YOU REALIZE THAT YOU'LL NEVER REALLY PUT THE NEEDS OF THE MANY BEFORE THE NEEDS OF THE FEW.
YOU REALIZE YOU'D DO ANYTHING TO KEEP THESE FEW FROM HARM.

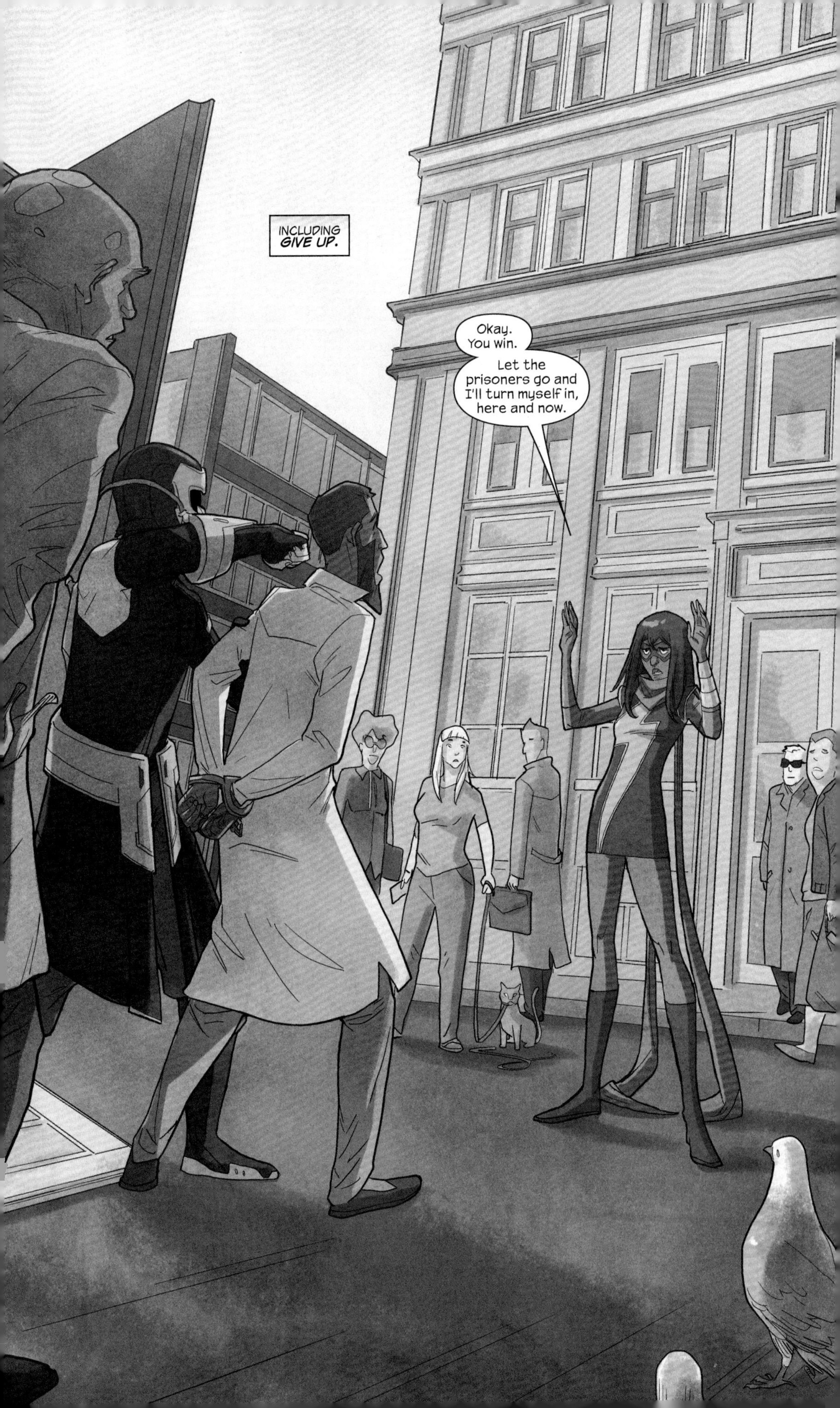
INCLUDING GIVE UP.
Okay. You win.
Let the prisoners go and I'll turn myself in, here and now.

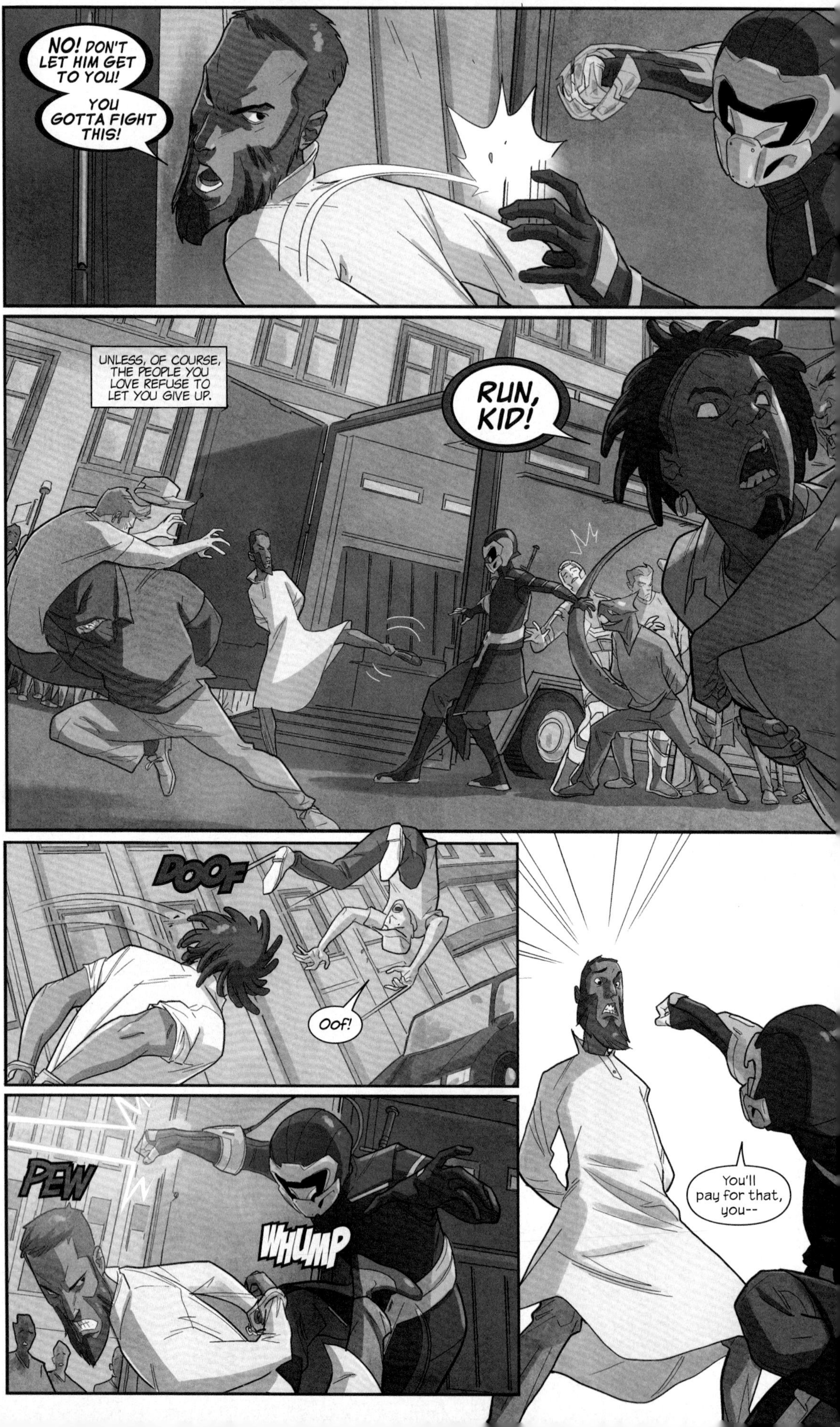
NO! DON'T LET HIM GET TO YOU!
YOU GOTTA FIGHT THIS!
UNLESS, OF COURSE, THE PEOPLE YOU LOVE REFUSE TO LET YOU GIVE UP.
RUN, KID!
DOOF
Oof!
PEW
WHUMP
You'll pay for that, you--

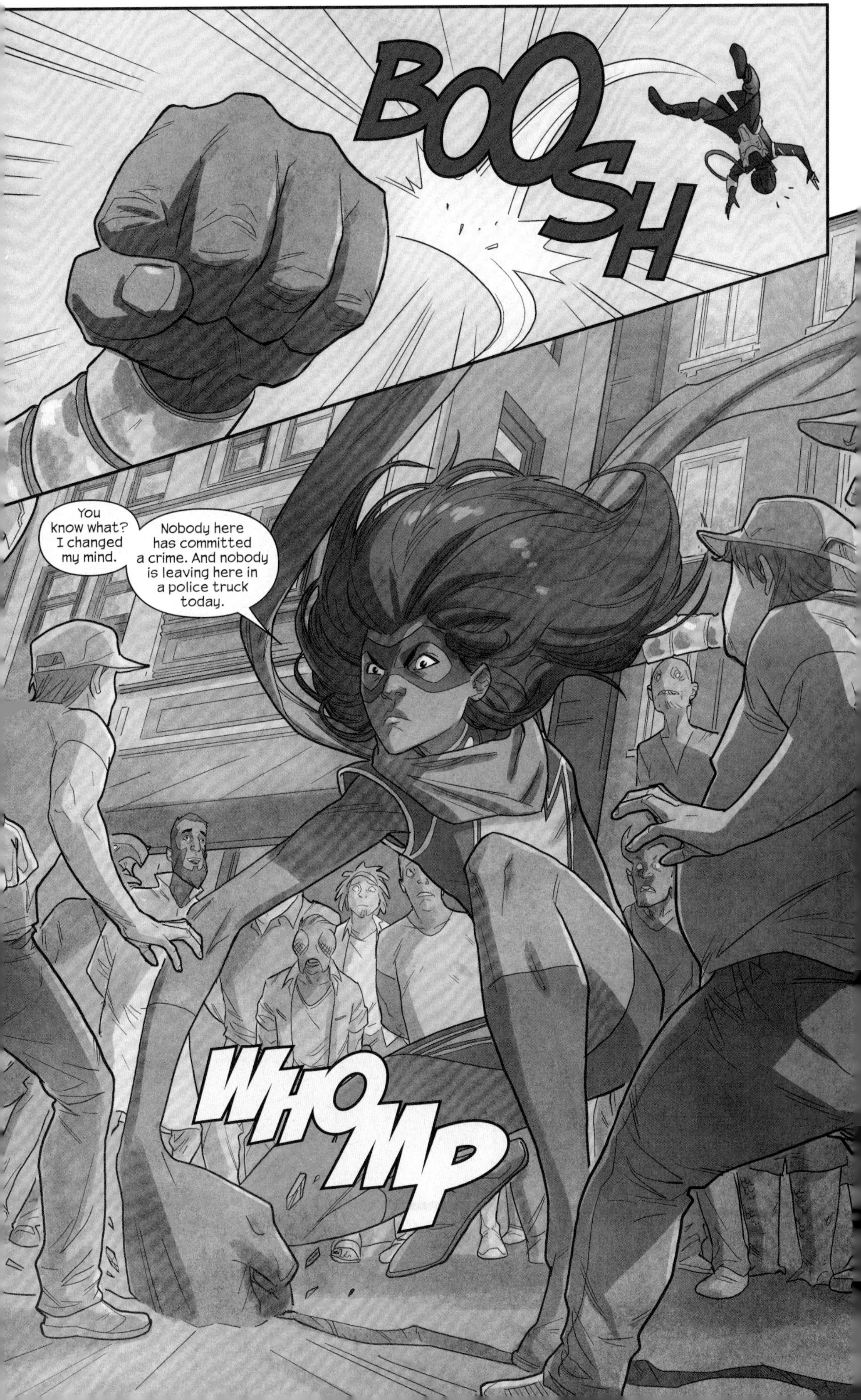
BOOOSH
You know what? I changed my mind.
Nobody here has committed a crime. And nobody is leaving here in a police truck today.
WHOMP

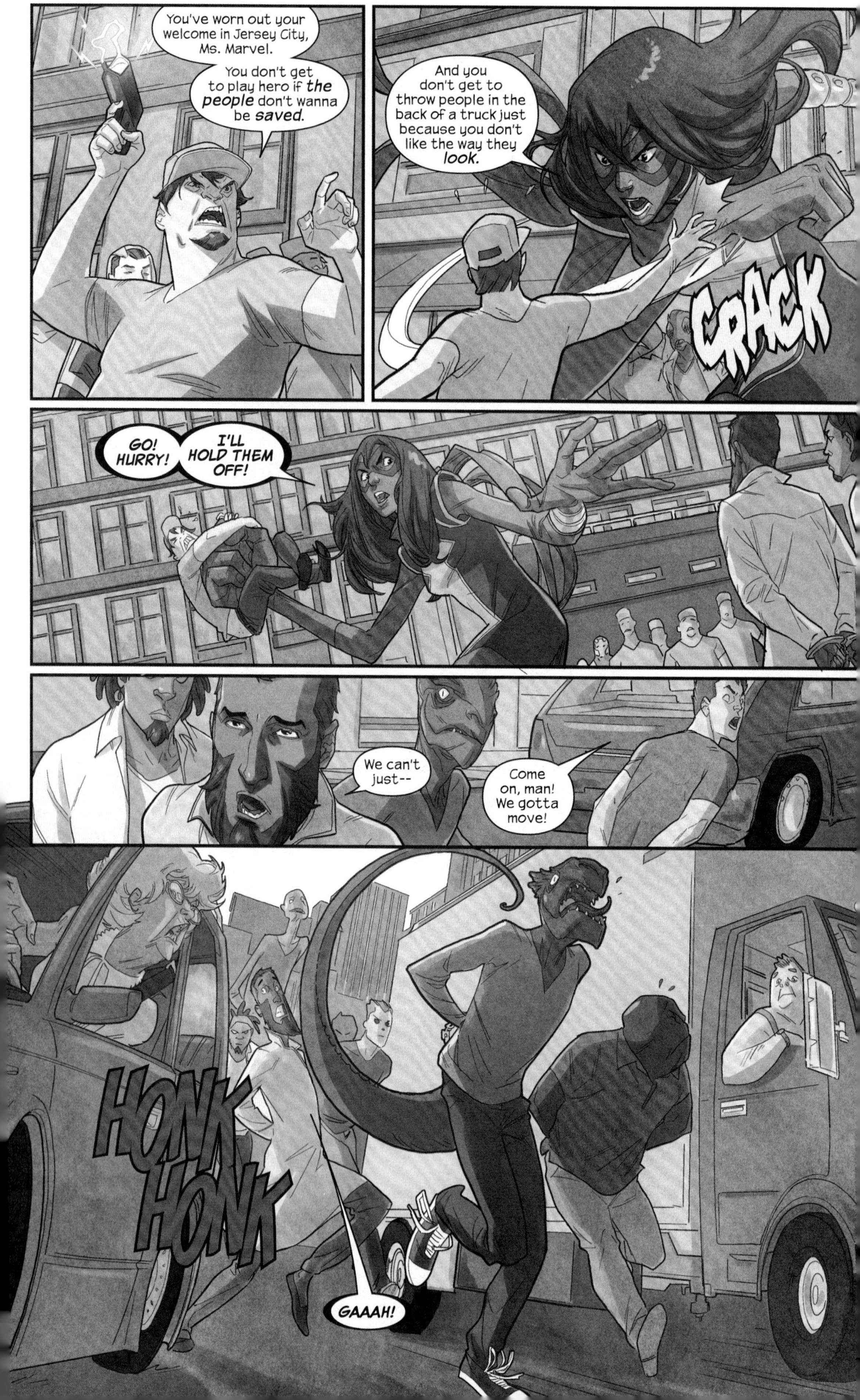

You've worn out your welcome in Jersey City, Ms. Marvel.
You don't get to play hero if *the people* don't wanna be *saved*.
And you don't get to throw people in the back of a truck just because you don't like the way they *look*.
CRACK
GO! HURRY!
I'LL HOLD THEM OFF!
We can't just--
Come on, man! We gotta move!
HONK HONK
GAAAH!

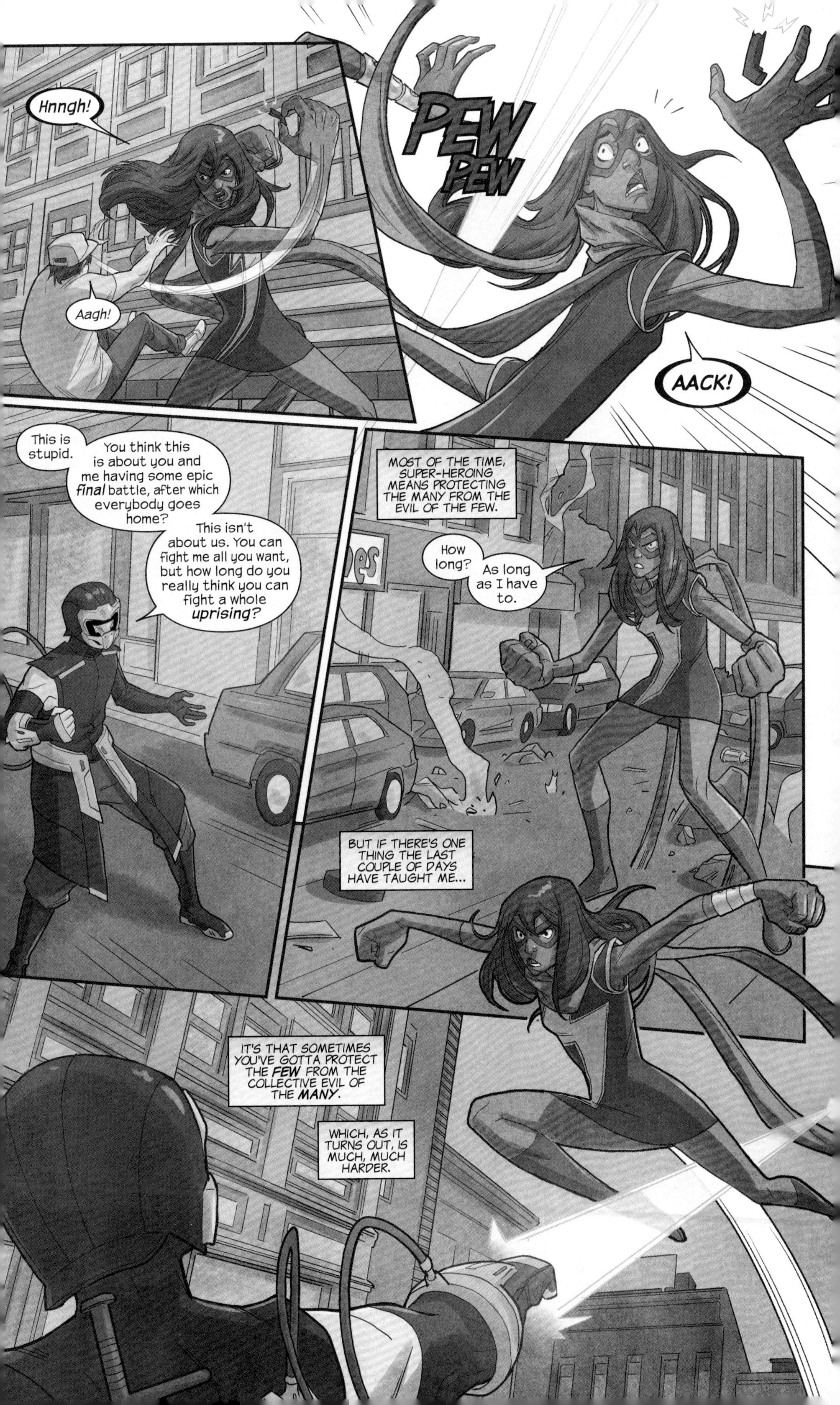
Hnngh!
Aagh!
PEW PEW
AACK!
This is stupid.
You think this is about you and me having some epic *final* battle, after which everybody goes home?
This isn't about us. You can fight me all you want, but how long do you really think you can fight a whole *uprising*?
MOST OF THE TIME, SUPER-HEROING MEANS PROTECTING THE MANY FROM THE EVIL OF THE FEW.
How long?
As long as I have to.
BUT IF THERE'S ONE THING THE LAST COUPLE OF DAYS HAVE TAUGHT ME...
IT'S THAT SOMETIMES YOU'VE GOTTA PROTECT THE *FEW* FROM THE COLLECTIVE EVIL OF THE *MANY*.
WHICH, AS IT TURNS OUT, IS MUCH, MUCH HARDER.

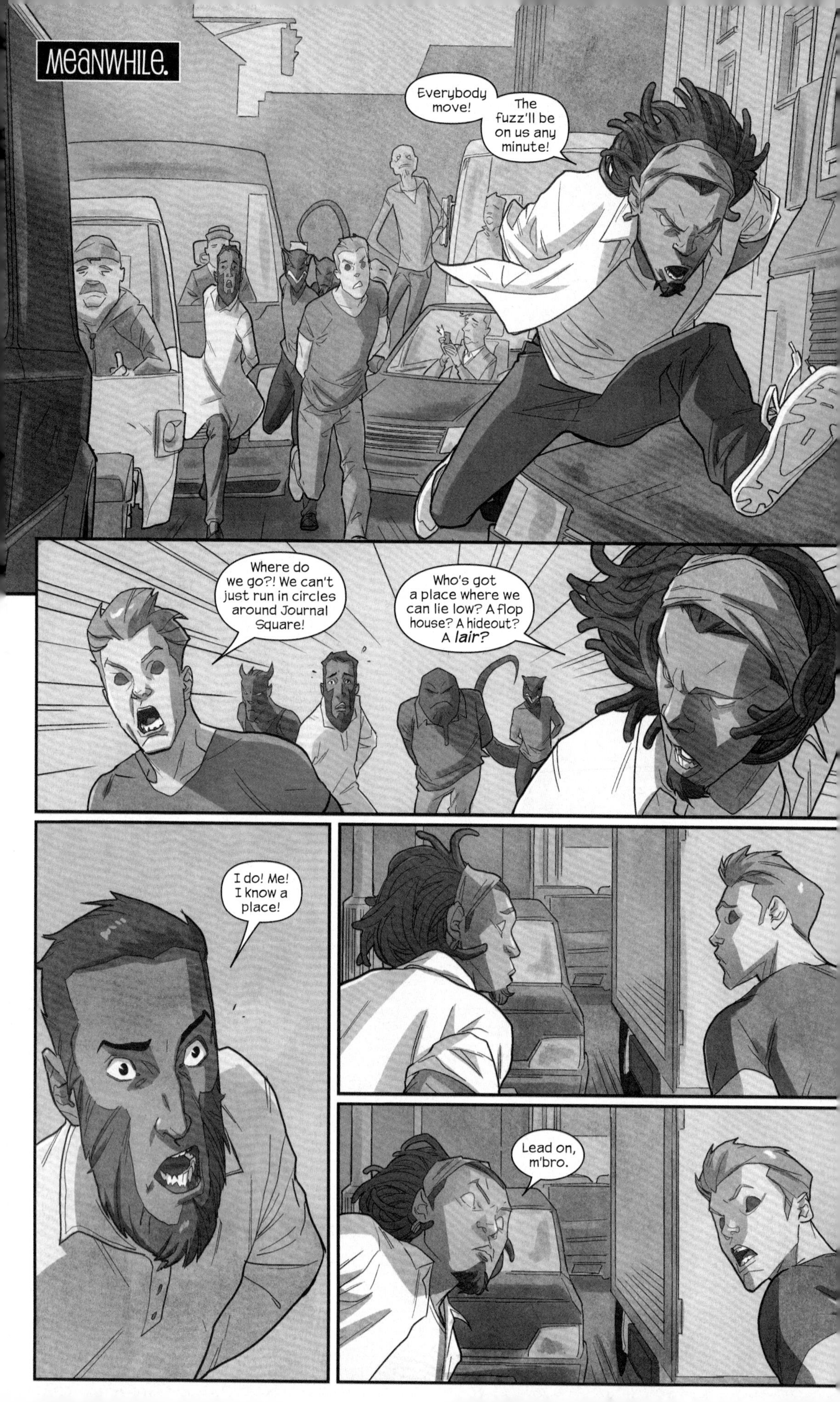
MEANWHILE.
Everybody move!
The fuzz'll be on us any minute!
Where do we go?! We can't just run in circles around Journal Square!
Who's got a place where we can lie low? A flop house? A hideout? A *lair?*
I do! Me! I know a place!
Lead on, m'bro.

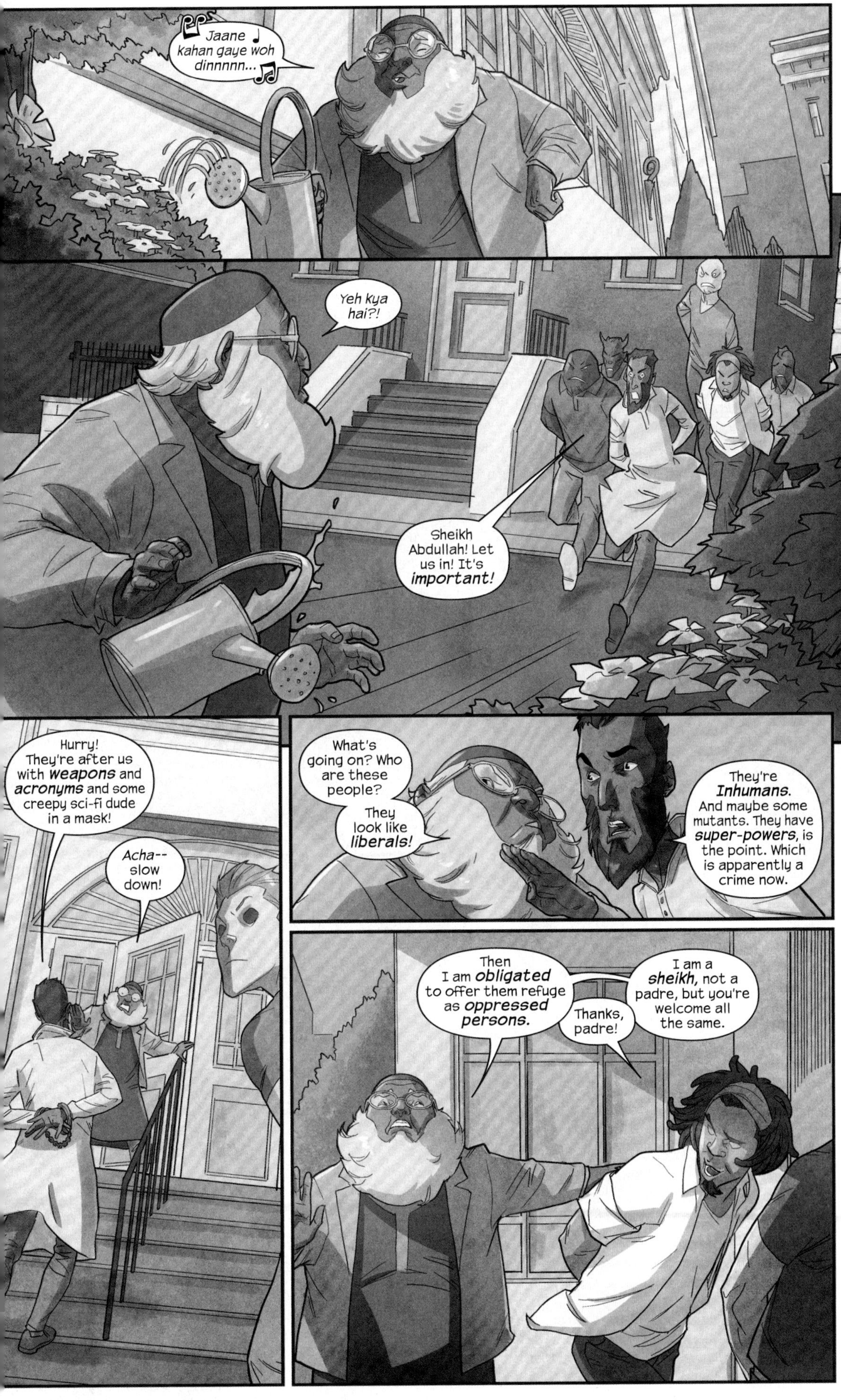
Jaane kahan gaye woh dinnnnn...
Yeh kya hai?!
Sheikh Abdullah! Let us in! It's important!
Hurry! They're after us with weapons and acronyms and some creepy sci-fi dude in a mask!
Acha-- slow down!
What's going on? Who are these people?
They look like liberals!
They're Inhumans. And maybe some mutants. They have super-powers, is the point. Which is apparently a crime now.
Then I am obligated to offer them refuge as oppressed persons.
Thanks, padre!
I am a sheikh, not a padre, but you're welcome all the same.

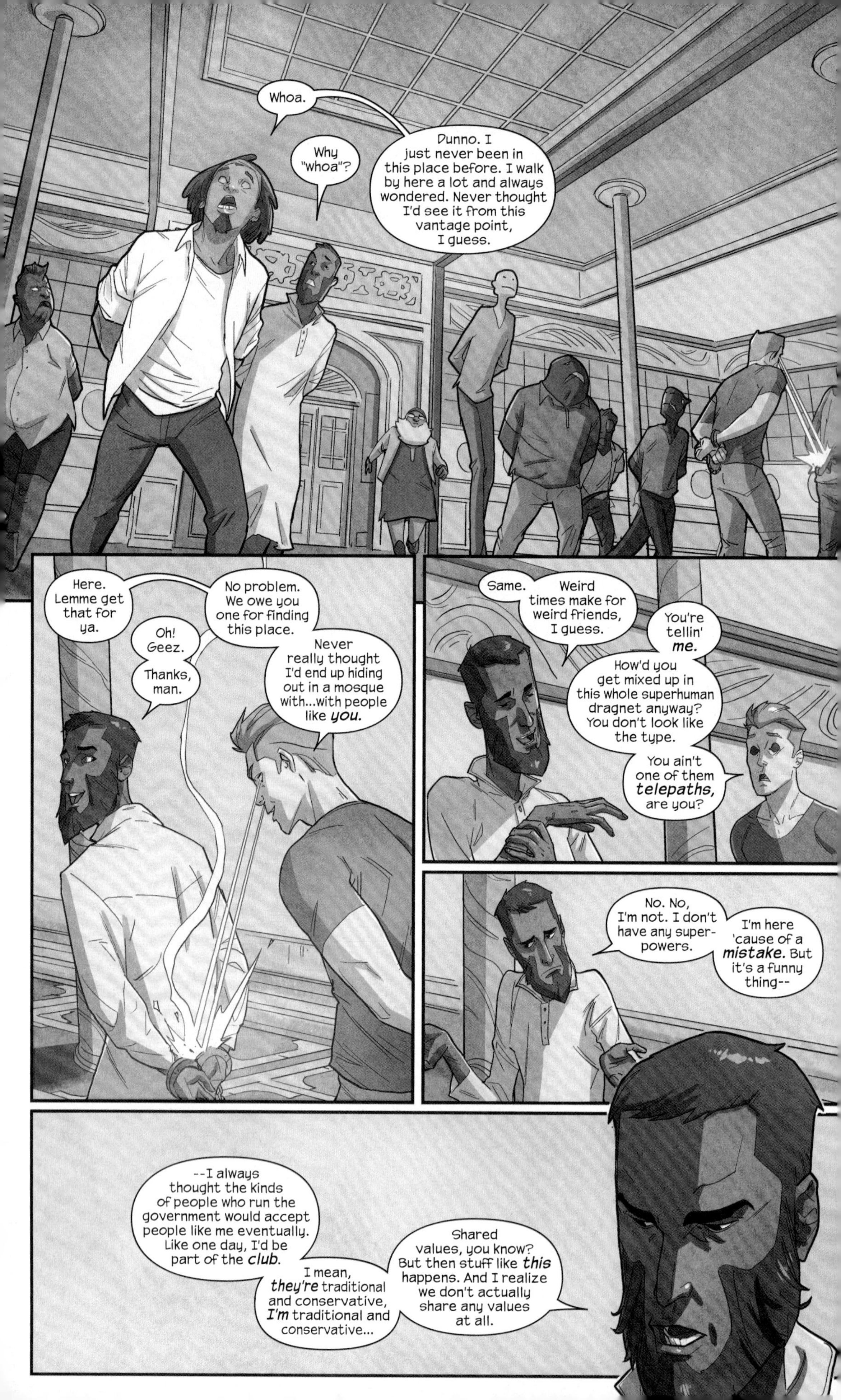
Whoa.
Why "whoa"?
Dunno. I just never been in this place before. I walk by here a lot and always wondered. Never thought I'd see it from this vantage point, I guess.
Here. Lemme get that for ya.
Oh! Geez.
Thanks, man.
No problem. We owe you one for finding this place.
Never really thought I'd end up hiding out in a mosque with...with people like *you.*
Same.
Weird times make for weird friends, I guess.
You're tellin' *me.*
How'd you get mixed up in this whole superhuman dragnet anyway? You don't look like the type.
You ain't one of them *telepaths,* are you?
No. No, I'm not. I don't have any super-powers.
I'm here 'cause of a *mistake.* But it's a funny thing--
--I always thought the kinds of people who run the government would accept people like me eventually. Like one day, I'd be part of the *club.*
I mean, *they're* traditional and conservative, *I'm* traditional and conservative...
Shared values, you know? But then stuff like *this* happens. And I realize we don't actually share any values at all.

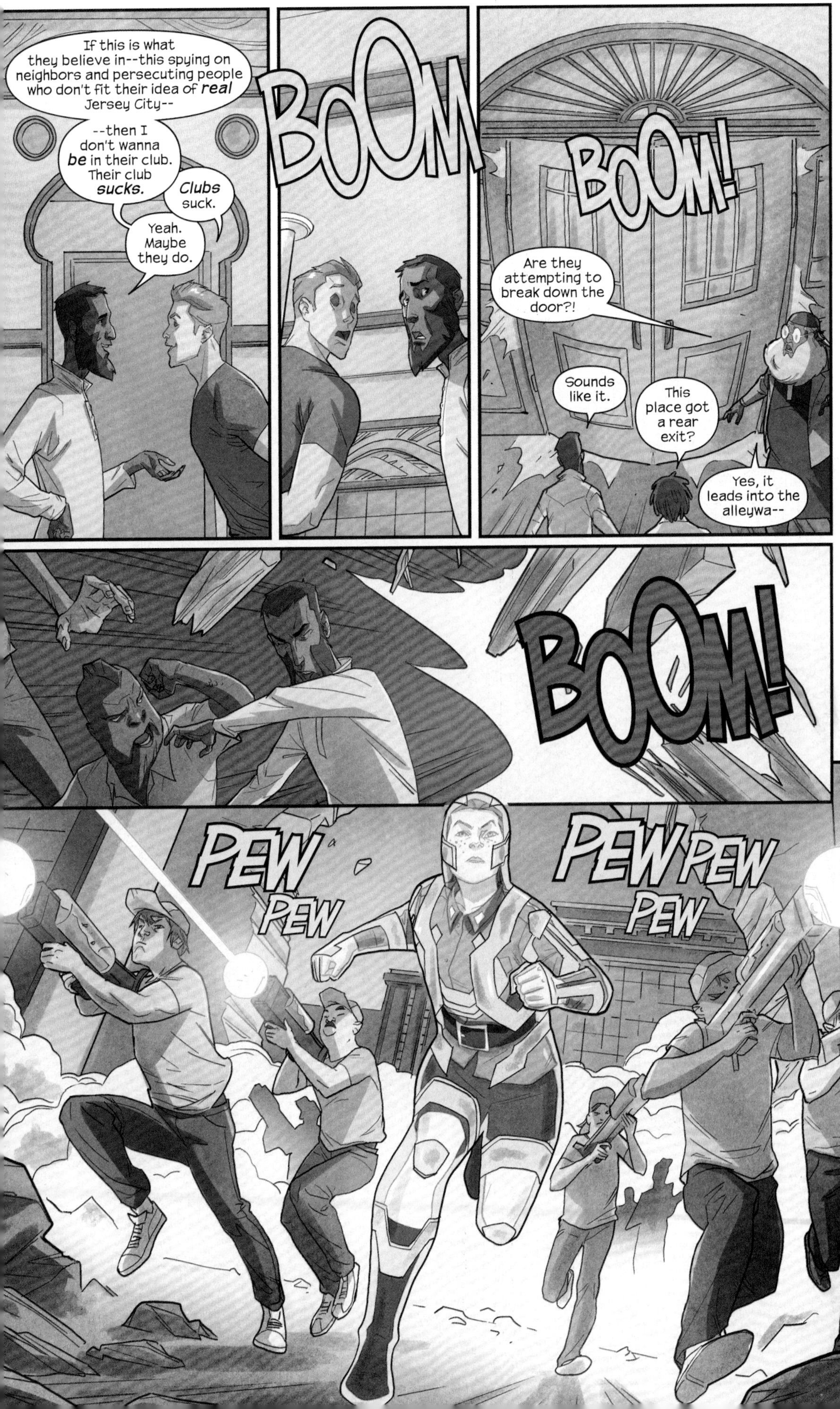
If this is what they believe in--this spying on neighbors and persecuting people who don't fit their idea of *real* Jersey City--
--then I don't wanna *be* in their club. Their club *sucks.*
Clubs suck.
Yeah. Maybe they do.
BOOM
BOOM!
Are they attempting to break down the door?!
Sounds like it.
This place got a rear exit?
Yes, it leads into the alleywa--
BOOM!
PEW PEW
PEW PEW PEW PEW

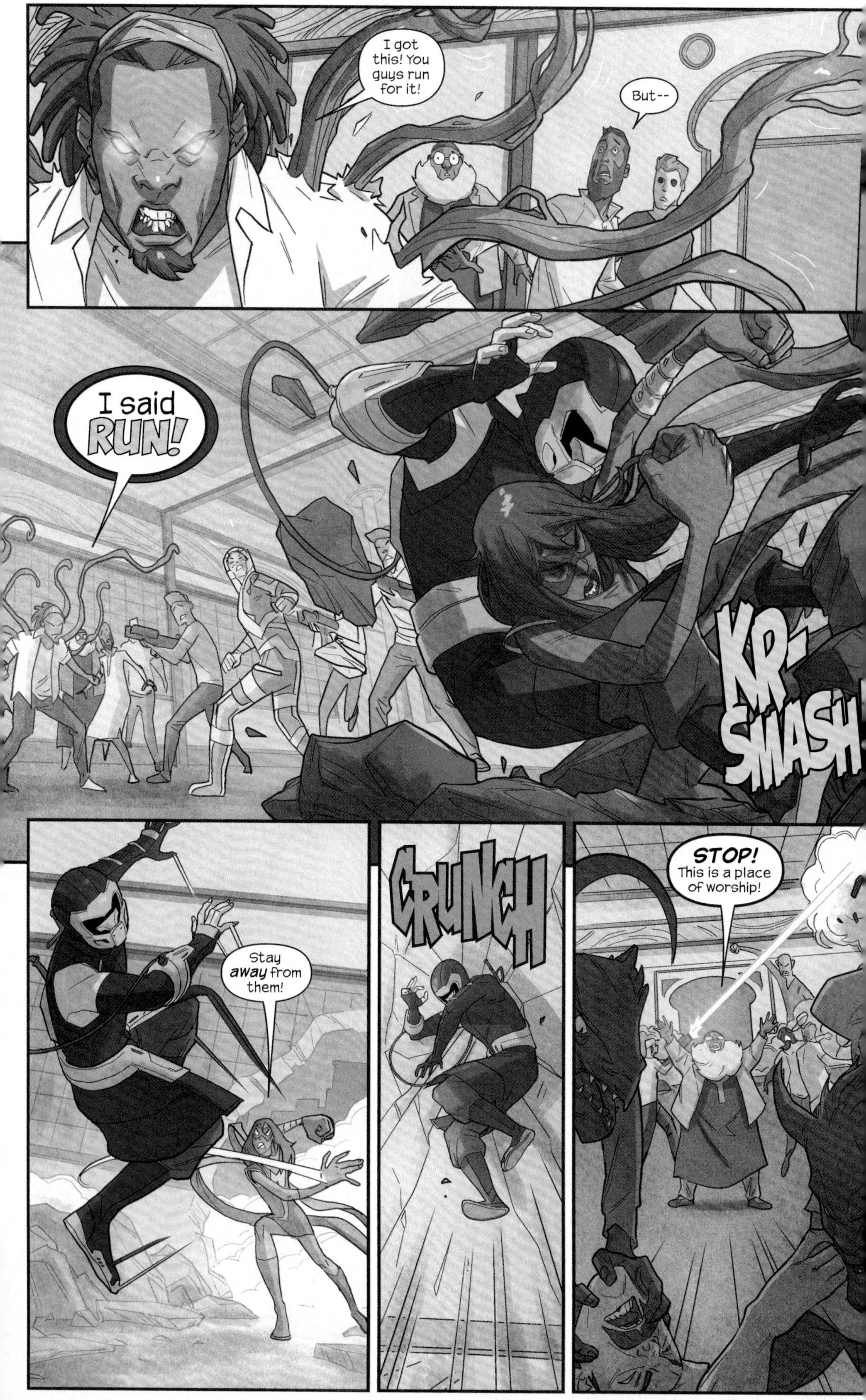

I got this! You guys run for it!
But--
I said RUN!
KR-SMASH
Stay away from them!
CRUNCH
STOP! This is a place of worship!

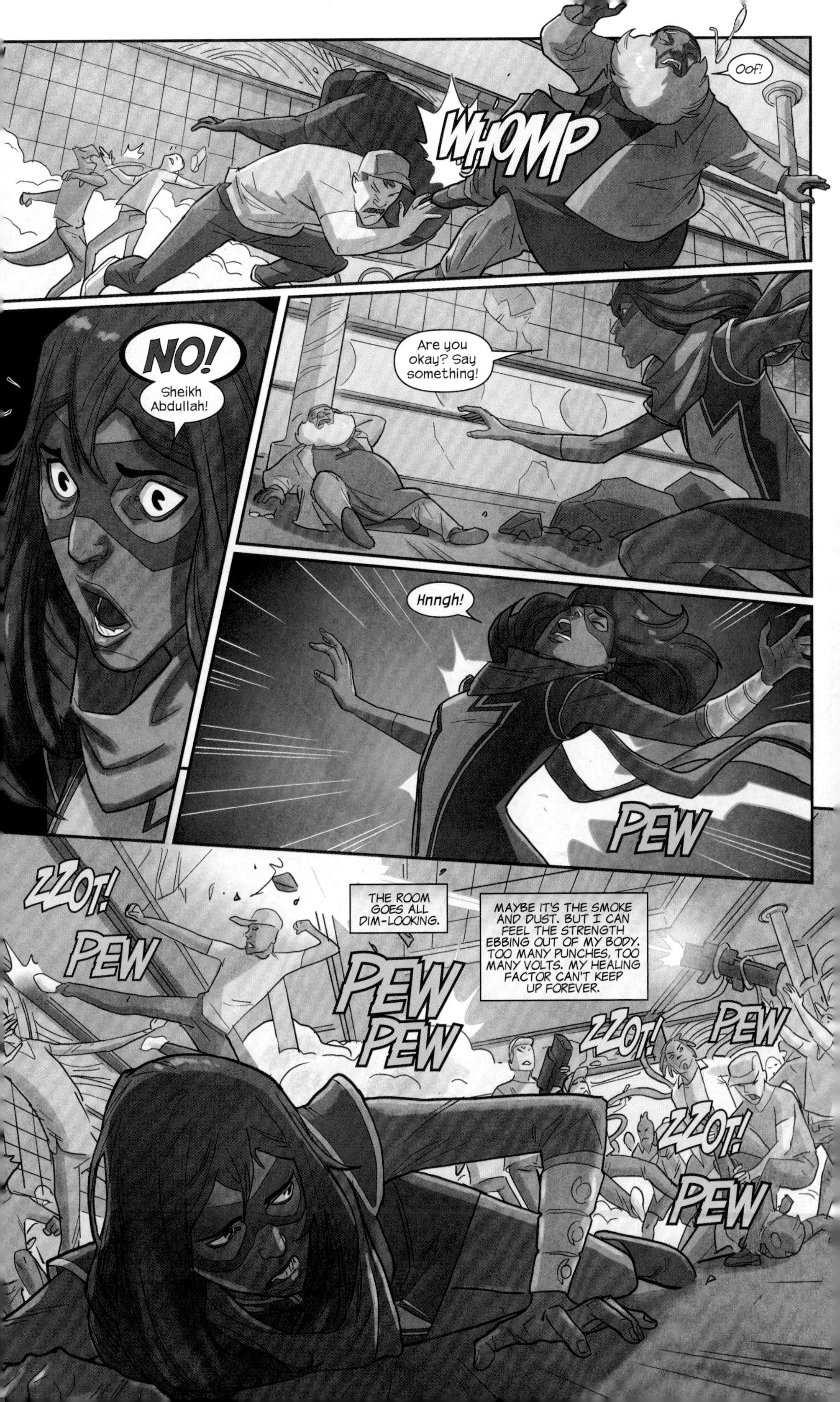

Oof!
WHOMP
NO!
Sheikh Abdullah!
Are you okay? Say something!
Hnngh!
PEW
ZZOT!
PEW
THE ROOM GOES ALL DIM-LOOKING.
MAYBE IT'S THE SMOKE AND DUST. BUT I CAN FEEL THE STRENGTH EBBING OUT OF MY BODY. TOO MANY PUNCHES, TOO MANY VOLTS. MY HEALING FACTOR CAN'T KEEP UP FOREVER.
PEW PEW
ZZOT!
PEW
ZZOT!
PEW

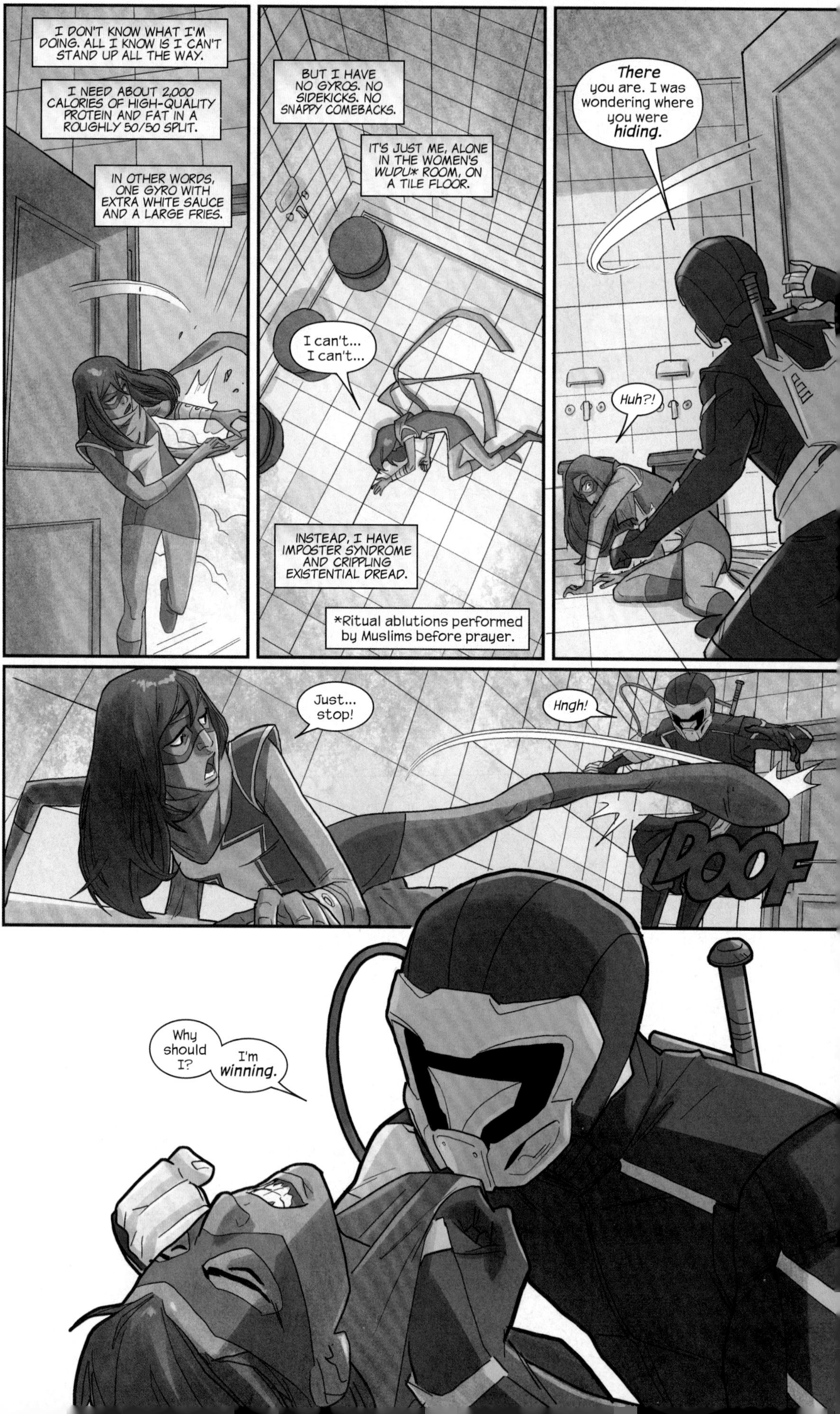

I DON'T KNOW WHAT I'M DOING. ALL I KNOW IS I CAN'T STAND UP ALL THE WAY.
I NEED ABOUT 2,000 CALORIES OF HIGH-QUALITY PROTEIN AND FAT IN A ROUGHLY 50/50 SPLIT.
IN OTHER WORDS, ONE GYRO WITH EXTRA WHITE SAUCE AND A LARGE FRIES.
BUT I HAVE NO GYROS. NO SIDEKICKS. NO SNAPPY COMEBACKS.
IT'S JUST ME, ALONE IN THE WOMEN'S WUDU* ROOM, ON A TILE FLOOR.
I can't... I can't...
INSTEAD, I HAVE IMPOSTER SYNDROME AND CRIPPLING EXISTENTIAL DREAD.
*Ritual ablutions performed by Muslims before prayer.
There you are. I was wondering where you were hiding.
Huh?!
Just... stop!
Hngh!
DOOF
Why should I?
I'm winning.

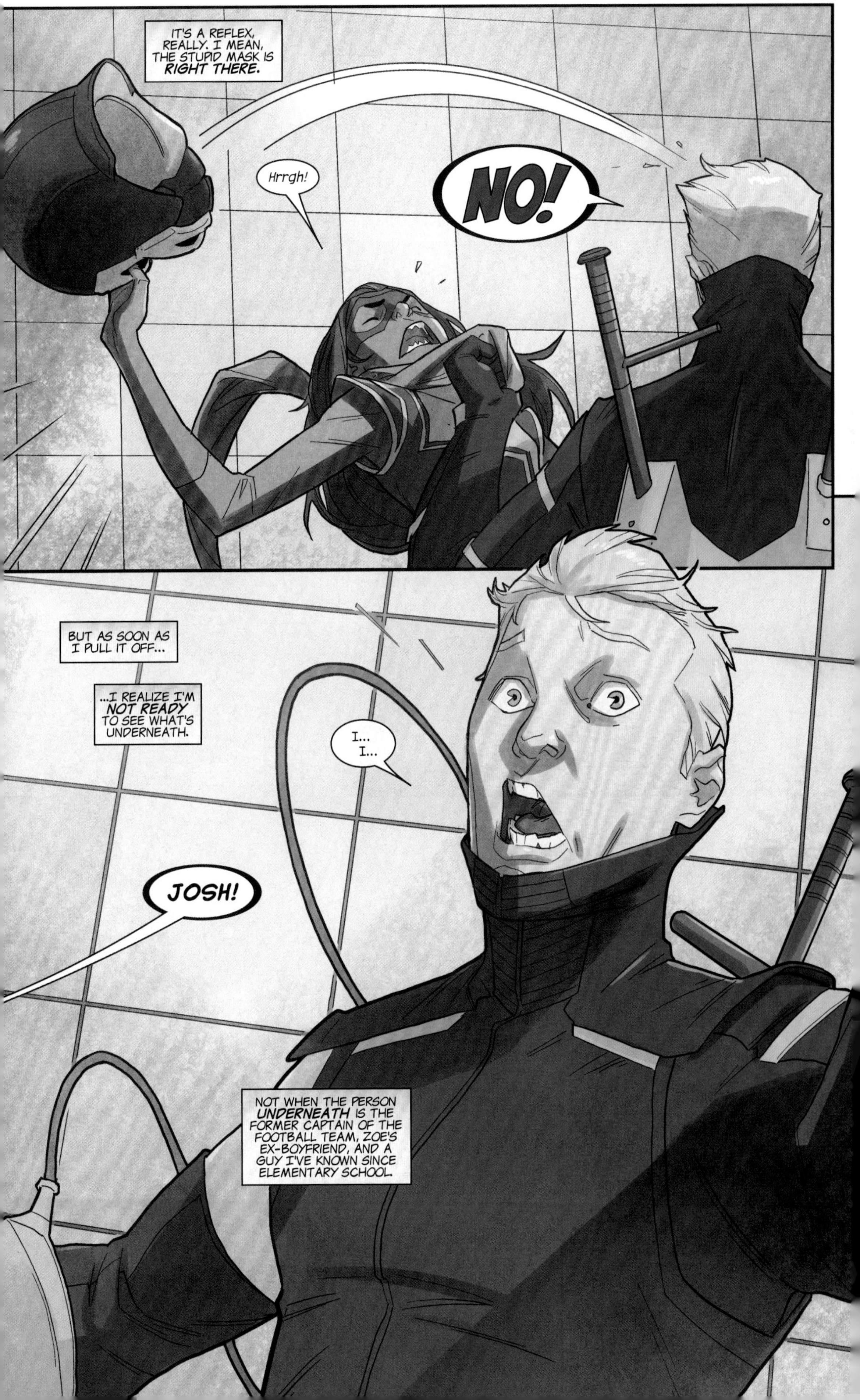
IT'S A REFLEX, REALLY. I MEAN, THE STUPID MASK IS RIGHT THERE.
Hrrgh!
NO!
BUT AS SOON AS I PULL IT OFF...
...I REALIZE I'M NOT READY TO SEE WHAT'S UNDERNEATH.
I... I...
JOSH!
NOT WHEN THE PERSON UNDERNEATH IS THE FORMER CAPTAIN OF THE FOOTBALL TEAM, ZOE'S EX-BOYFRIEND, AND A GUY I'VE KNOWN SINCE ELEMENTARY SCHOOL.

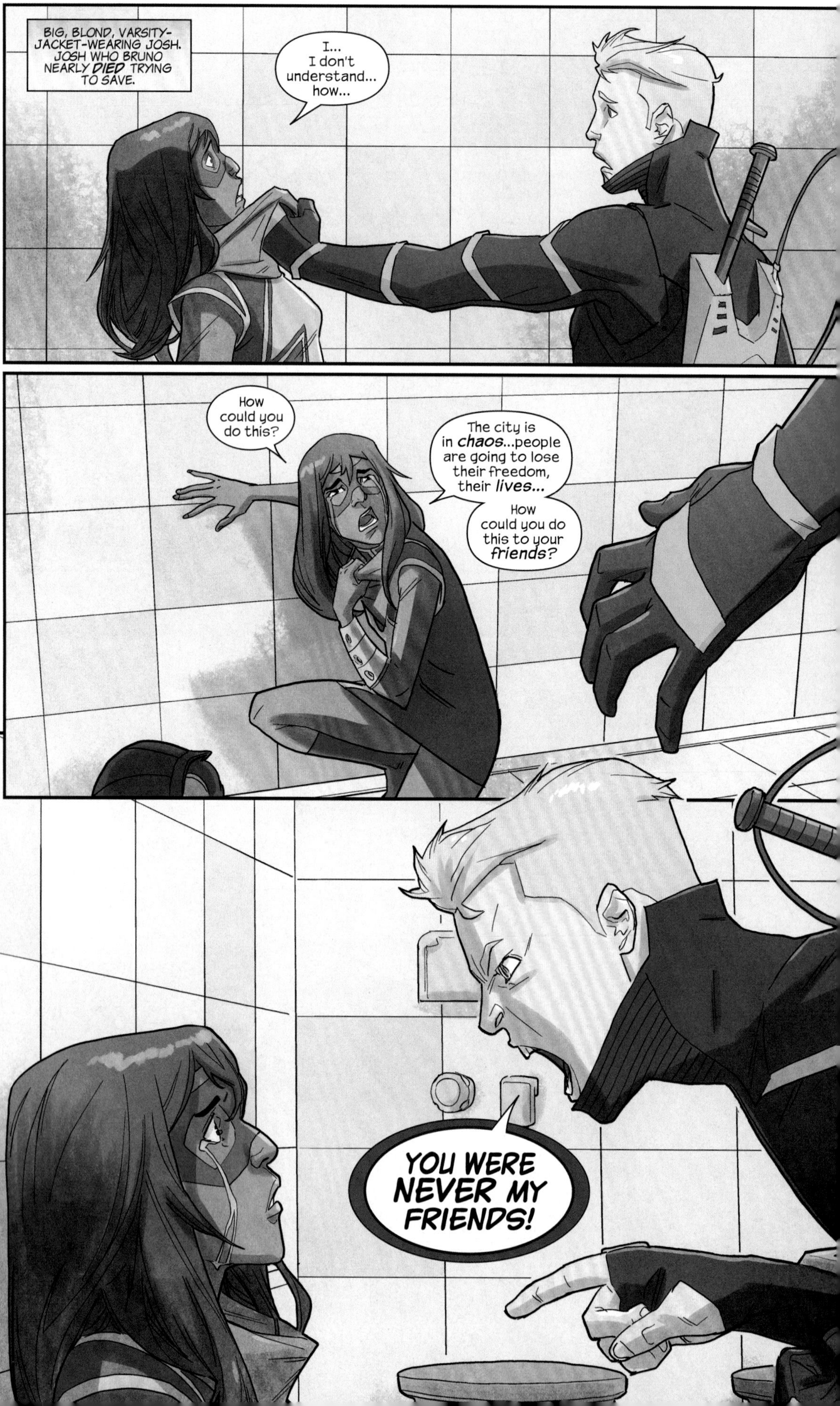

BIG, BLOND, VARSITY-JACKET-WEARING JOSH. JOSH WHO BRUNO NEARLY DIED TRYING TO SAVE.
I... I don't understand... how...
How could you do this?
The city is in chaos...people are going to lose their freedom, their lives...
How could you do this to your friends?
YOU WERE NEVER MY FRIENDS!

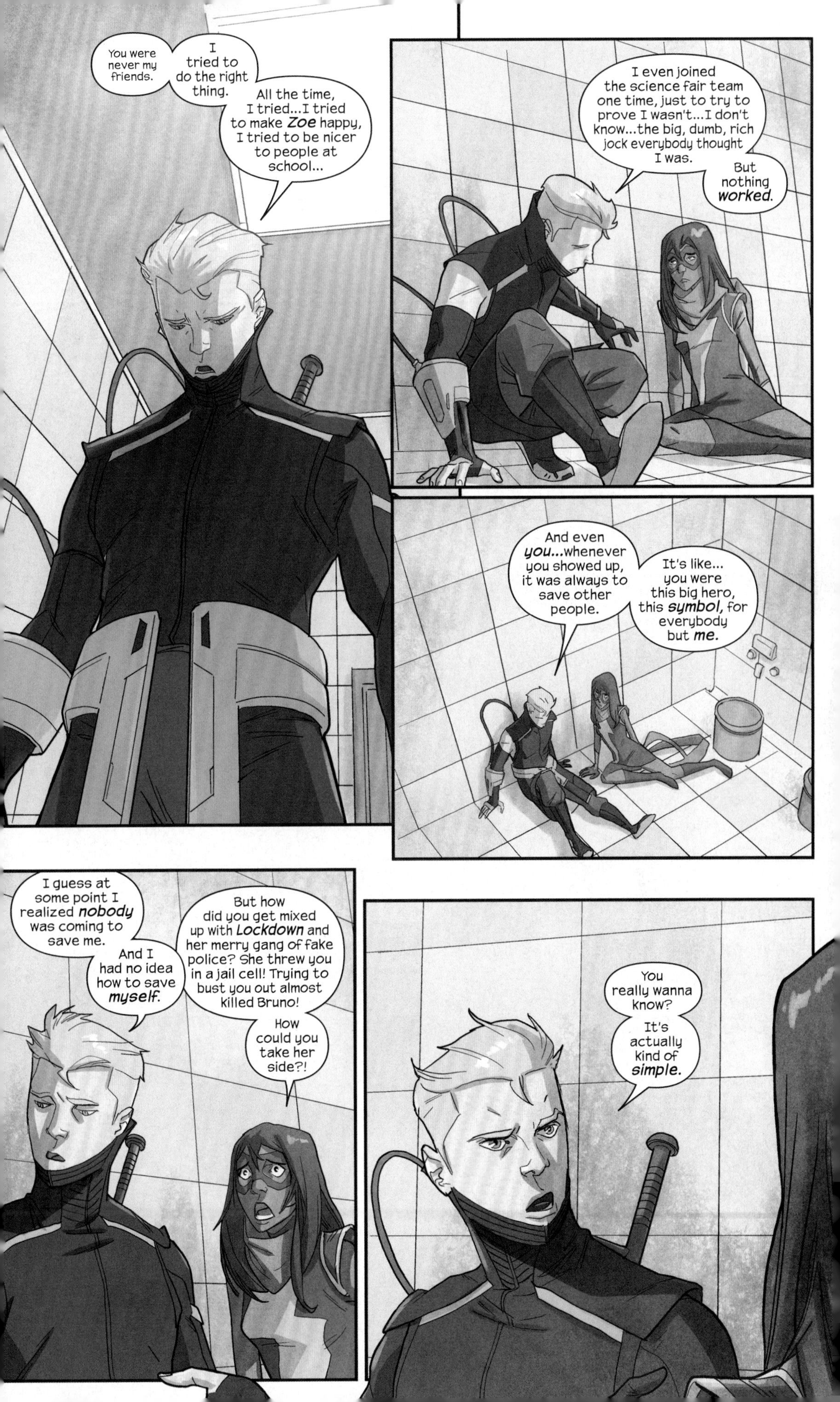
You were never my friends.
I tried to do the right thing.
All the time, I tried...I tried to make Zoe happy, I tried to be nicer to people at school...
I even joined the science fair team one time, just to try to prove I wasn't...I don't know...the big, dumb, rich jock everybody thought I was.
But nothing worked.
And even you...whenever you showed up, it was always to save other people.
It's like... you were this big hero, this symbol, for everybody but me.
I guess at some point I realized nobody was coming to save me.
And I had no idea how to save myself.
But how did you get mixed up with Lockdown and her merry gang of fake police? She threw you in a jail cell! Trying to bust you out almost killed Bruno!
How could you take her side?!
You really wanna know?
It's actually kind of simple.

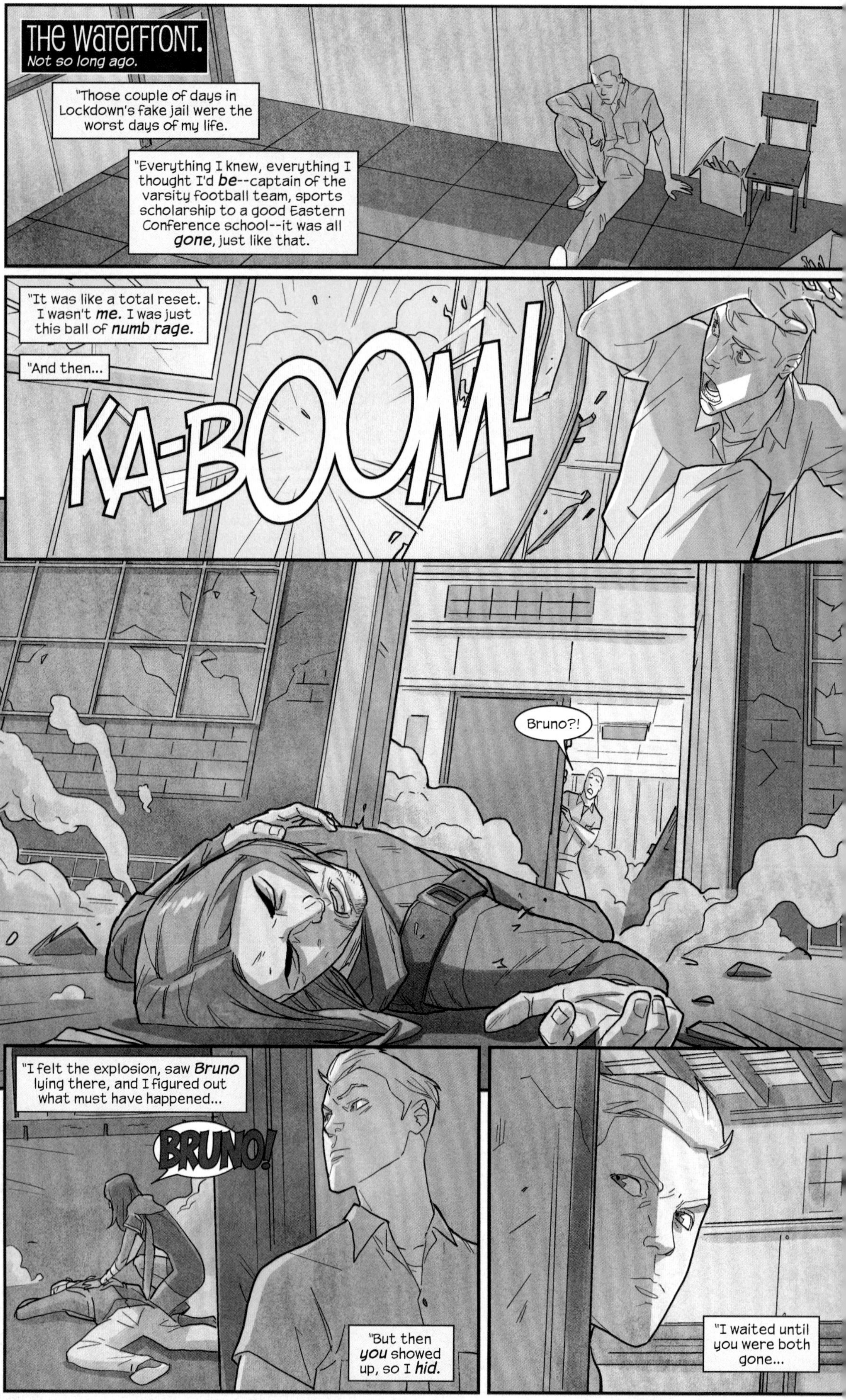

THE WATERFRONT.
Not so long ago.
"Those couple of days in Lockdown's fake jail were the worst days of my life.
"Everything I knew, everything I thought I'd be--captain of the varsity football team, sports scholarship to a good Eastern Conference school--it was all gone, just like that.
"It was like a total reset. I wasn't me. I was just this ball of numb rage.
"And then...
KA-BOOM!
Bruno?!
"I felt the explosion, saw Bruno lying there, and I figured out what must have happened...
BRUNO!
"But then you showed up, so I hid.
"I waited until you were both gone...

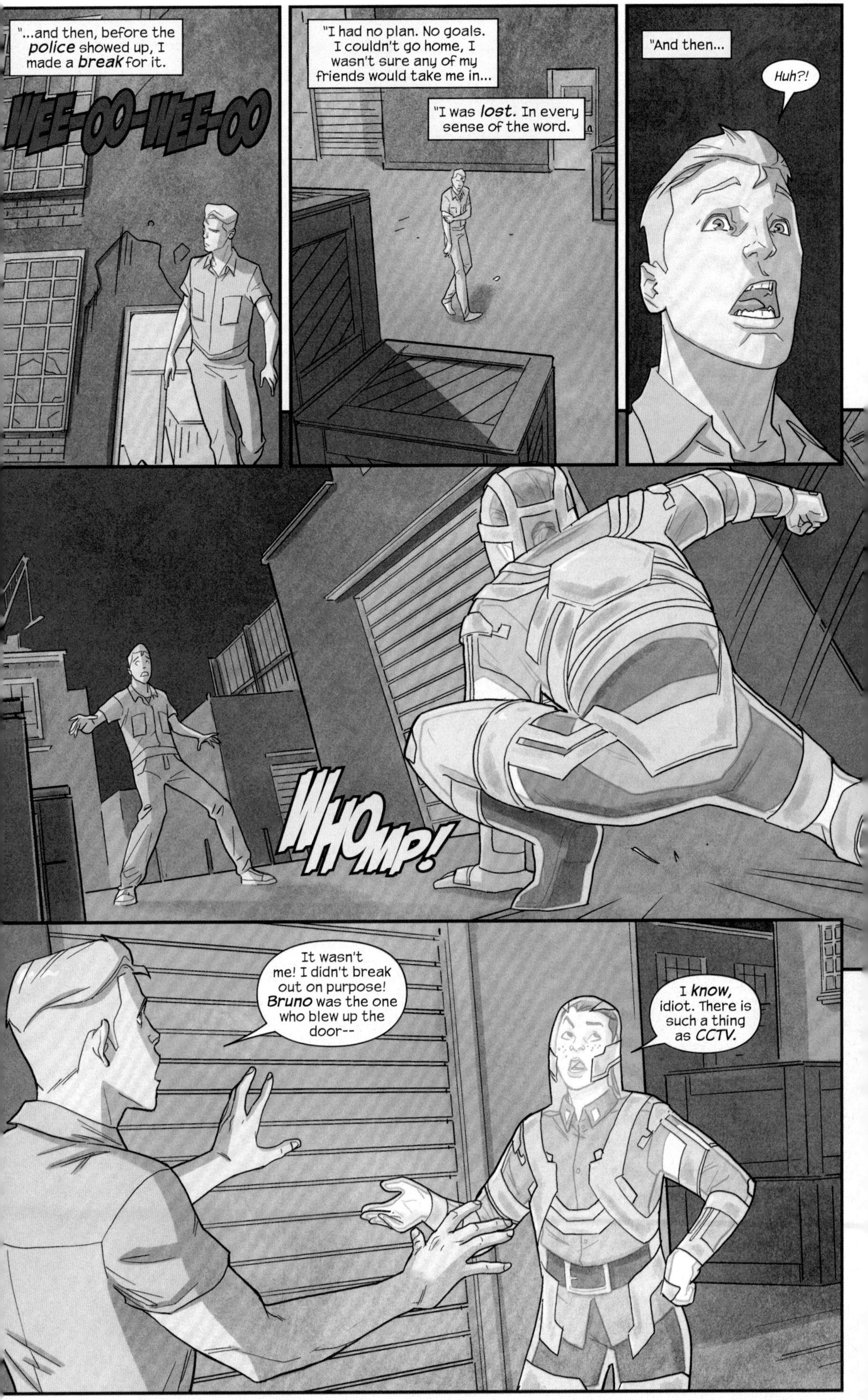

"...and then, before the *police* showed up, I made a *break* for it.
WEE-OO-WEE-OO
"I had no plan. No goals. I couldn't go home, I wasn't sure any of my friends would take me in...
"I was *lost.* In every sense of the word.
"And then...
Huh?!
WHOMP!
It wasn't me! I didn't break out on purpose! *Bruno* was the one who blew up the door--
I *know,* idiot. There is such a thing as *CCTV.*

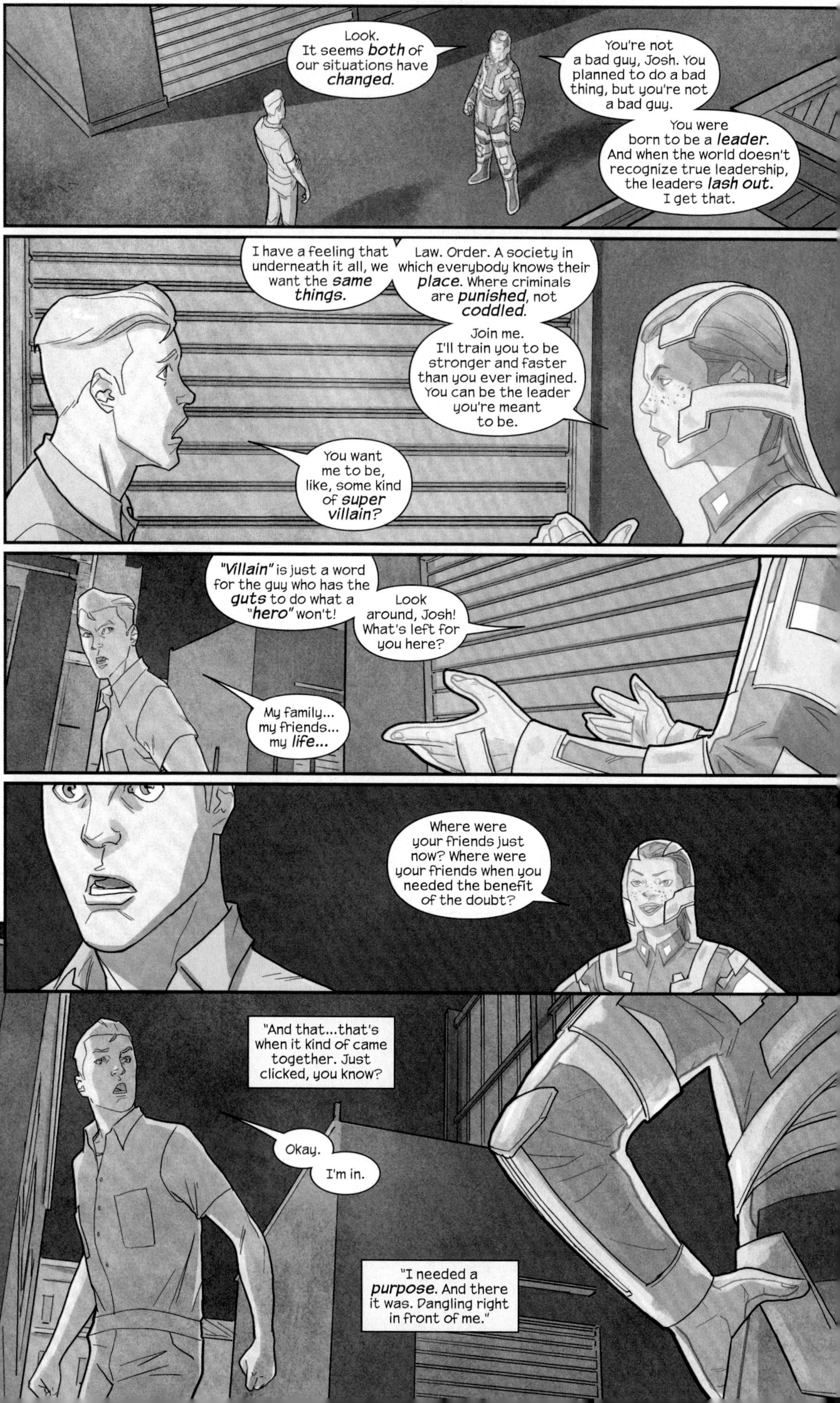
Look. It seems both of our situations have changed.
You're not a bad guy, Josh. You planned to do a bad thing, but you're not a bad guy.
You were born to be a leader. And when the world doesn't recognize true leadership, the leaders lash out. I get that.
I have a feeling that underneath it all, we want the same things.
Law. Order. A society in which everybody knows their place. Where criminals are punished, not coddled.
Join me. I'll train you to be stronger and faster than you ever imagined. You can be the leader you're meant to be.
You want me to be, like, some kind of super villain?
"Villain" is just a word for the guy who has the guts to do what a "hero" won't!
Look around, Josh! What's left for you here?
My family... my friends... my life...
Where were your friends just now? Where were your friends when you needed the benefit of the doubt?
"And that...that's when it kind of came together. Just clicked, you know?
Okay.
I'm in.
"I needed a purpose. And there it was. Dangling right in front of me."

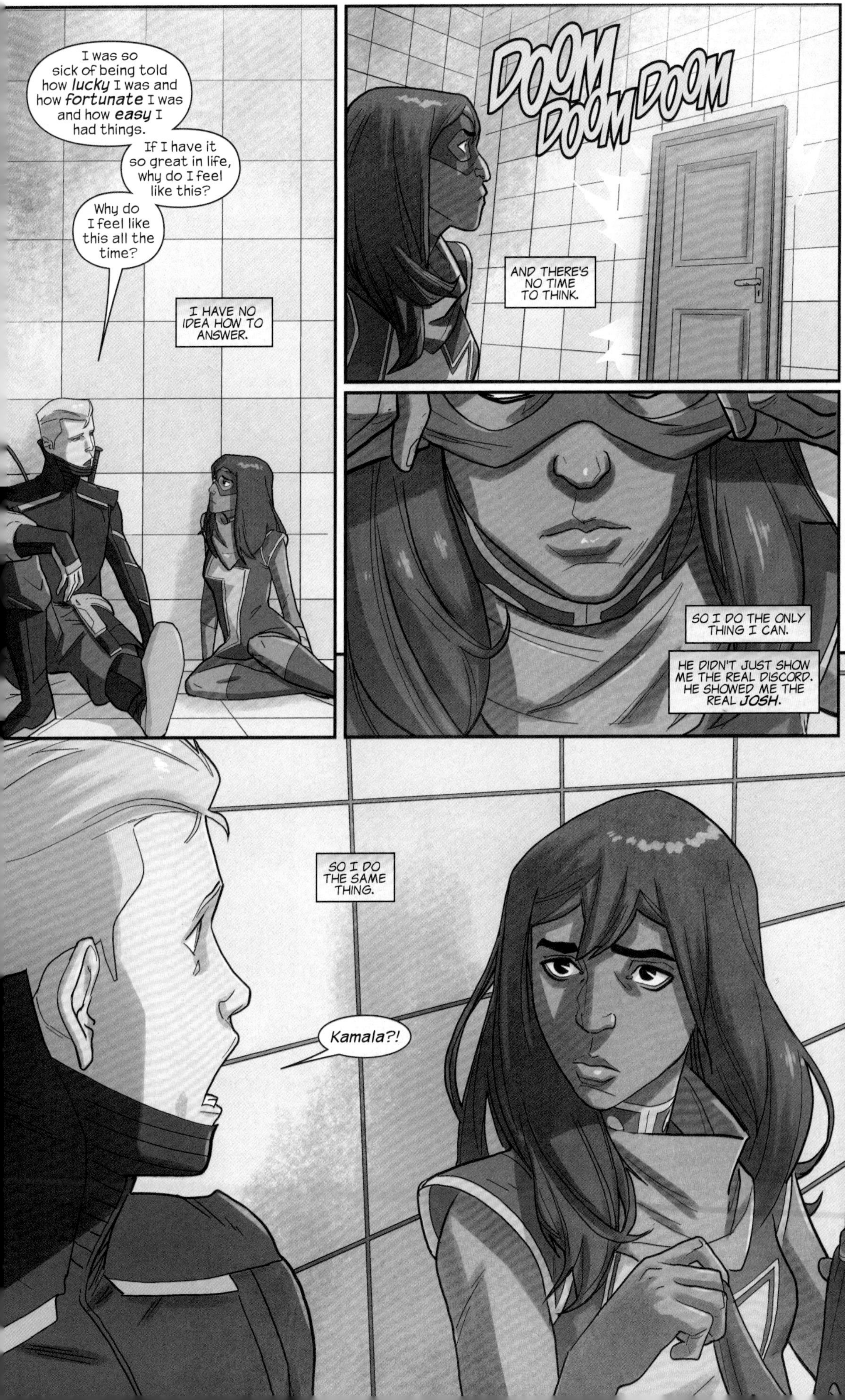
I was so sick of being told how *lucky* I was and how *fortunate* I was and how *easy* I had things.
If I have it so great in life, why do I feel like this?
Why do I feel like this all the time?
I HAVE NO IDEA HOW TO ANSWER.
DOOM DOOM DOOM
AND THERE'S NO TIME TO THINK.
SO I DO THE ONLY THING I CAN.
HE DIDN'T JUST SHOW ME THE REAL DISCORD. HE SHOWED ME THE REAL *JOSH*.
SO I DO THE SAME THING.
Kamala?!

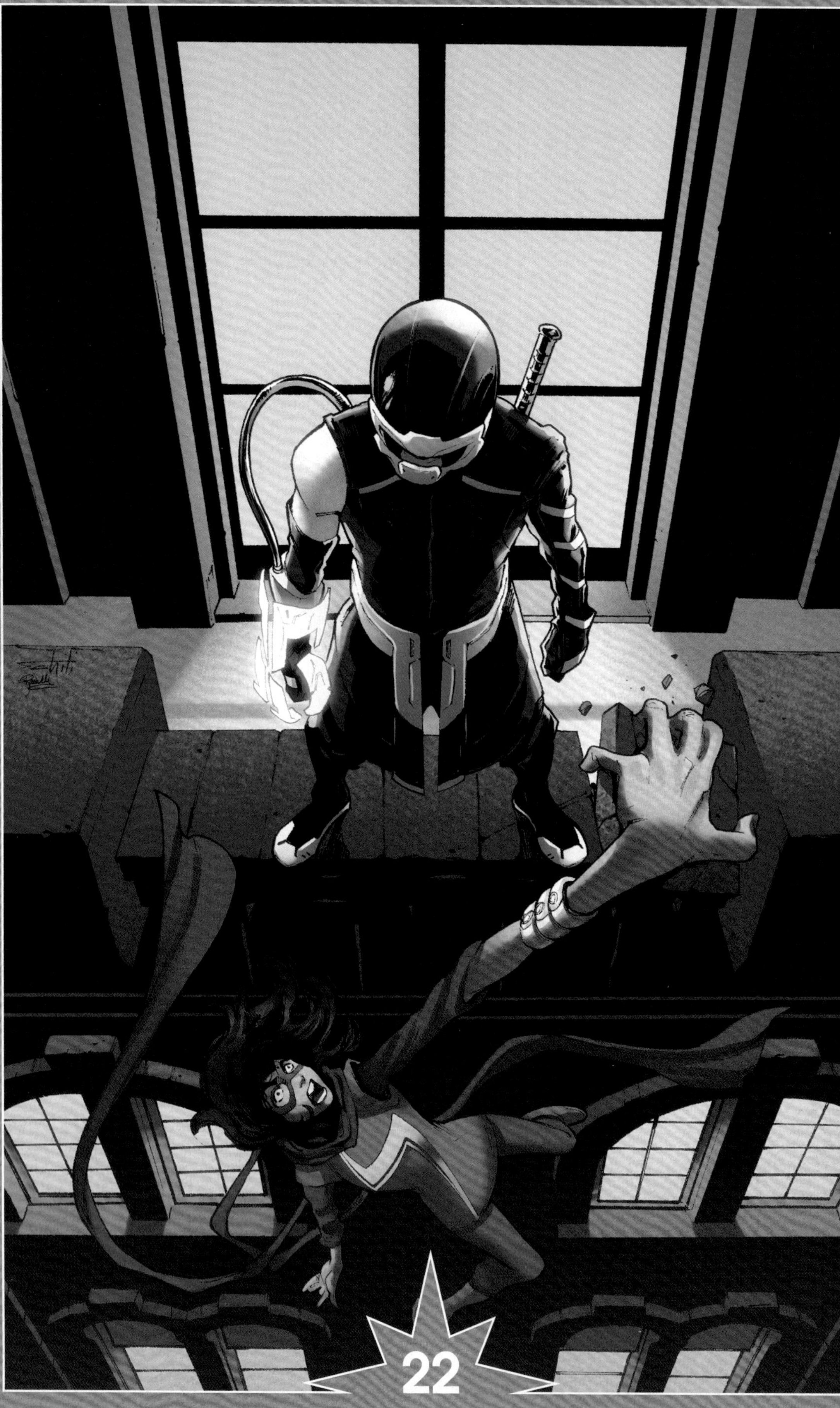
22

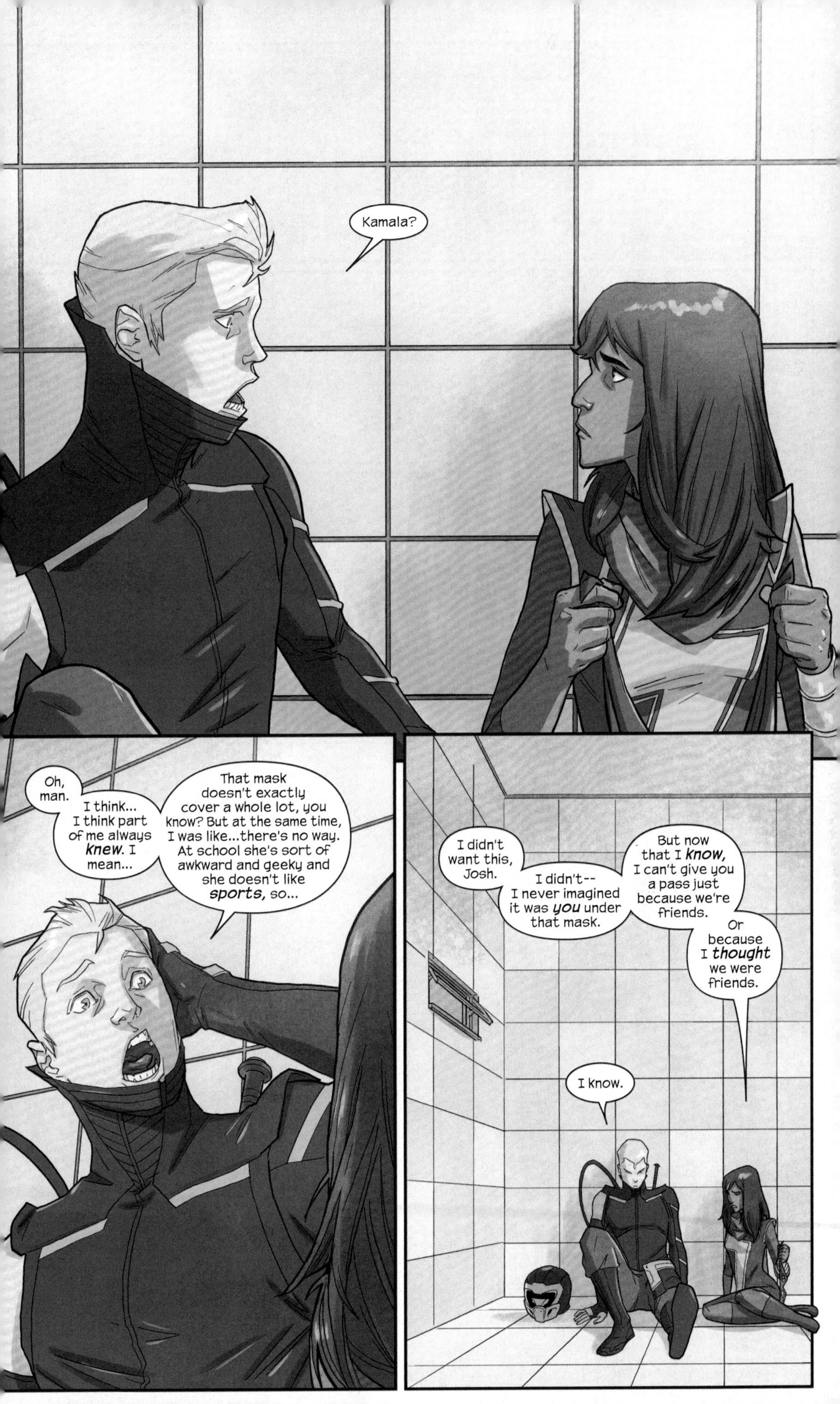

Kamala?
Oh, man.
I think... I think part of me always *knew*. I mean...
That mask doesn't exactly cover a whole lot, you know? But at the same time, I was like...there's no way. At school she's sort of awkward and geeky and she doesn't like *sports*, so...
I didn't want this, Josh.
I didn't-- I never imagined it was *you* under that mask.
But now that I *know*, I can't give you a pass just because we're friends.
Or because I *thought* we were friends.
I know.

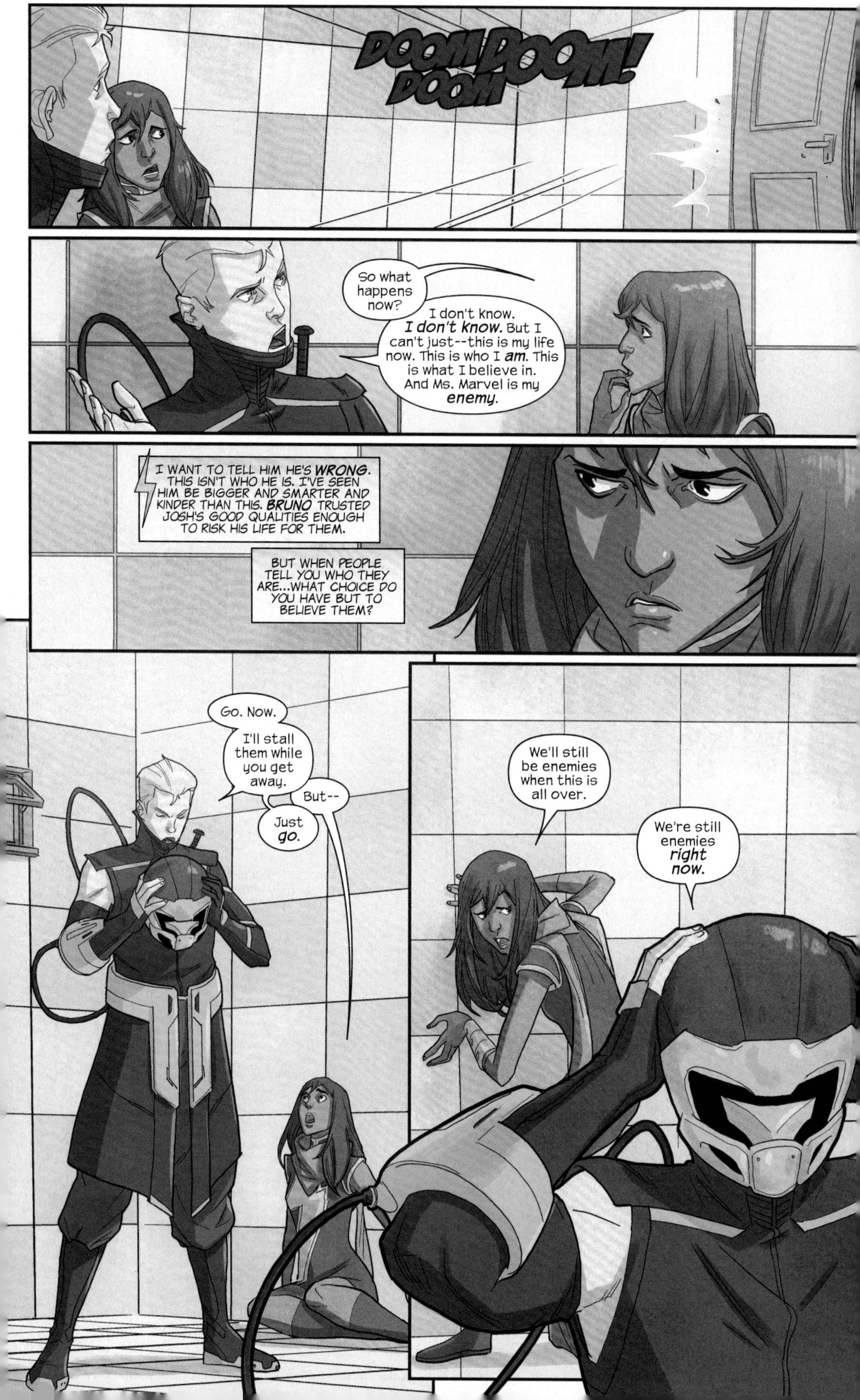
DOOM DOOM DOOM!
So what happens now?
I don't know. *I don't know.* But I can't just--this is my life now. This is who I *am*. This is what I believe in. And Ms. Marvel is my *enemy*.
I WANT TO TELL HIM HE'S *WRONG*. THIS ISN'T WHO HE IS. I'VE SEEN HIM BE BIGGER AND SMARTER AND KINDER THAN THIS. *BRUNO* TRUSTED JOSH'S GOOD QUALITIES ENOUGH TO RISK HIS LIFE FOR THEM.
BUT WHEN PEOPLE TELL YOU WHO THEY ARE...WHAT CHOICE DO YOU HAVE BUT TO BELIEVE THEM?
Go. Now.
I'll stall them while you get away.
But--
Just *go*.
We'll still be enemies when this is all over.
We're still enemies *right now.*

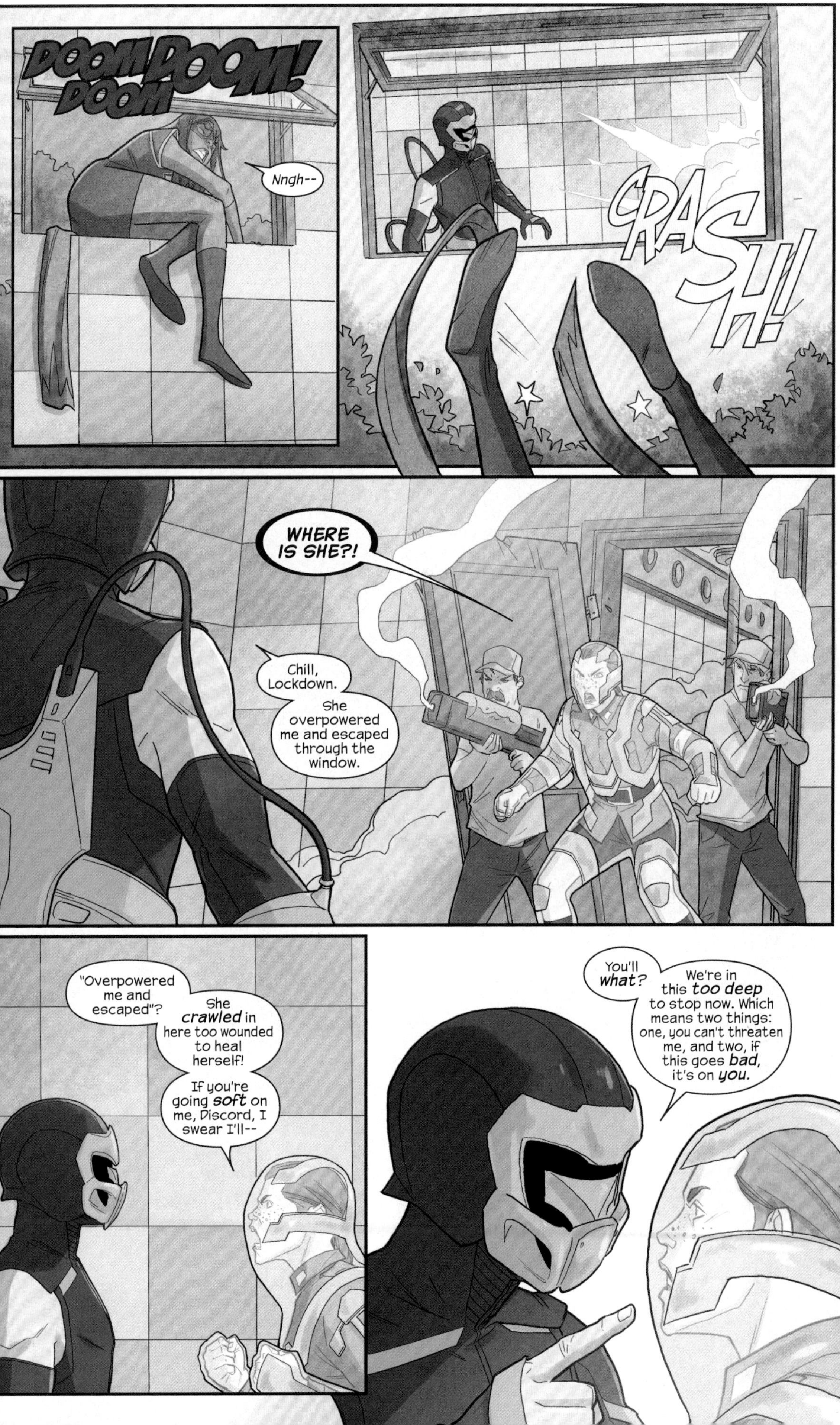
DOOM DOOM DOOM!
Nngh--
CRASH!
WHERE IS SHE?!
Chill, Lockdown.
She overpowered me and escaped through the window.
"Overpowered me and escaped"?
She crawled in here too wounded to heal herself!
If you're going soft on me, Discord, I swear I'll--
You'll what?
We're in this too deep to stop now. Which means two things: one, you can't threaten me, and two, if this goes bad, it's on you.

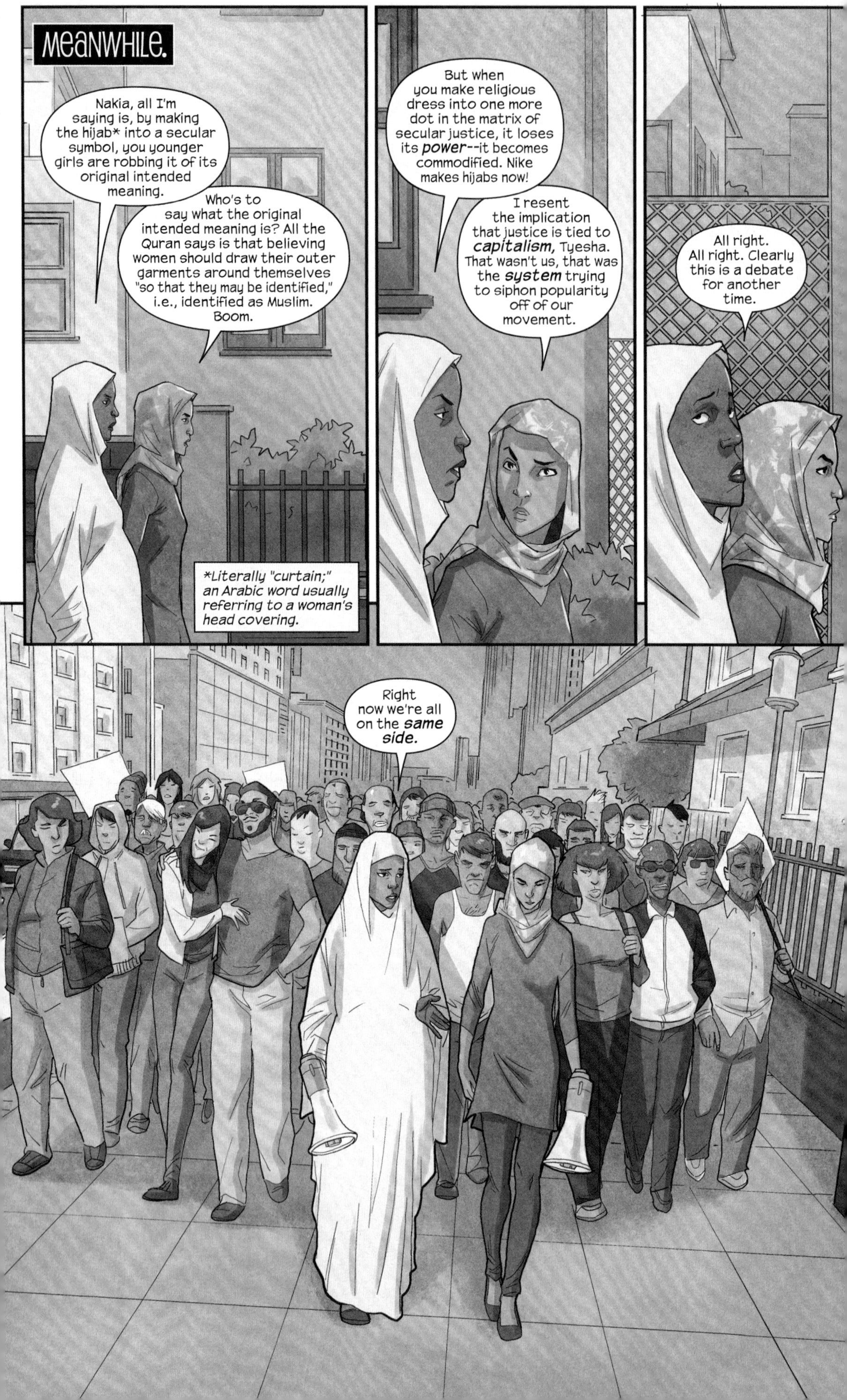
MEANWHILE.
Nakia, all I'm saying is, by making the hijab* into a secular symbol, you younger girls are robbing it of its original intended meaning.
Who's to say what the original intended meaning is? All the Quran says is that believing women should draw their outer garments around themselves "so that they may be identified," i.e., identified as Muslim. Boom.
*Literally "curtain;" an Arabic word usually referring to a woman's head covering.
But when you make religious dress into one more dot in the matrix of secular justice, it loses its power--it becomes commodified. Nike makes hijabs now!
I resent the implication that justice is tied to capitalism, Tyesha. That wasn't us, that was the system trying to siphon popularity off of our movement.
All right. All right. Clearly this is a debate for another time.
Right now we're all on the same side.

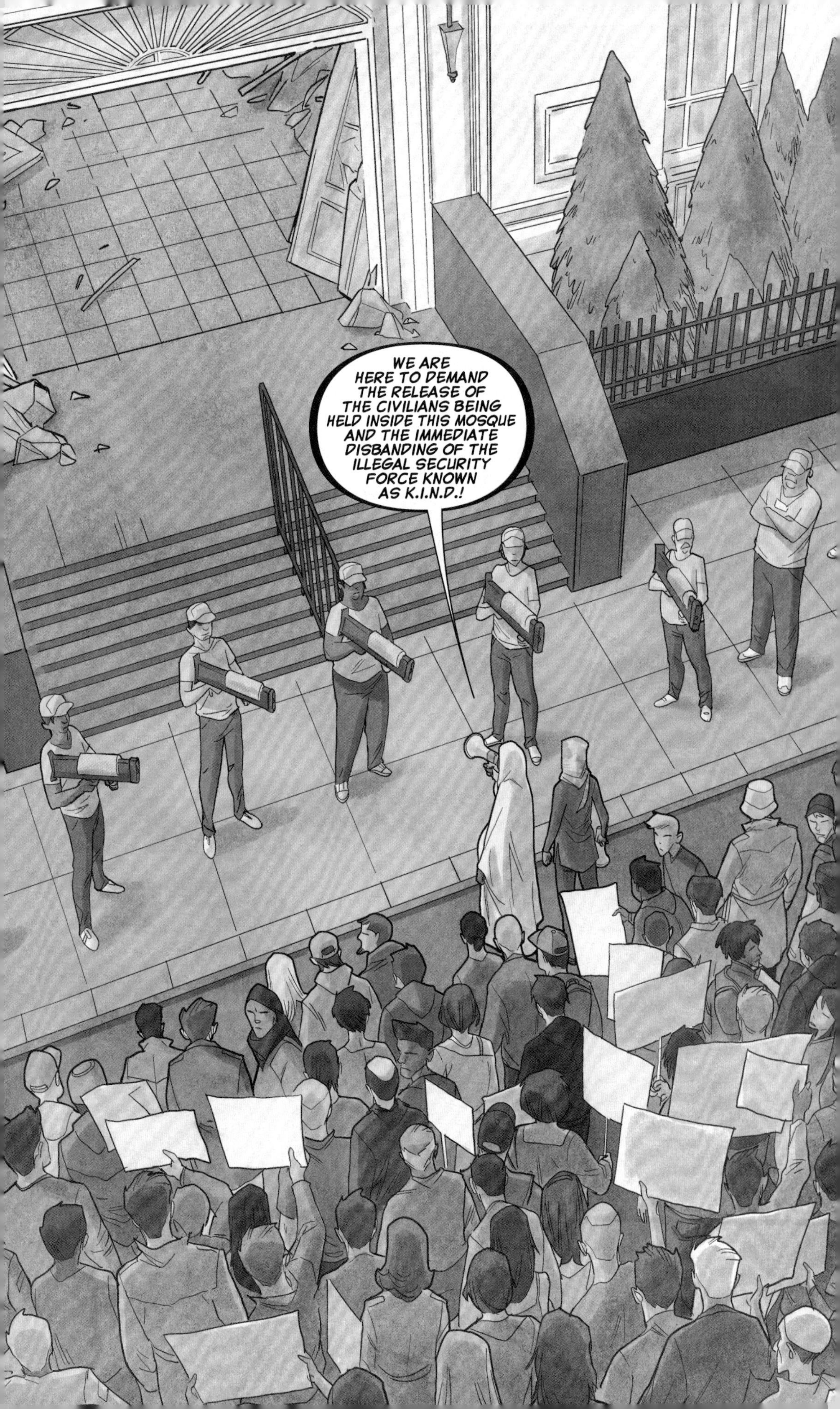
WE ARE HERE TO DEMAND THE RELEASE OF THE CIVILIANS BEING HELD INSIDE THIS MOSQUE AND THE IMMEDIATE DISBANDING OF THE ILLEGAL SECURITY FORCE KNOWN AS K.I.N.D.!

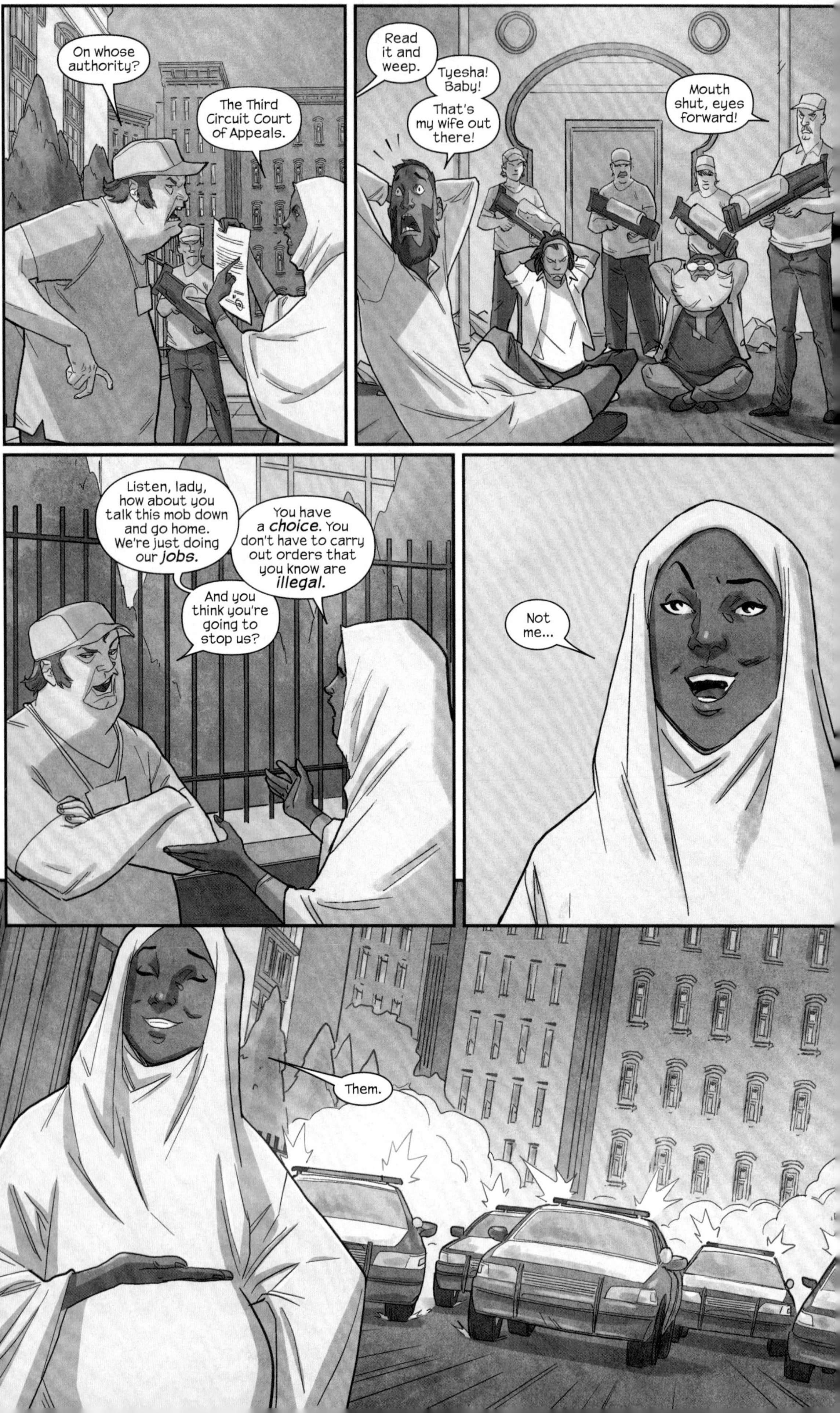
On whose authority?
The Third Circuit Court of Appeals.
Read it and weep.
Tyesha! Baby!
That's my wife out there!
Mouth shut, eyes forward!
Listen, lady, how about you talk this mob down and go home. We're just doing our *jobs.*
You have a *choice.* You don't have to carry out orders that you know are *illegal.*
And you think you're going to stop us?
Not me...
Them.

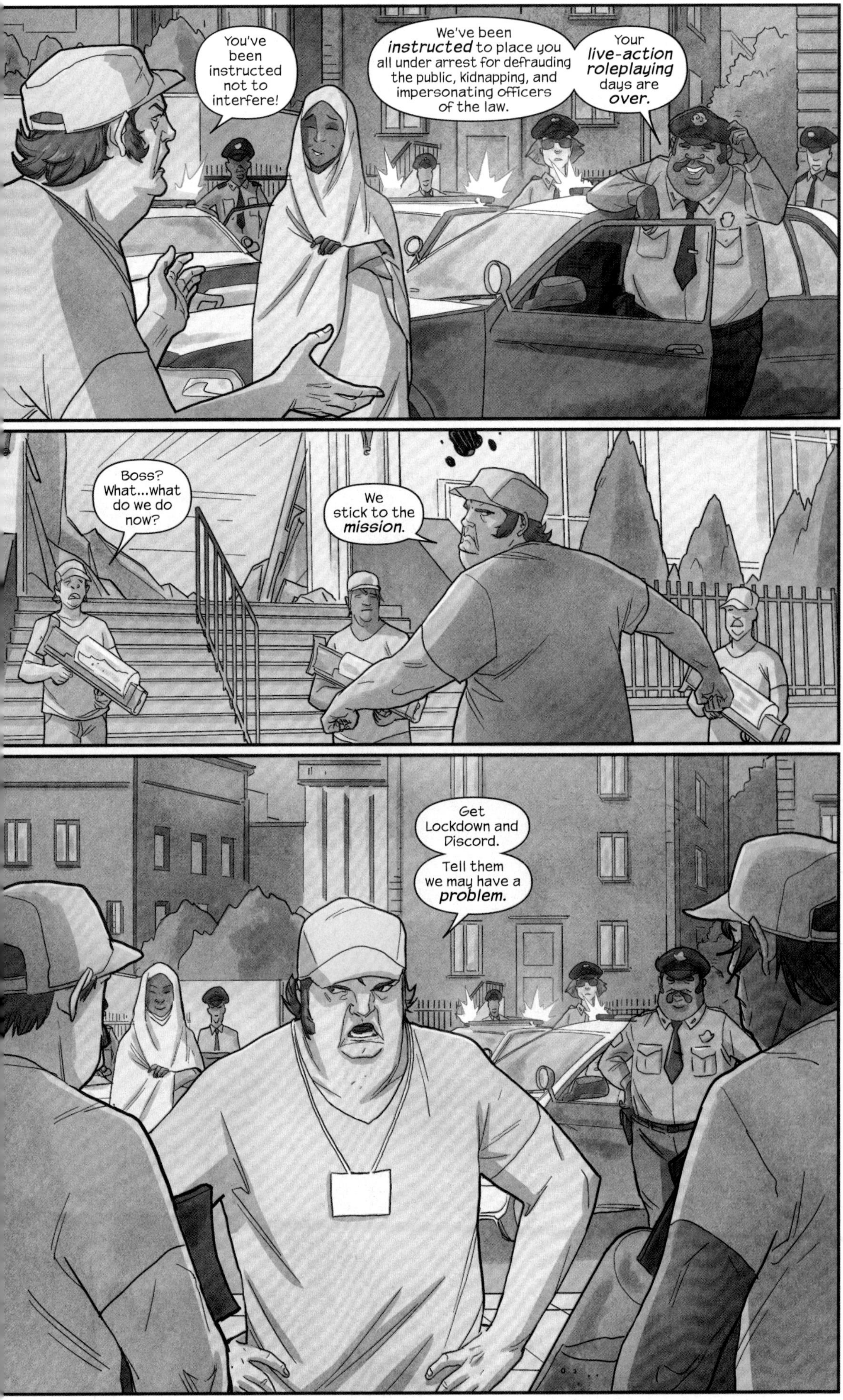
You've been instructed not to interfere!
We've been instructed to place you all under arrest for defrauding the public, kidnapping, and impersonating officers of the law.
Your live-action roleplaying days are over.
Boss? What...what do we do now?
We stick to the mission.
Get Lockdown and Discord.
Tell them we may have a problem.

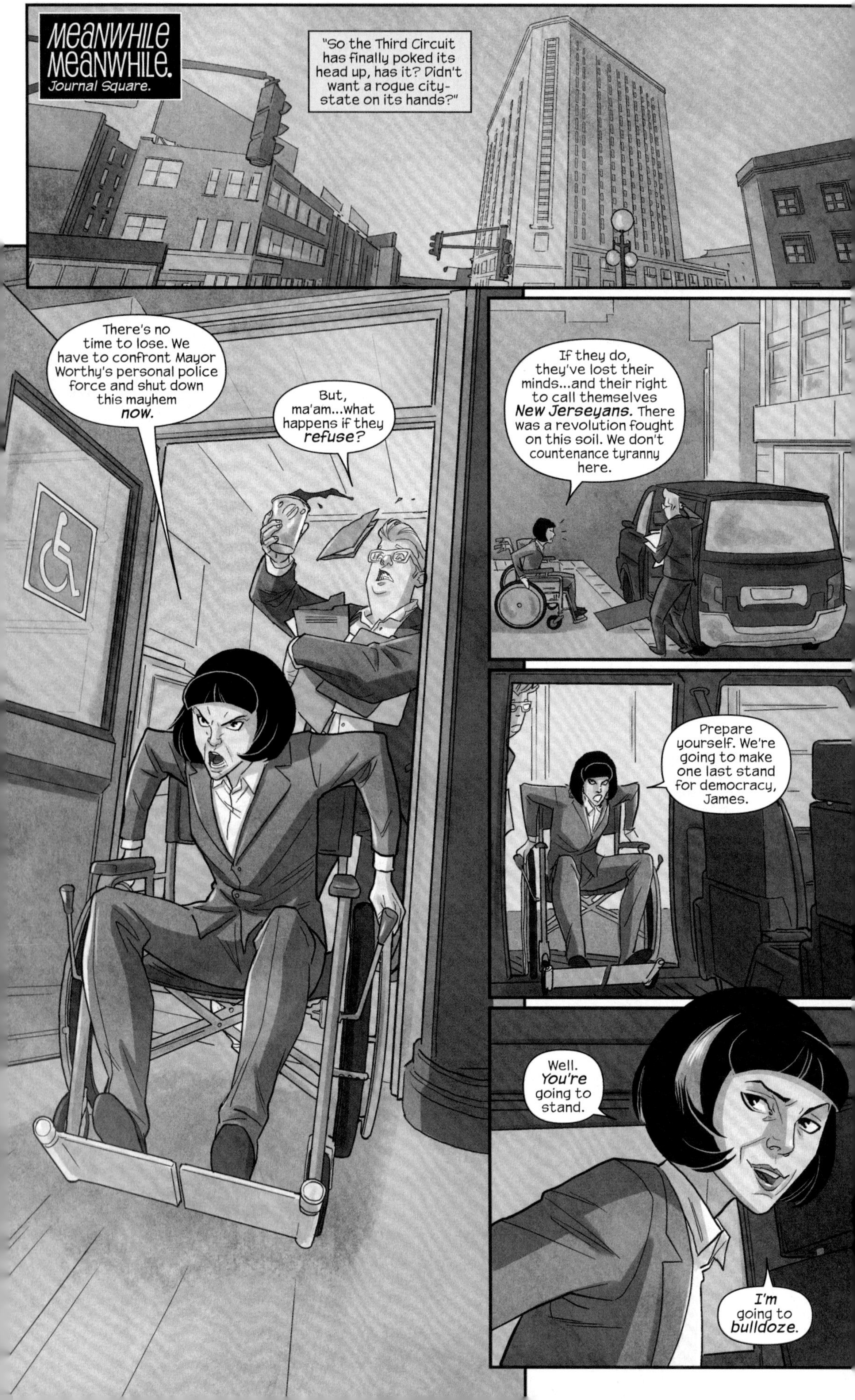
MEANWHILE MEANWHILE.
Journal Square.
"So the Third Circuit has finally poked its head up, has it? Didn't want a rogue city-state on its hands?"
There's no time to lose. We have to confront Mayor Worthy's personal police force and shut down this mayhem *now.*
But, ma'am...what happens if they *refuse?*
If they do, they've lost their minds...and their right to call themselves *New Jerseyans.* There was a revolution fought on this soil. We don't countenance tyranny here.
Prepare yourself. We're going to make one last stand for democracy, James.
Well. *You're* going to stand.
I'm going to *bulldoze.*

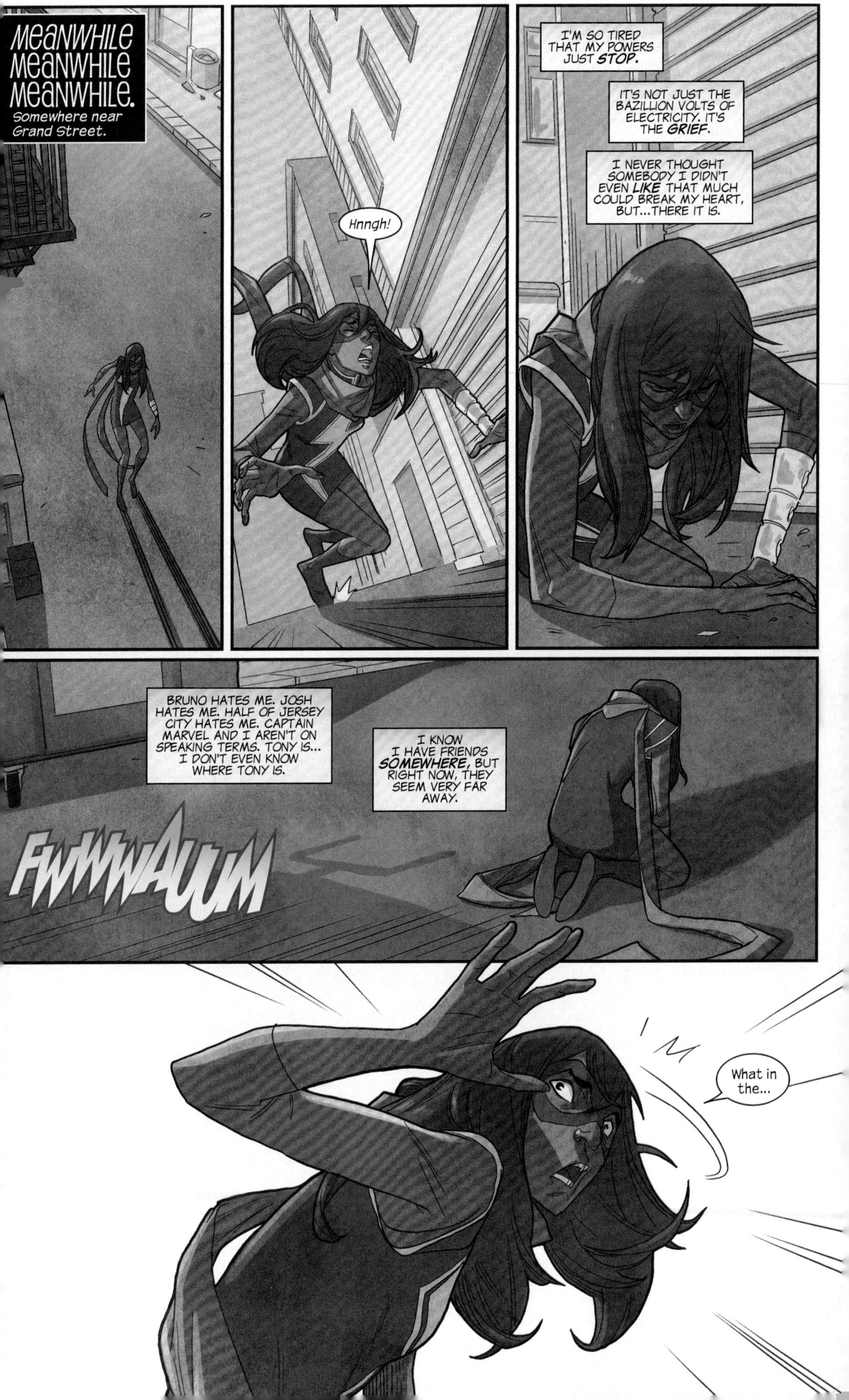
MEANWHILE
MEANWHILE
MEANWHILE.
Somewhere near Grand Street.
Hnngh!
I'M SO TIRED THAT MY POWERS JUST STOP.
IT'S NOT JUST THE BAZILLION VOLTS OF ELECTRICITY. IT'S THE GRIEF.
I NEVER THOUGHT SOMEBODY I DIDN'T EVEN LIKE THAT MUCH COULD BREAK MY HEART, BUT...THERE IT IS.
BRUNO HATES ME. JOSH HATES ME. HALF OF JERSEY CITY HATES ME. CAPTAIN MARVEL AND I AREN'T ON SPEAKING TERMS. TONY IS... I DON'T EVEN KNOW WHERE TONY IS.
I KNOW I HAVE FRIENDS SOMEWHERE, BUT RIGHT NOW, THEY SEEM VERY FAR AWAY.
FWWWAUUM
What in the...

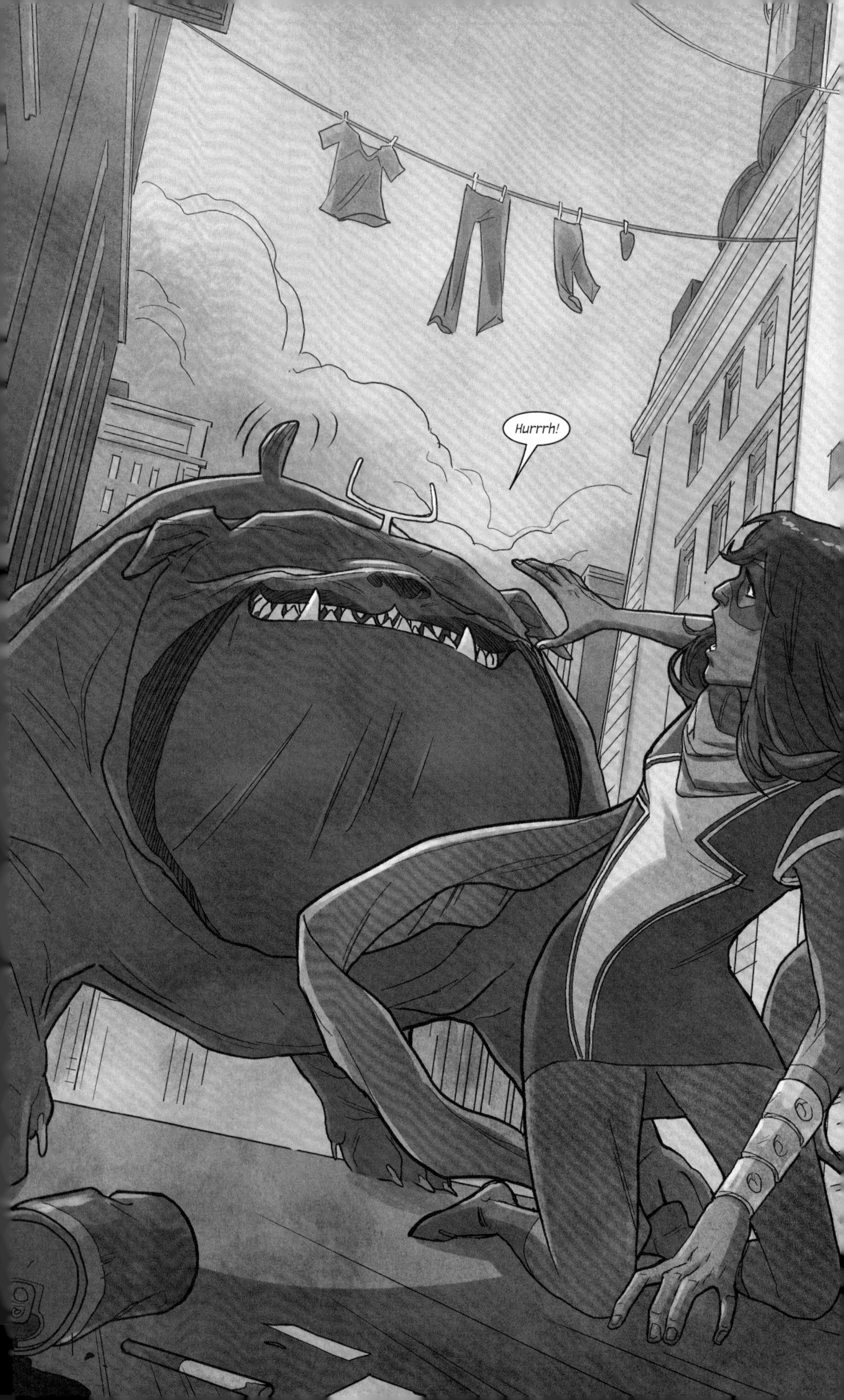
Hurrrh!

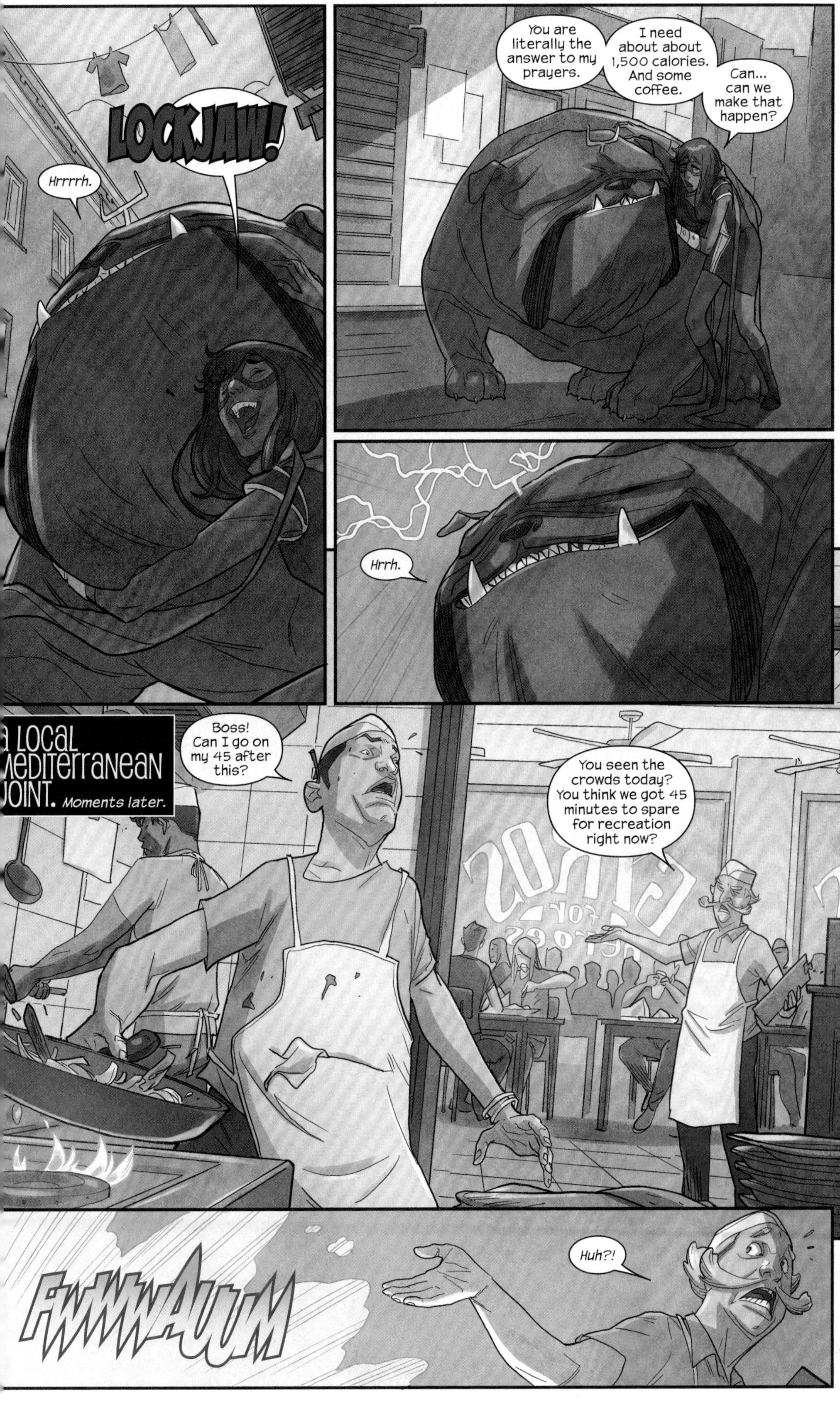
LOCKJAW!
Hrrrrh.
You are literally the answer to my prayers.
I need about about 1,500 calories. And some coffee.
Can... can we make that happen?
Hrrh.
A LOCAL MEDITERRANEAN JOINT. Moments later.
Boss! Can I go on my 45 after this?
You seen the crowds today? You think we got 45 minutes to spare for recreation right now?
Huh?!
FWWWAUUM

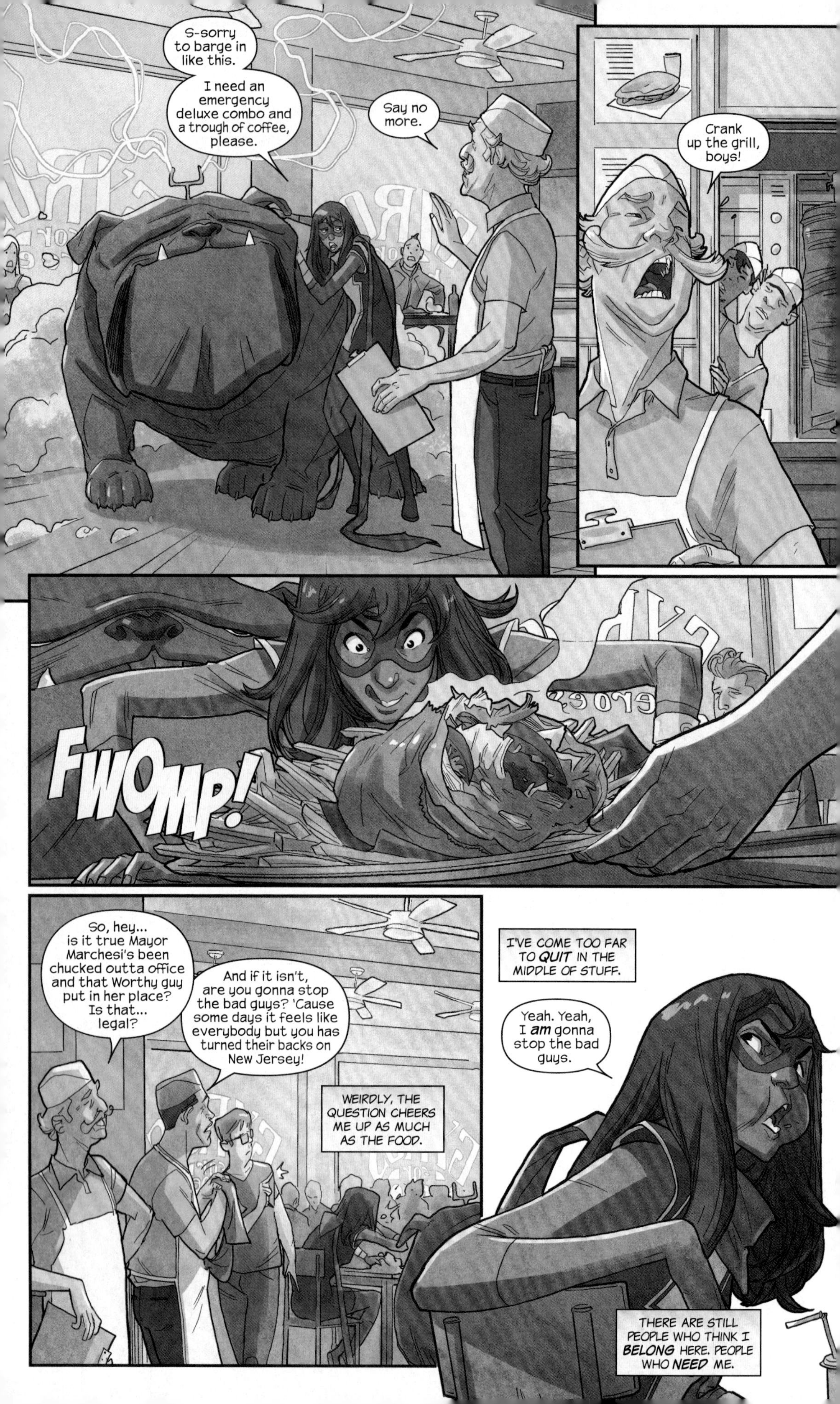
S-sorry to barge in like this.
I need an emergency deluxe combo and a trough of coffee, please.
Say no more.
Crank up the grill, boys!
FWOMP!
So, hey... is it true Mayor Marchesi's been chucked outta office and that Worthy guy put in her place? Is that... legal?
And if it isn't, are you gonna stop the bad guys? 'Cause some days it feels like everybody but you has turned their backs on New Jersey!
WEIRDLY, THE QUESTION CHEERS ME UP AS MUCH AS THE FOOD.
I'VE COME TOO FAR TO QUIT IN THE MIDDLE OF STUFF.
Yeah. Yeah, I am gonna stop the bad guys.
THERE ARE STILL PEOPLE WHO THINK I BELONG HERE. PEOPLE WHO NEED ME.

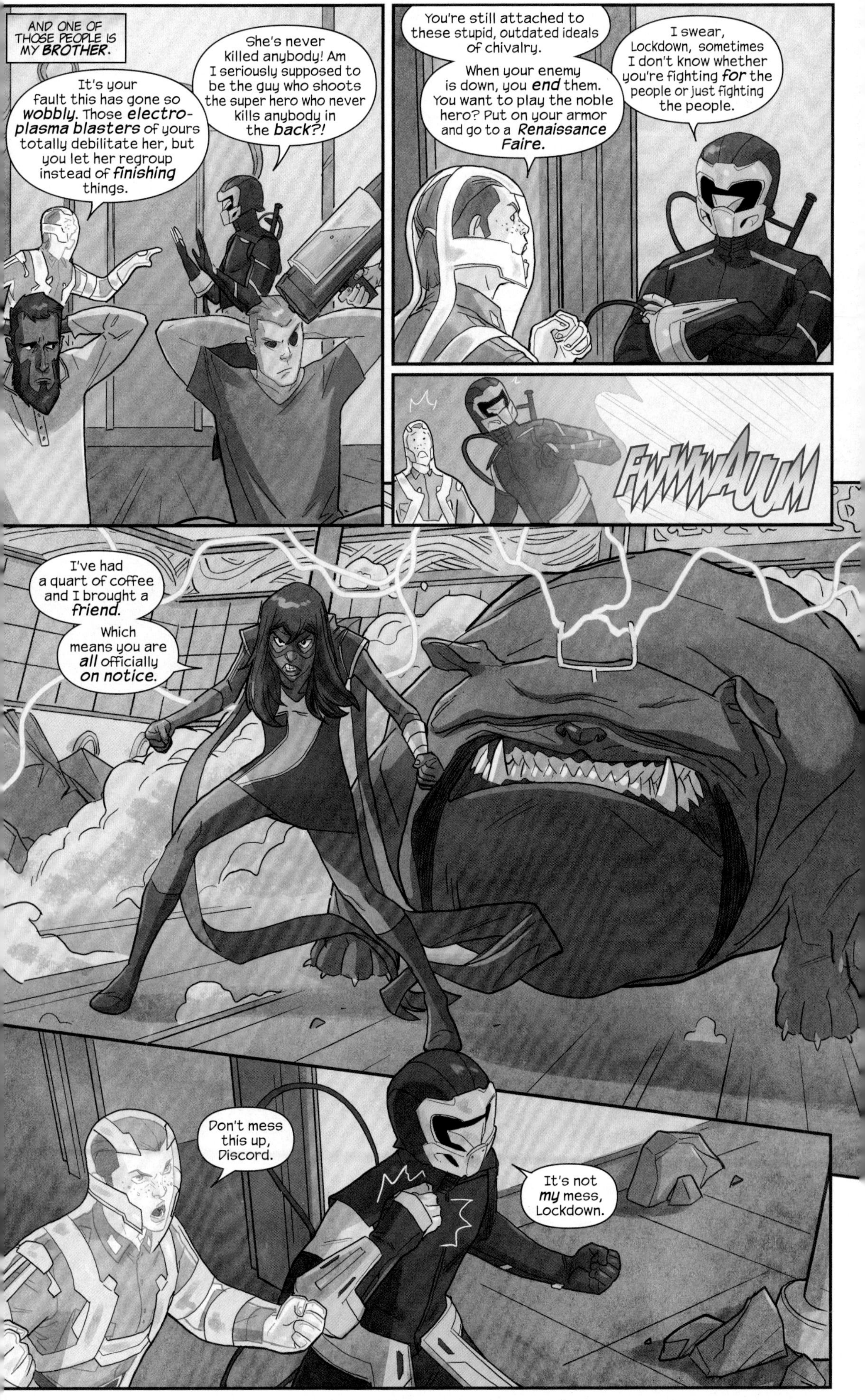
AND ONE OF THOSE PEOPLE IS MY BROTHER.
It's your fault this has gone so wobbly. Those electro-plasma blasters of yours totally debilitate her, but you let her regroup instead of finishing things.
She's never killed anybody! Am I seriously supposed to be the guy who shoots the super hero who never kills anybody in the back?!
You're still attached to these stupid, outdated ideals of chivalry.
When your enemy is down, you end them. You want to play the noble hero? Put on your armor and go to a Renaissance Faire.
I swear, Lockdown, sometimes I don't know whether you're fighting for the people or just fighting the people.
FWWWAUUM
I've had a quart of coffee and I brought a friend.
Which means you are all officially on notice.
Don't mess this up, Discord.
It's not my mess, Lockdown.

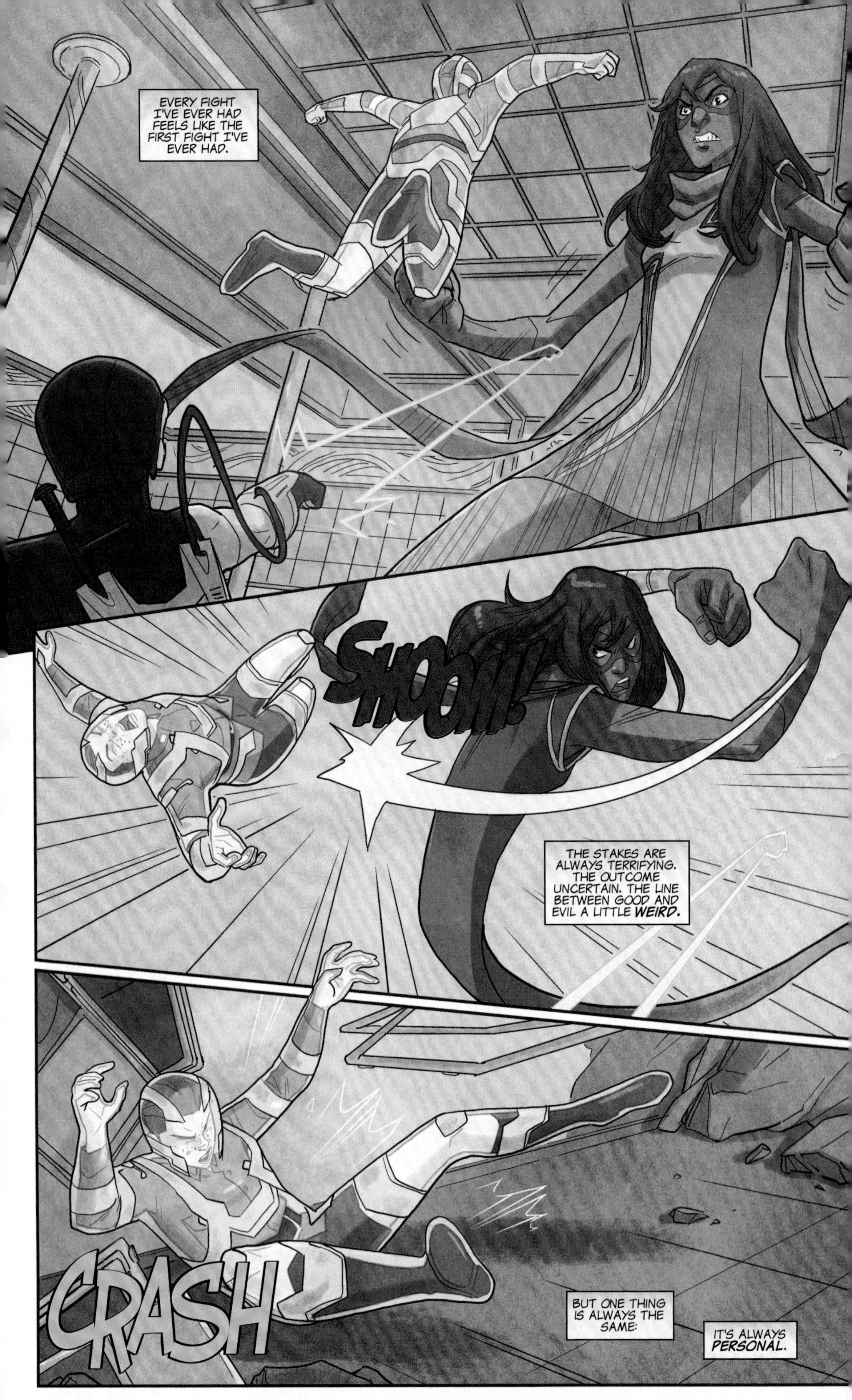
EVERY FIGHT I'VE EVER HAD FEELS LIKE THE FIRST FIGHT I'VE EVER HAD.
SHOOM!
THE STAKES ARE ALWAYS TERRIFYING. THE OUTCOME UNCERTAIN. THE LINE BETWEEN GOOD AND EVIL A LITTLE WEIRD.
CRASH
BUT ONE THING IS ALWAYS THE SAME:
IT'S ALWAYS PERSONAL.

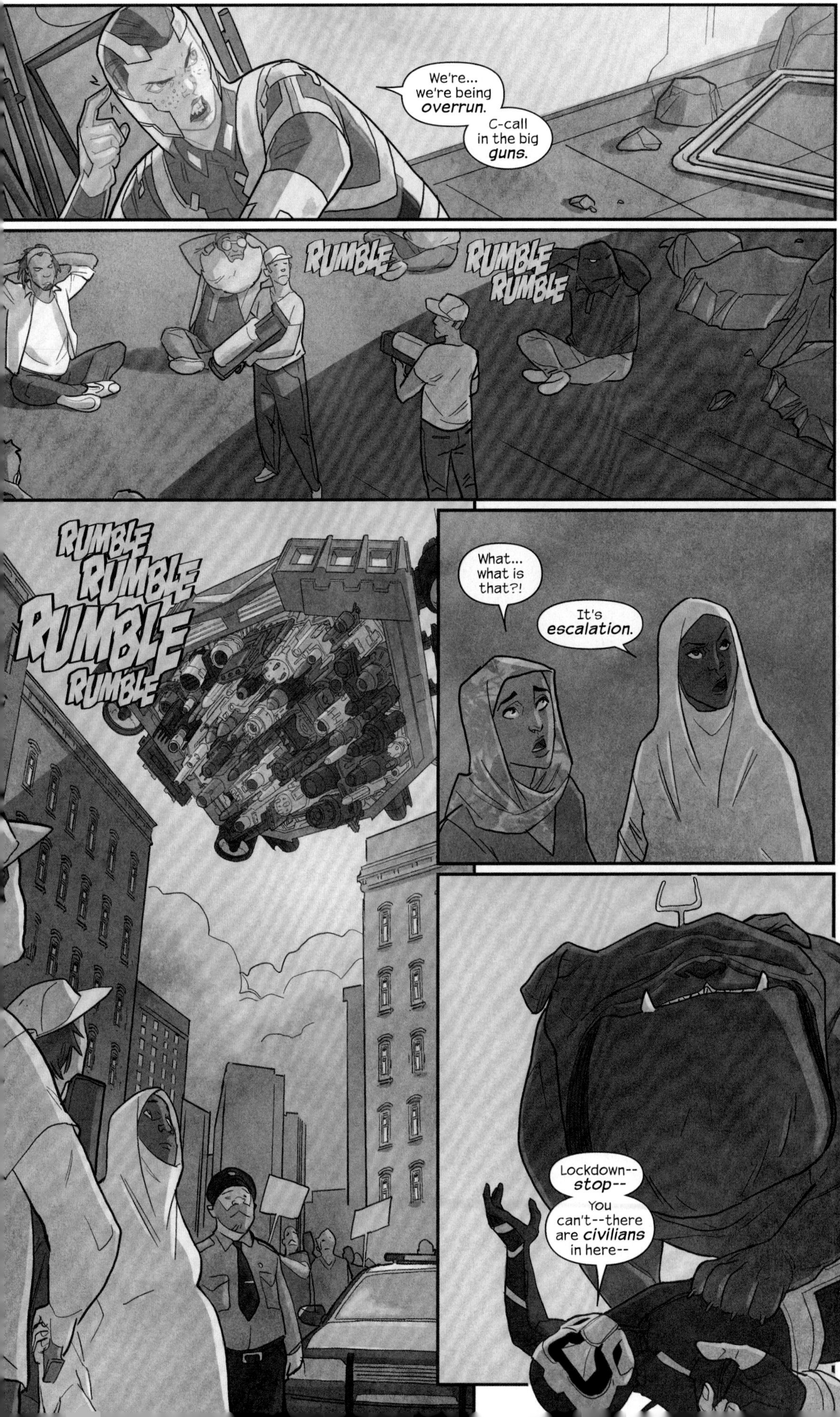

We're... we're being overrun.
C-call in the big guns.
RUMBLE
RUMBLE RUMBLE
RUMBLE RUMBLE RUMBLE RUMBLE
What... what is that?!
It's escalation.
Lockdown-- stop--
You can't--there are civilians in here--

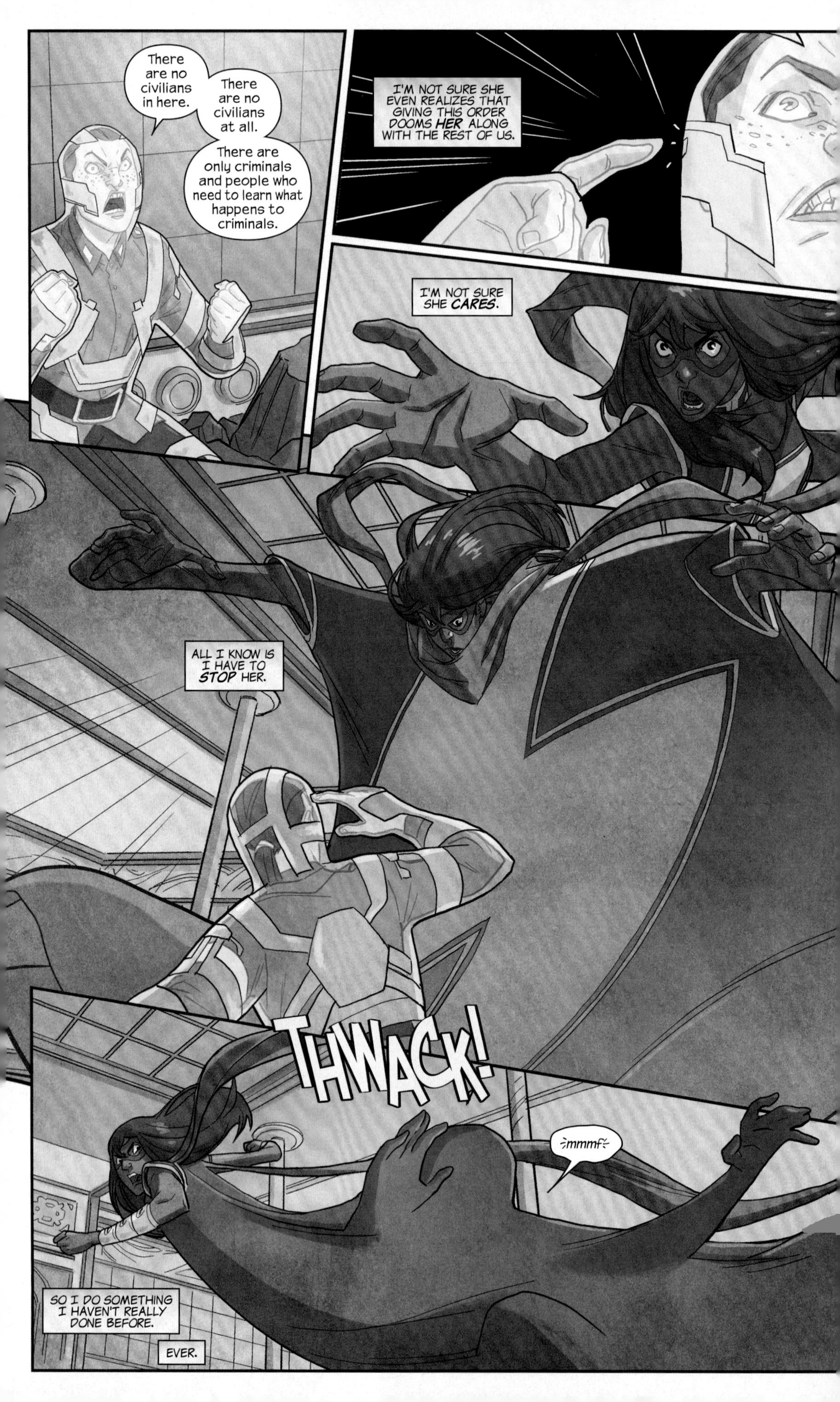
There are no civilians in here.
There are no civilians at all.
There are only criminals and people who need to learn what happens to criminals.
I'M NOT SURE SHE EVEN REALIZES THAT GIVING THIS ORDER DOOMS HER ALONG WITH THE REST OF US.
I'M NOT SURE SHE CARES.
ALL I KNOW IS I HAVE TO STOP HER.
THWACK!
mmmf
SO I DO SOMETHING I HAVEN'T REALLY DONE BEFORE.
EVER.

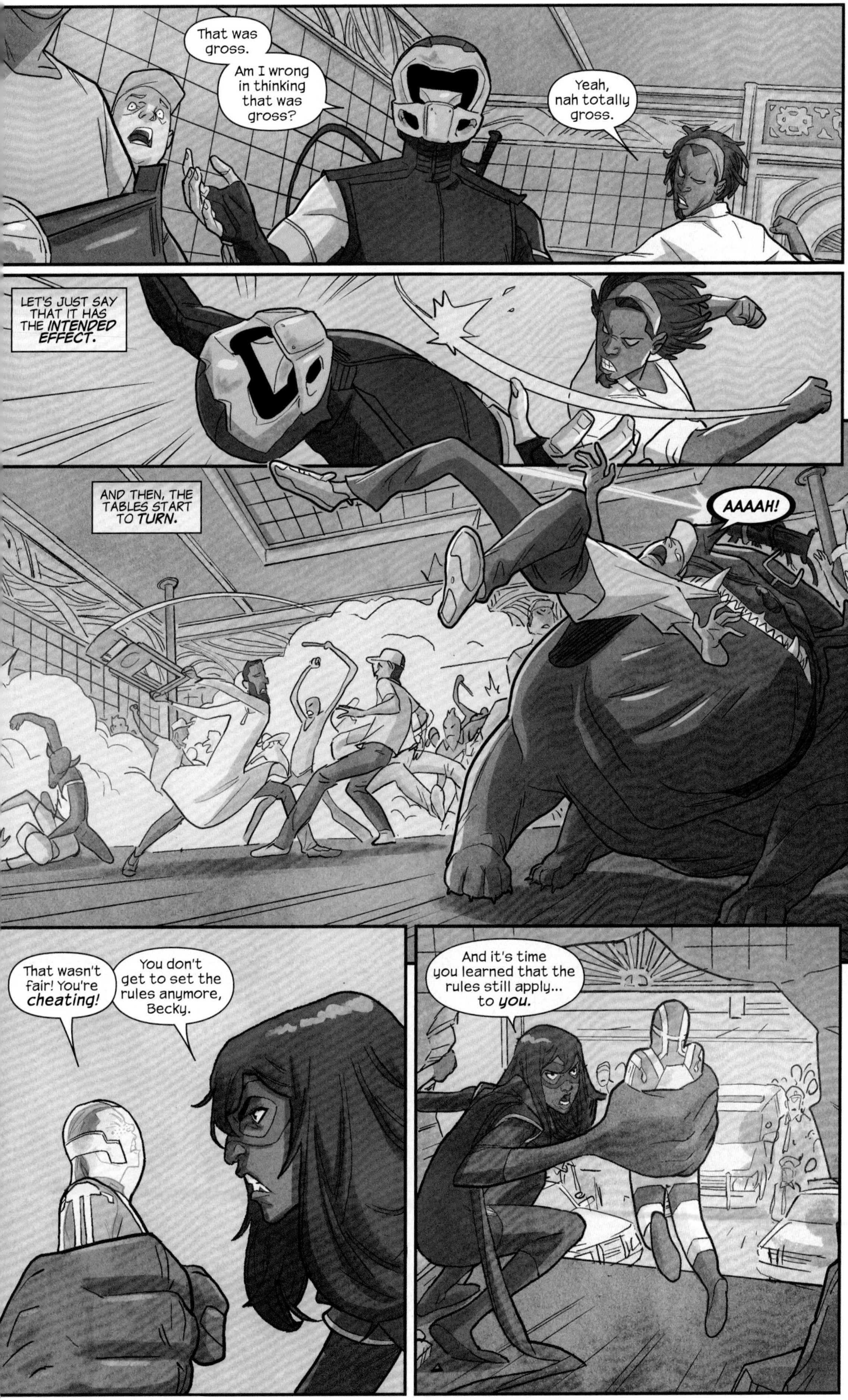

That was gross.
Am I wrong in thinking that was gross?
Yeah, nah totally gross.
LET'S JUST SAY THAT IT HAS THE *INTENDED EFFECT.*
AND THEN, THE TABLES START TO *TURN.*
AAAAH!
That wasn't fair! You're *cheating!*
You don't get to set the rules anymore, Becky.
And it's time you learned that the rules still apply... to *you.*

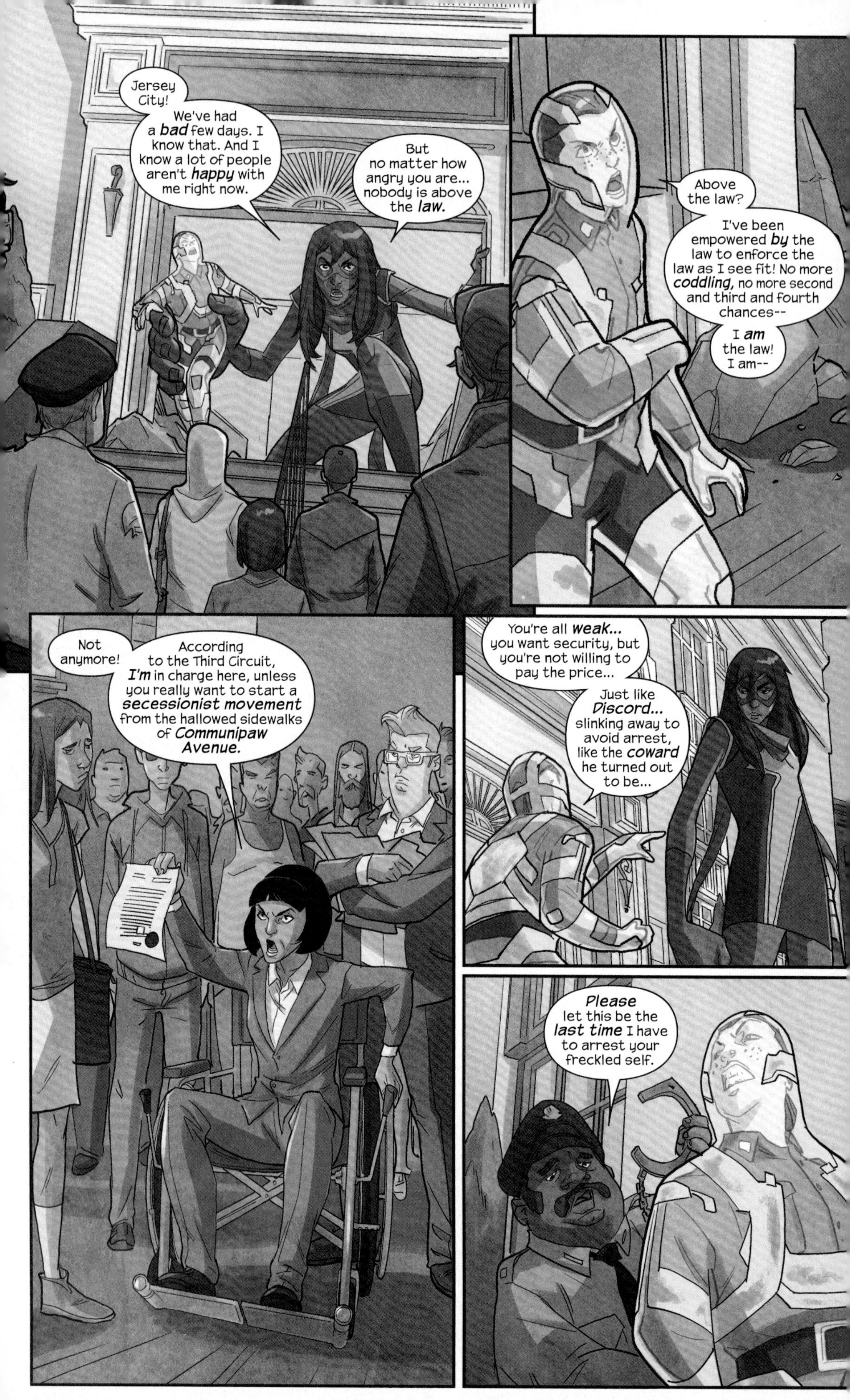

Jersey City!
We've had a bad few days. I know that. And I know a lot of people aren't happy with me right now.
But no matter how angry you are... nobody is above the law.
Above the law?
I've been empowered by the law to enforce the law as I see fit! No more coddling, no more second and third and fourth chances--
I am the law! I am--
Not anymore!
According to the Third Circuit, I'm in charge here, unless you really want to start a secessionist movement from the hallowed sidewalks of Communipaw Avenue.
You're all weak... you want security, but you're not willing to pay the price...
Just like Discord... slinking away to avoid arrest, like the coward he turned out to be...
Please let this be the last time I have to arrest your freckled self.

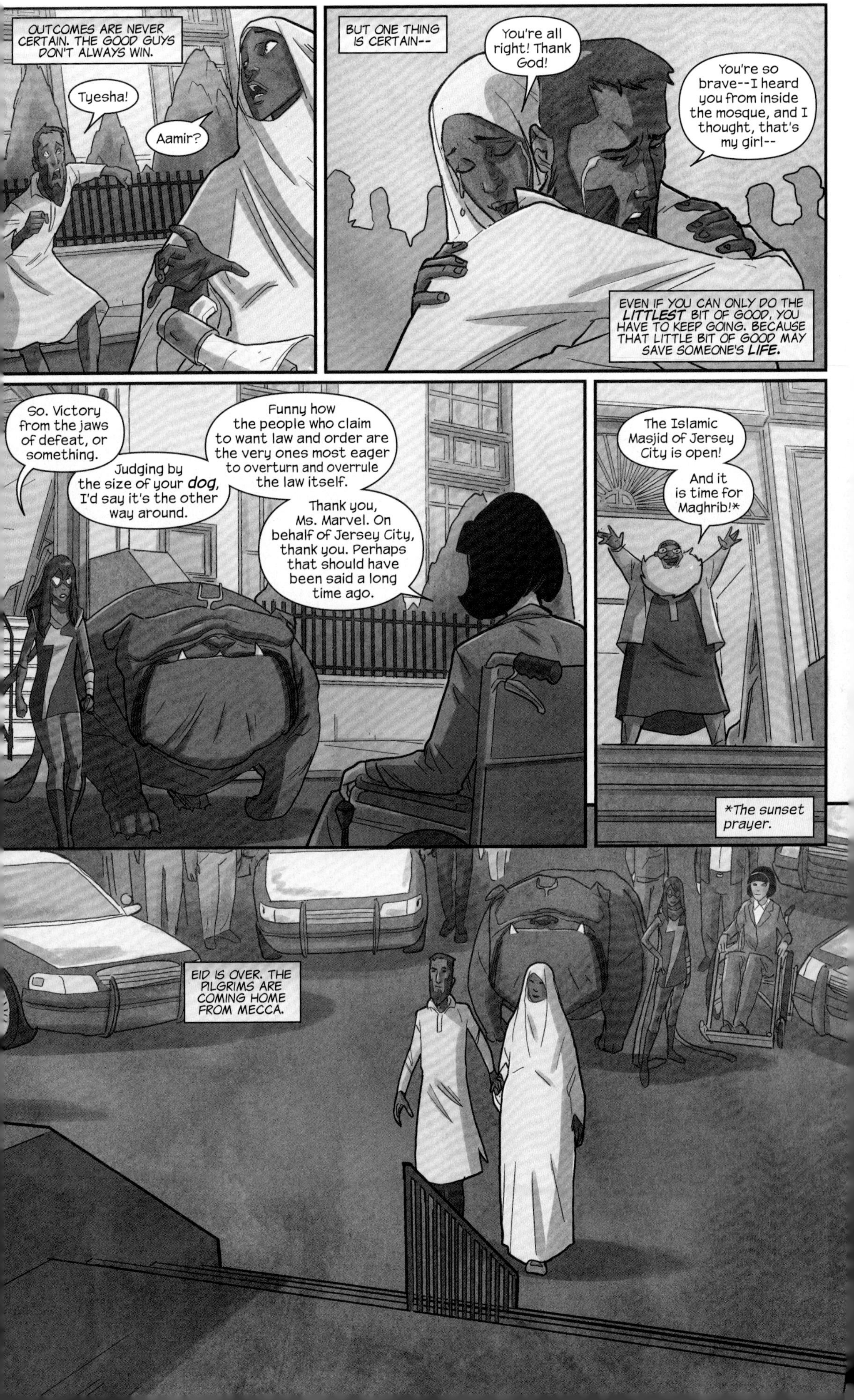

OUTCOMES ARE NEVER CERTAIN. THE GOOD GUYS DON'T ALWAYS WIN.
Tyesha!
Aamir?
BUT ONE THING IS CERTAIN--
You're all right! Thank God!
You're so brave--I heard you from inside the mosque, and I thought, that's my girl--
EVEN IF YOU CAN ONLY DO THE LITTLEST BIT OF GOOD, YOU HAVE TO KEEP GOING. BECAUSE THAT LITTLE BIT OF GOOD MAY SAVE SOMEONE'S LIFE.
So. Victory from the jaws of defeat, or something.
Judging by the size of your dog, I'd say it's the other way around.
Funny how the people who claim to want law and order are the very ones most eager to overturn and overrule the law itself.
Thank you, Ms. Marvel. On behalf of Jersey City, thank you. Perhaps that should have been said a long time ago.
The Islamic Masjid of Jersey City is open!
And it is time for Maghrib!*
*The sunset prayer.
EID IS OVER. THE PILGRIMS ARE COMING HOME FROM MECCA.

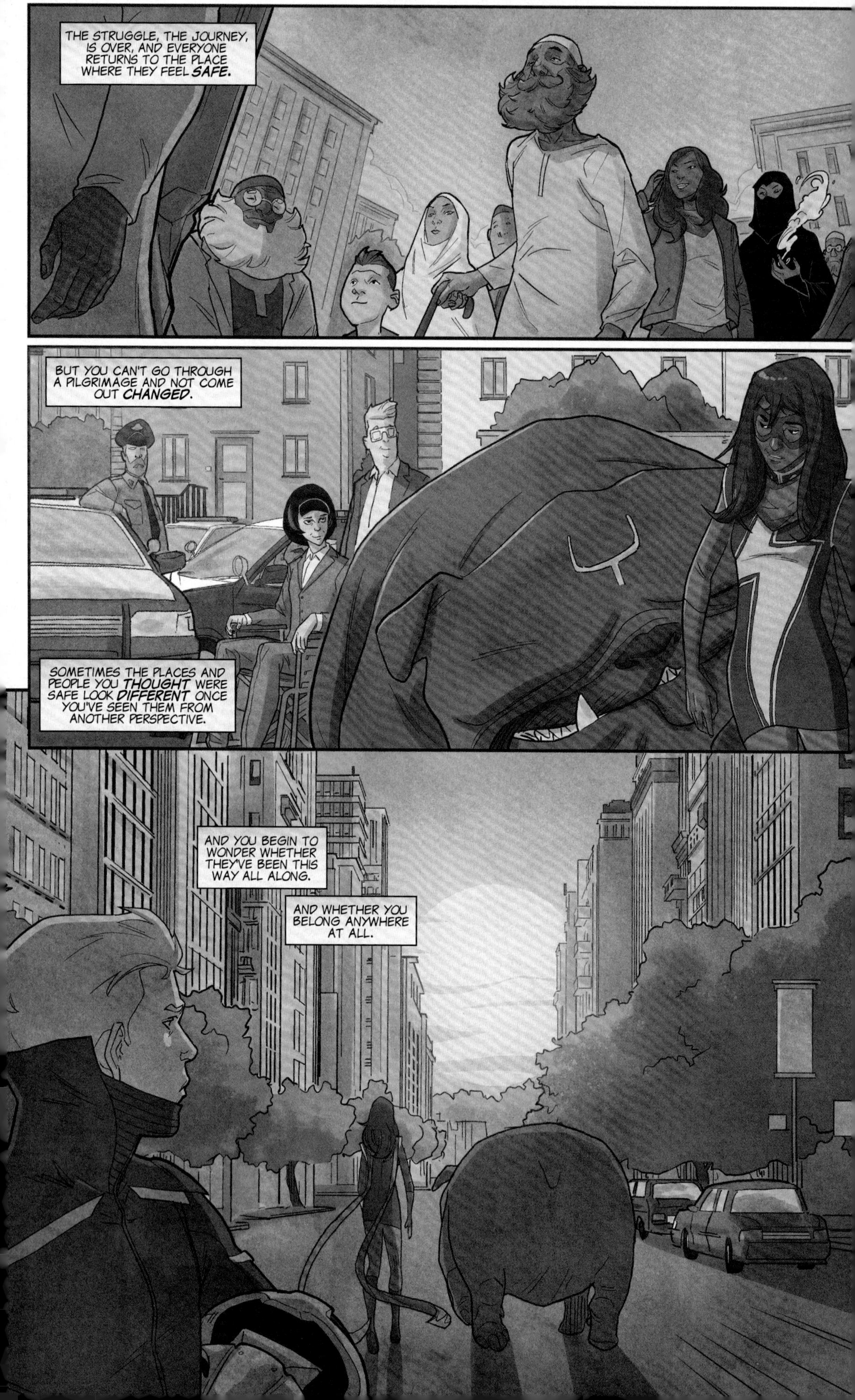

THE STRUGGLE, THE JOURNEY, IS OVER, AND EVERYONE RETURNS TO THE PLACE WHERE THEY FEEL SAFE.
BUT YOU CAN'T GO THROUGH A PILGRIMAGE AND NOT COME OUT CHANGED.
SOMETIMES THE PLACES AND PEOPLE YOU THOUGHT WERE SAFE LOOK DIFFERENT ONCE YOU'VE SEEN THEM FROM ANOTHER PERSPECTIVE.
AND YOU BEGIN TO WONDER WHETHER THEY'VE BEEN THIS WAY ALL ALONG.
AND WHETHER YOU BELONG ANYWHERE AT ALL.

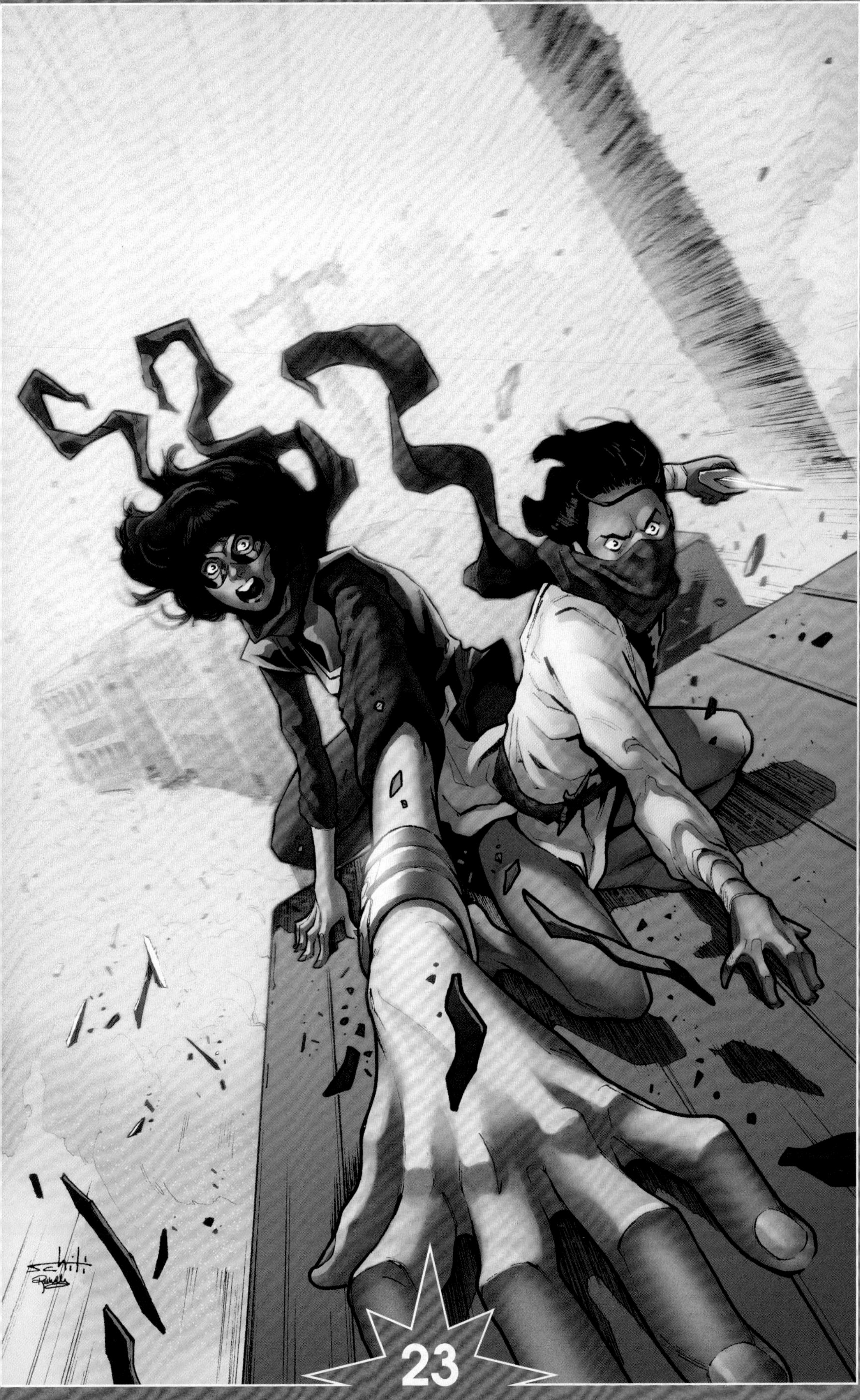
23

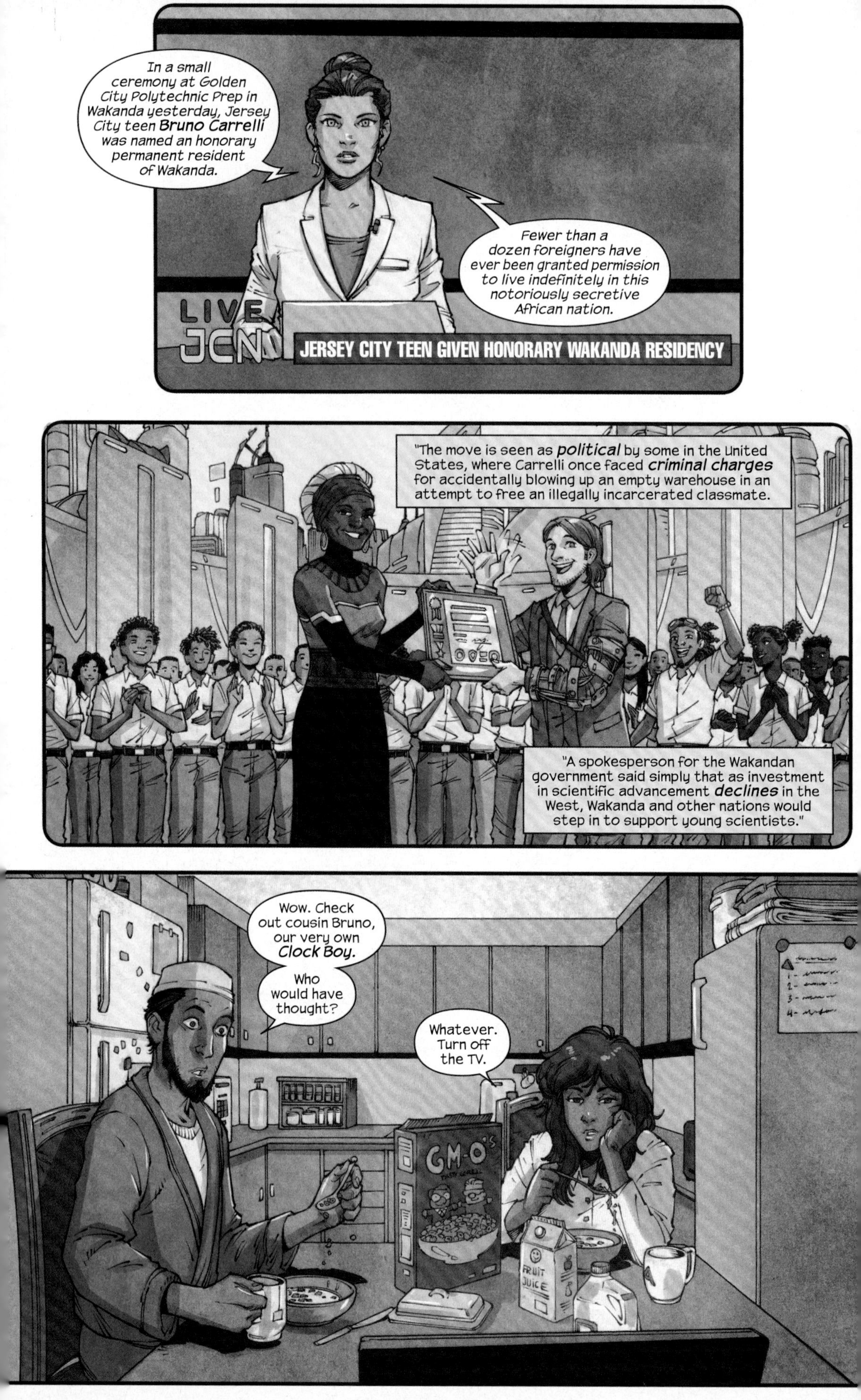
In a small ceremony at Golden City Polytechnic Prep in Wakanda yesterday, Jersey City teen Bruno Carrelli was named an honorary permanent resident of Wakanda.
Fewer than a dozen foreigners have ever been granted permission to live indefinitely in this notoriously secretive African nation.
LIVE
JCN
JERSEY CITY TEEN GIVEN HONORARY WAKANDA RESIDENCY
"The move is seen as political by some in the United States, where Carrelli once faced criminal charges for accidentally blowing up an empty warehouse in an attempt to free an illegally incarcerated classmate.
"A spokesperson for the Wakandan government said simply that as investment in scientific advancement declines in the West, Wakanda and other nations would step in to support young scientists."
Wow. Check out cousin Bruno, our very own Clock Boy.
Who would have thought?
Whatever. Turn off the TV.
GM-O's
FRUIT JUICE

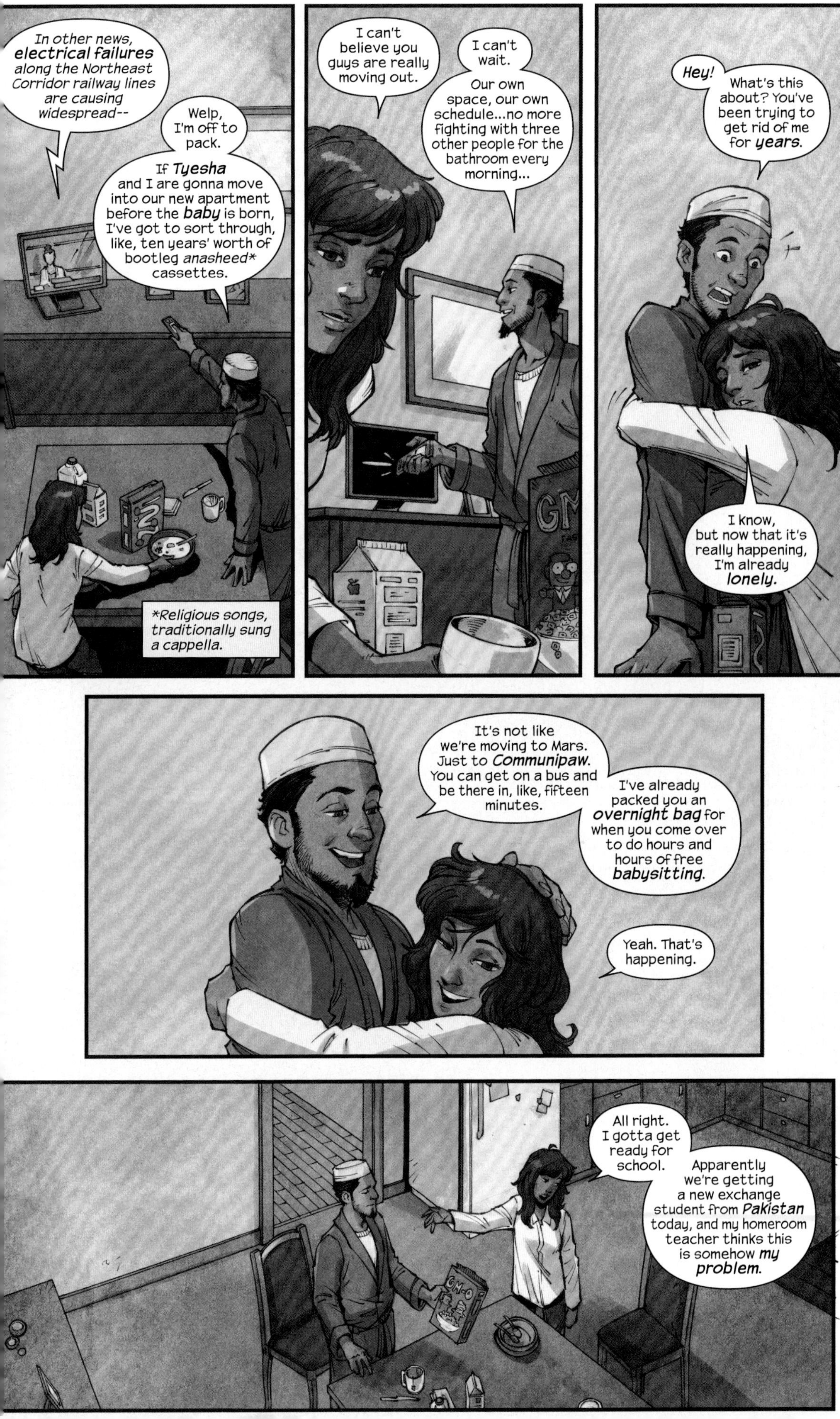
In other news, electrical failures along the Northeast Corridor railway lines are causing widespread--
Welp, I'm off to pack.
If Tyesha and I are gonna move into our new apartment before the baby is born, I've got to sort through, like, ten years' worth of bootleg anasheed* cassettes.
*Religious songs, traditionally sung a cappella.
I can't believe you guys are really moving out.
I can't wait.
Our own space, our own schedule...no more fighting with three other people for the bathroom every morning...
Hey!
What's this about? You've been trying to get rid of me for years.
I know, but now that it's really happening, I'm already lonely.
It's not like we're moving to Mars. Just to Communipaw. You can get on a bus and be there in, like, fifteen minutes.
I've already packed you an overnight bag for when you come over to do hours and hours of free babysitting.
Yeah. That's happening.
All right. I gotta get ready for school.
Apparently we're getting a new exchange student from Pakistan today, and my homeroom teacher thinks this is somehow my problem.

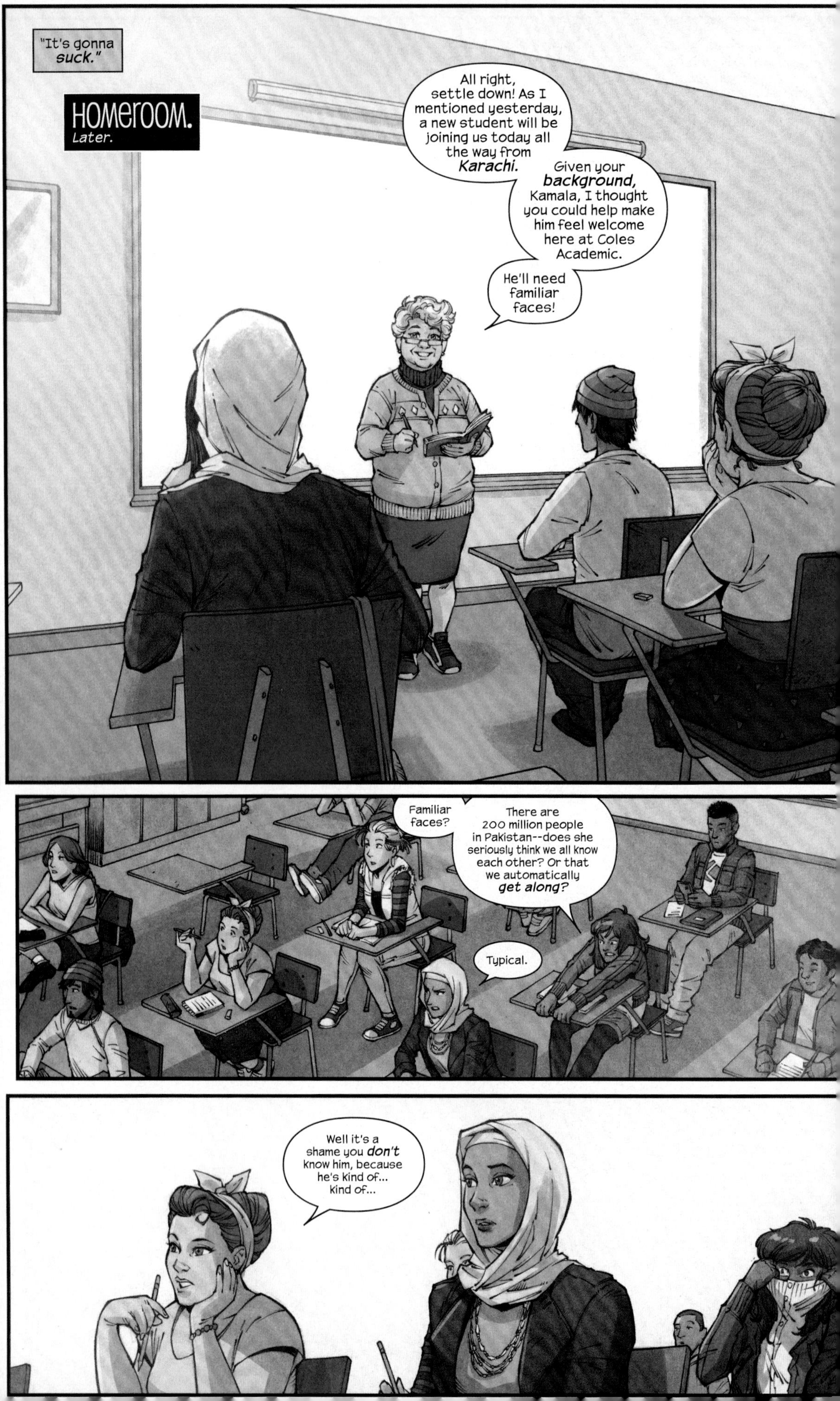
"It's gonna suck."
HOMEROOM. Later.
All right, settle down! As I mentioned yesterday, a new student will be joining us today all the way from Karachi.
Given your background, Kamala, I thought you could help make him feel welcome here at Coles Academic.
He'll need familiar faces!
Familiar faces?
There are 200 million people in Pakistan--does she seriously think we all know each other? Or that we automatically get along?
Typical.
Well it's a shame you don't know him, because he's kind of... kind of...

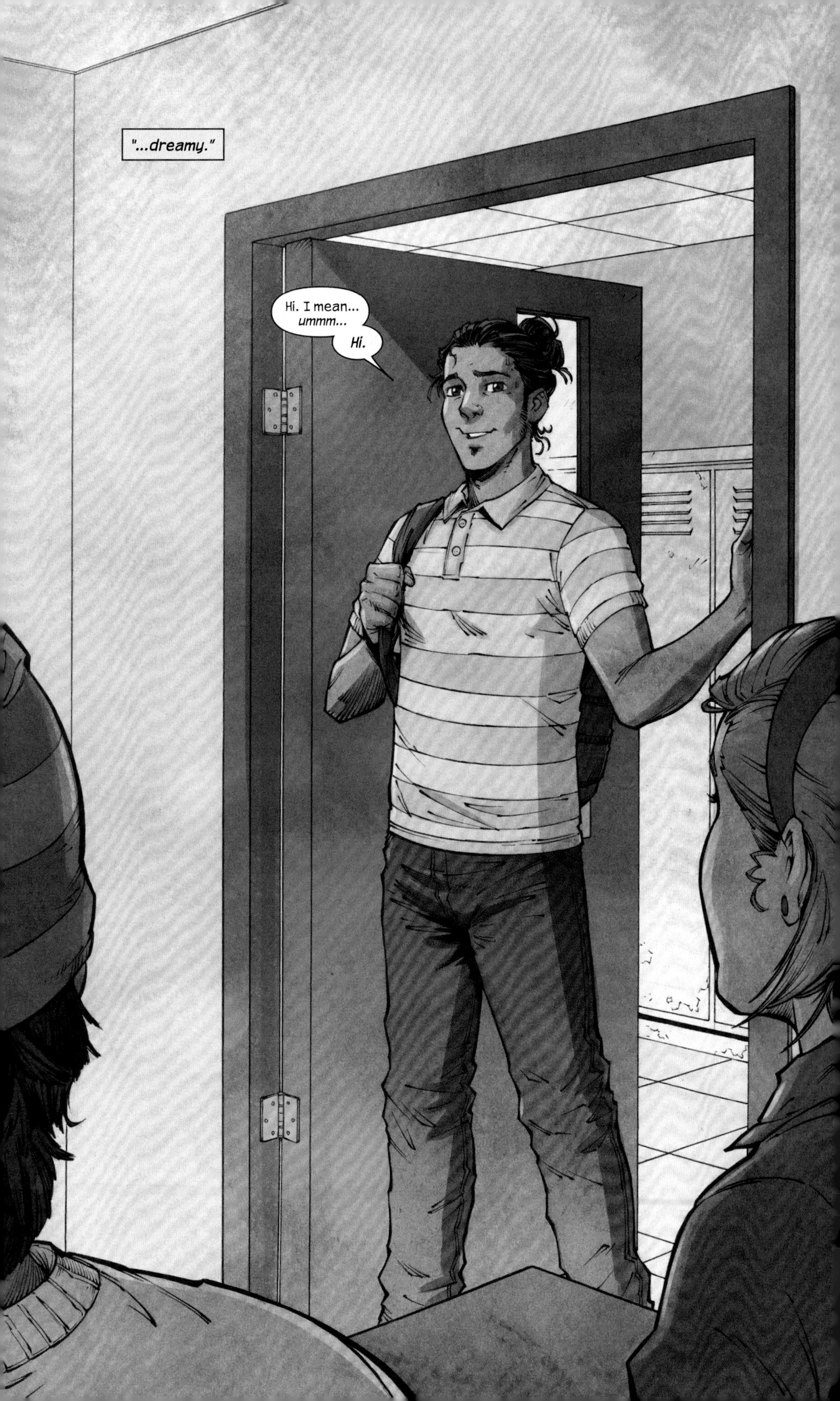
"...dreamy."
Hi. I mean... ummm... Hi.

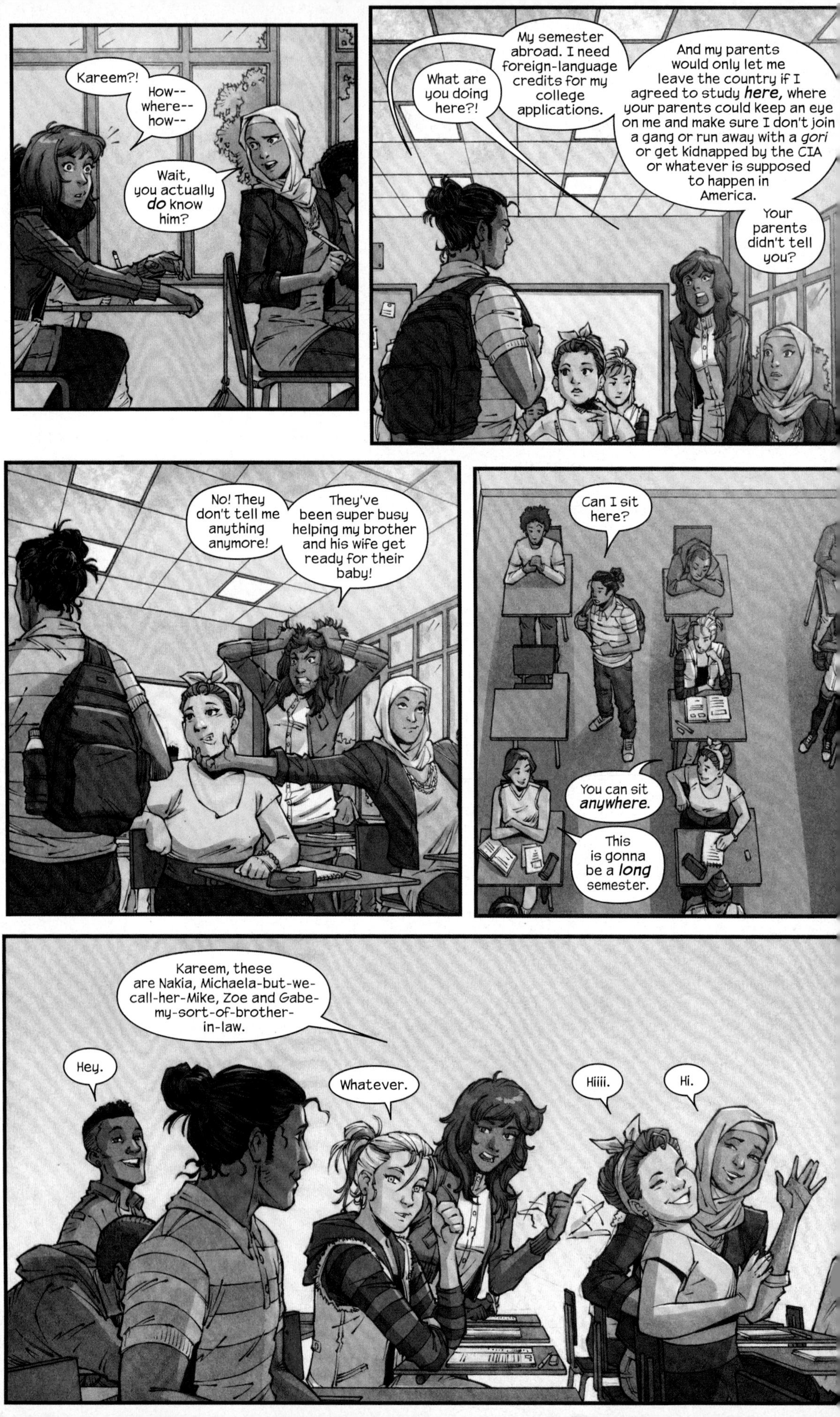
Kareem?!
How--
where--
how--
Wait, you actually *do* know him?
What are you doing here?!
My semester abroad. I need foreign-language credits for my college applications.
And my parents would only let me leave the country if I agreed to study *here,* where your parents could keep an eye on me and make sure I don't join a gang or run away with a *gori* or get kidnapped by the CIA or whatever is supposed to happen in America.
Your parents didn't tell you?
No! They don't tell me anything anymore!
They've been super busy helping my brother and his wife get ready for their baby!
Can I sit here?
You can sit *anywhere*.
This is gonna be a *long* semester.
Kareem, these are Nakia, Michaela-but-we-call-her-Mike, Zoe and Gabe-my-sort-of-brother-in-law.
Hey.
Whatever.
Hiiii.
Hi.

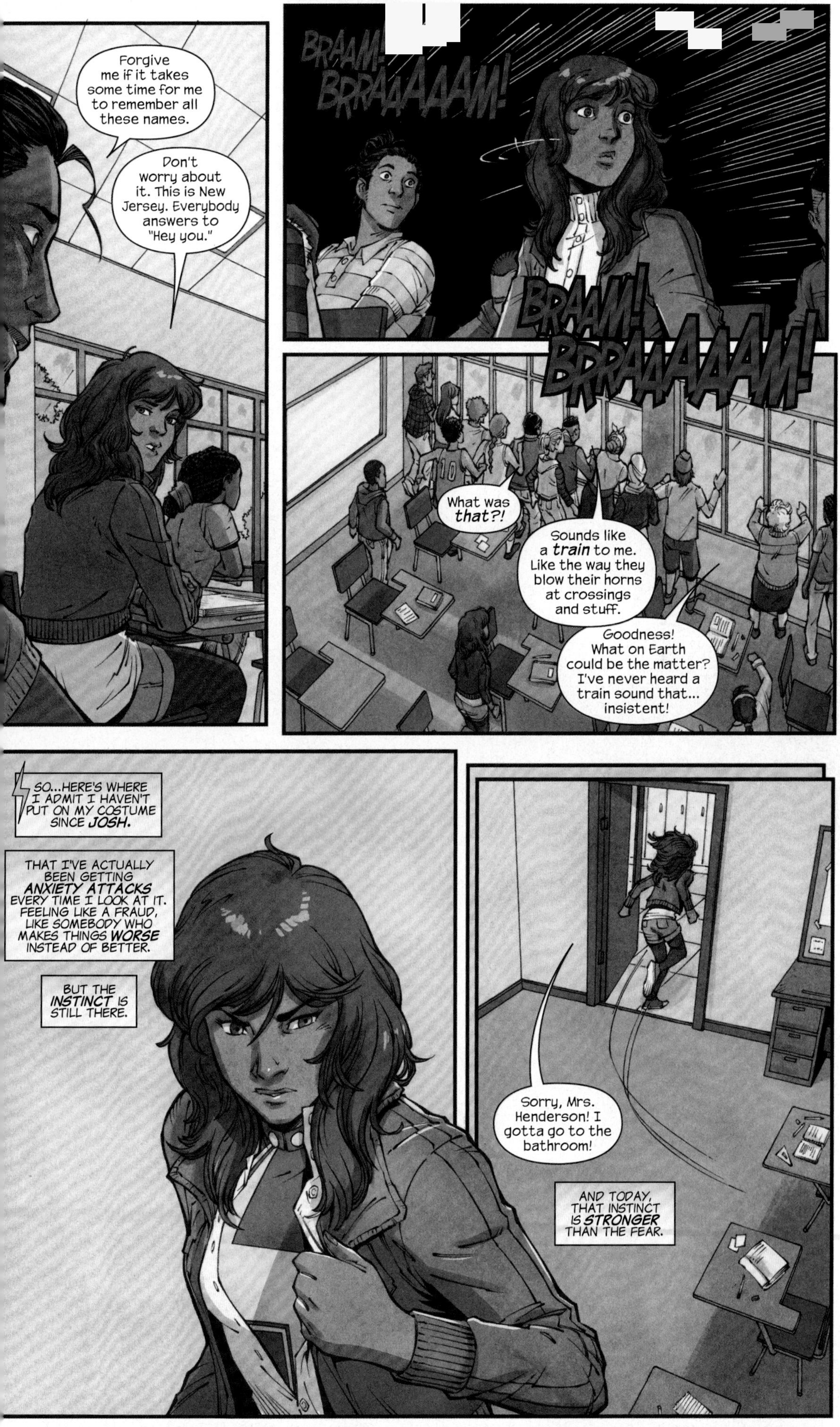

Forgive me if it takes some time for me to remember all these names.
Don't worry about it. This is New Jersey. Everybody answers to "Hey you."
BRAAM! BRRAAAAAM!
BRAAM! BRRAAAAAM!
What was *that?!*
Sounds like a *train* to me. Like the way they blow their horns at crossings and stuff.
Goodness! What on Earth could be the matter? I've never heard a train sound that... insistent!
SO...HERE'S WHERE I ADMIT I HAVEN'T PUT ON MY COSTUME SINCE *JOSH.*
THAT I'VE ACTUALLY BEEN GETTING *ANXIETY ATTACKS* EVERY TIME I LOOK AT IT. FEELING LIKE A FRAUD, LIKE SOMEBODY WHO MAKES THINGS *WORSE* INSTEAD OF BETTER.
BUT THE *INSTINCT* IS STILL THERE.
Sorry, Mrs. Henderson! I gotta go to the bathroom!
AND TODAY, THAT INSTINCT IS *STRONGER* THAN THE FEAR.

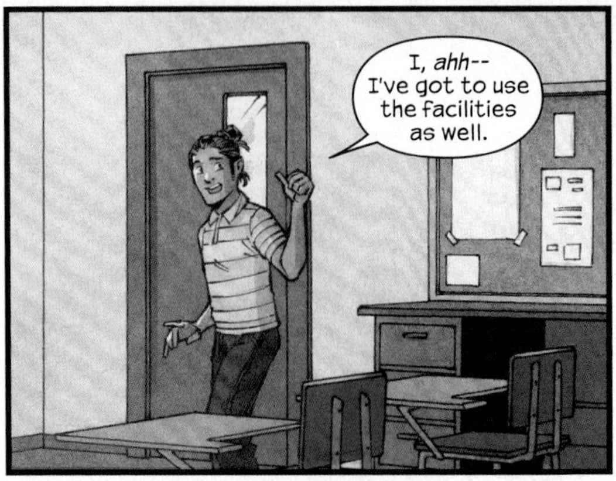
I, *ahh*--
I've got to use the facilities as well.

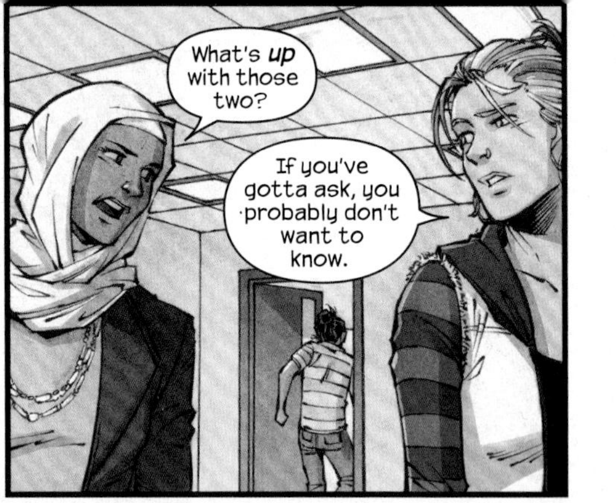
What's **up** with those two?
If you've gotta ask, you probably don't want to know.

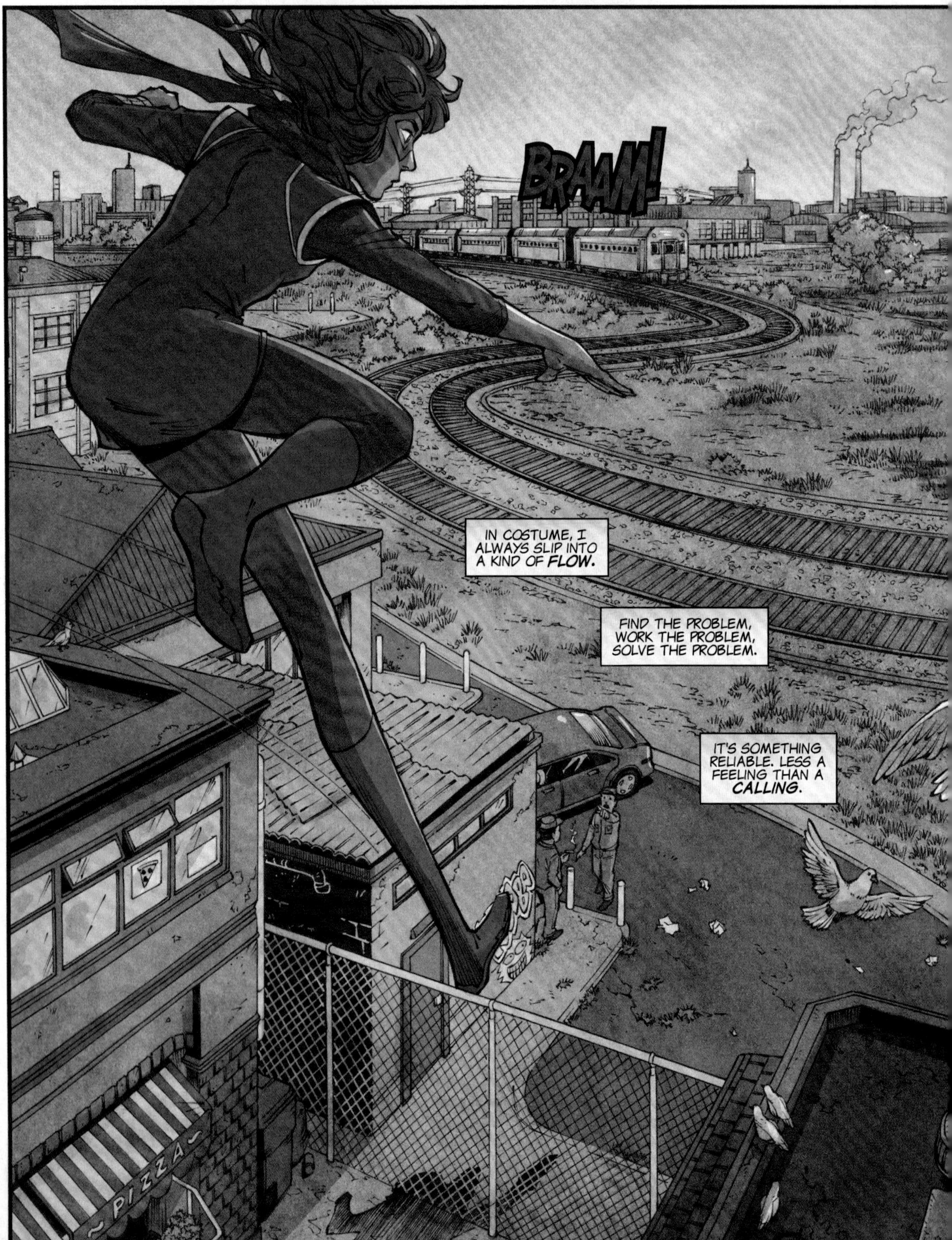
BRAAM!
IN COSTUME, I ALWAYS SLIP INTO A KIND OF **FLOW**.
FIND THE PROBLEM, WORK THE PROBLEM, SOLVE THE PROBLEM.
IT'S SOMETHING RELIABLE. LESS A FEELING THAN A **CALLING**.
PIZZA

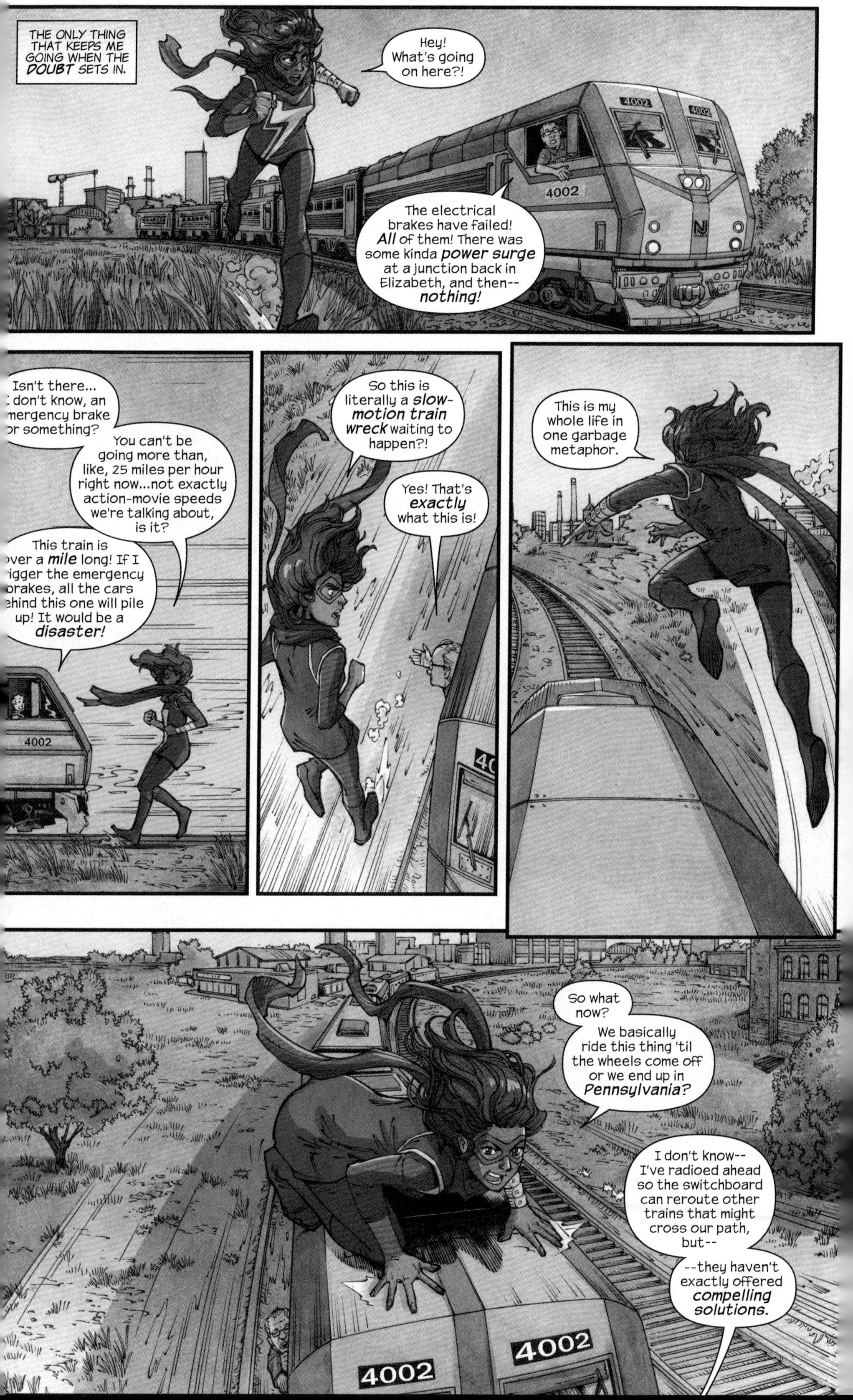
THE ONLY THING THAT KEEPS ME GOING WHEN THE DOUBT SETS IN.
Hey! What's going on here?!
The electrical brakes have failed! All of them! There was some kinda power surge at a junction back in Elizabeth, and then-- nothing!
Isn't there... I don't know, an emergency brake or something?
You can't be going more than, like, 25 miles per hour right now...not exactly action-movie speeds we're talking about, is it?
This train is over a mile long! If I trigger the emergency brakes, all the cars behind this one will pile up! It would be a disaster!
So this is literally a slow-motion train wreck waiting to happen?!
Yes! That's exactly what this is!
This is my whole life in one garbage metaphor.
So what now?
We basically ride this thing 'til the wheels come off or we end up in Pennsylvania?
I don't know-- I've radioed ahead so the switchboard can reroute other trains that might cross our path, but--
--they haven't exactly offered compelling solutions.

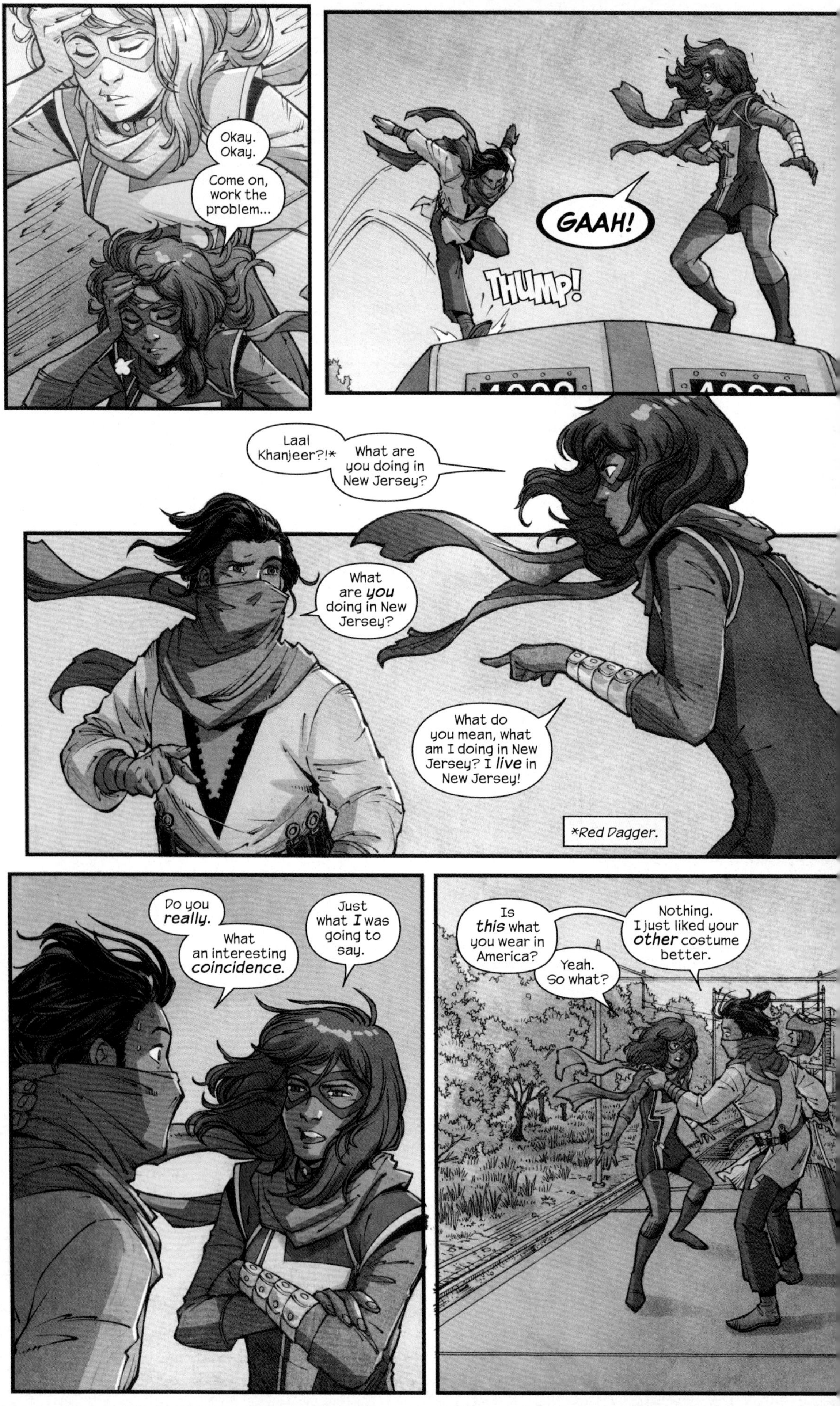

Okay. Okay.
Come on, work the problem...
GAAH!
THUMP!
Laal Khanjeer?!*
What are you doing in New Jersey?
What are *you* doing in New Jersey?
What do you mean, what am I doing in New Jersey? I *live* in New Jersey!
*Red Dagger.
Do you *really*.
What an interesting *coincidence*.
Just what *I* was going to say.
Is *this* what you wear in America?
Yeah. So what?
Nothing. I just liked your *other* costume better.

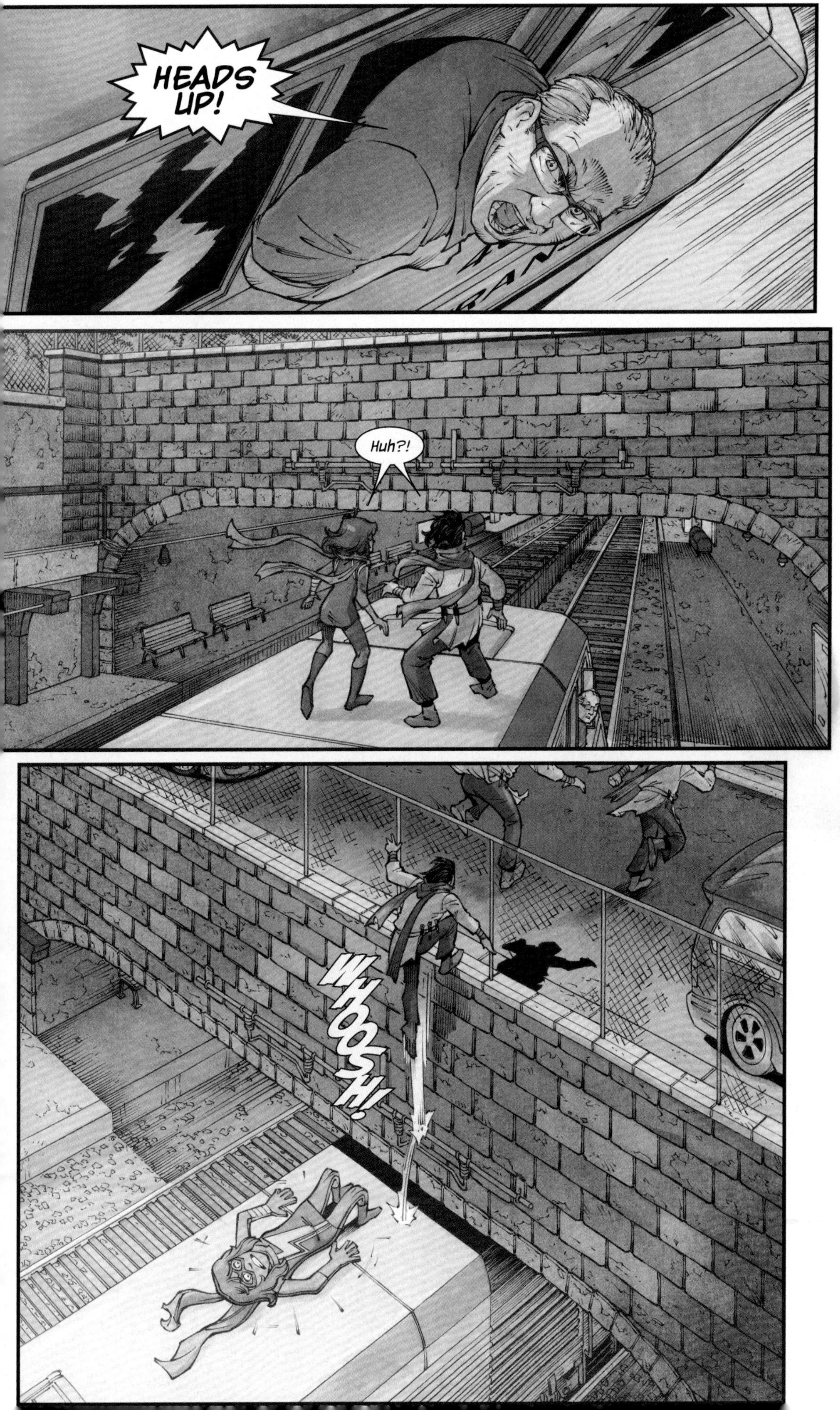
HEADS UP!
Huh?!
WHOOOSH!

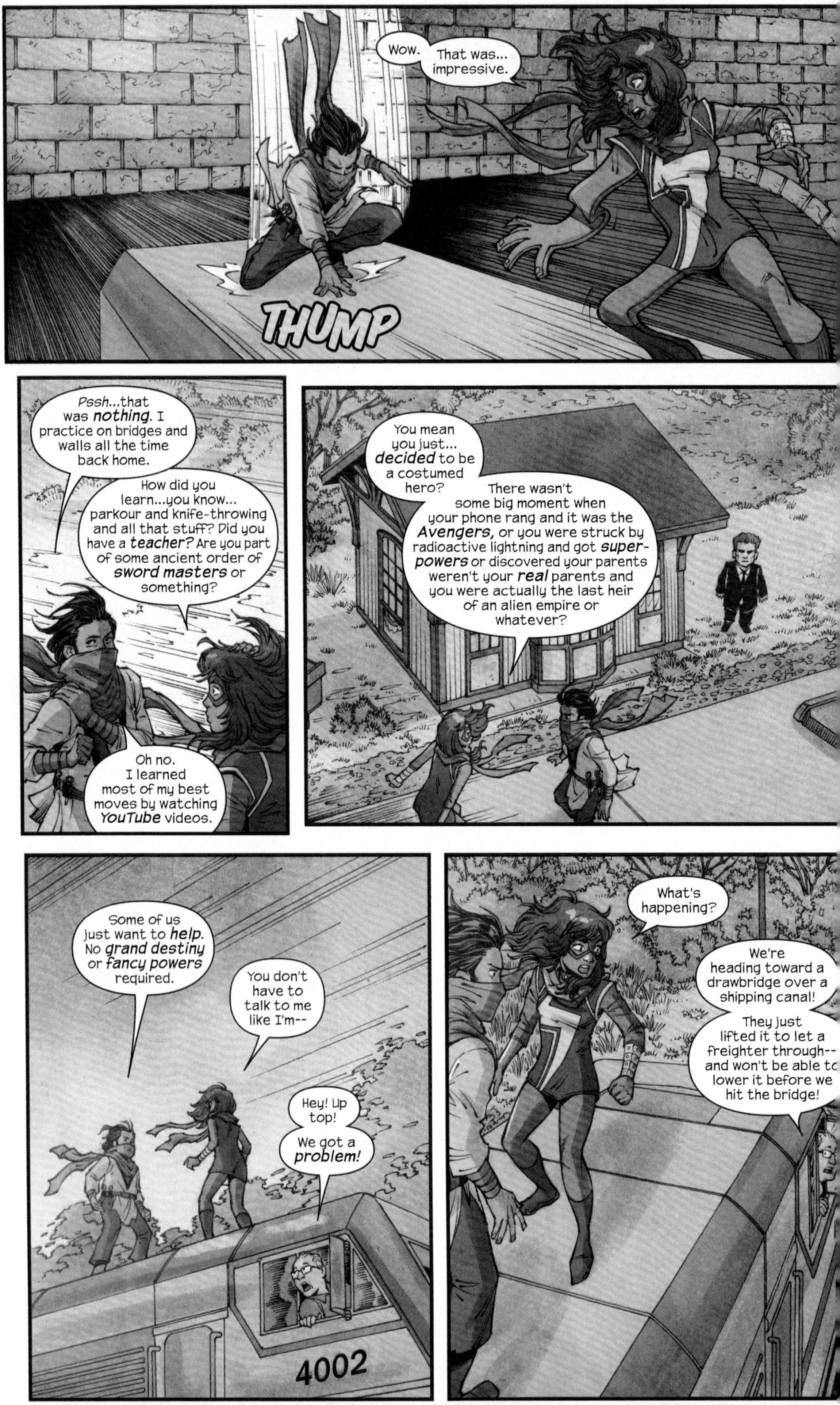

Wow.
That was... impressive.
THUMP
Pssh...that was nothing. I practice on bridges and walls all the time back home.
How did you learn...you know... parkour and knife-throwing and all that stuff? Did you have a teacher? Are you part of some ancient order of sword masters or something?
Oh no. I learned most of my best moves by watching YouTube videos.
You mean you just... decided to be a costumed hero?
There wasn't some big moment when your phone rang and it was the Avengers, or you were struck by radioactive lightning and got super-powers or discovered your parents weren't your real parents and you were actually the last heir of an alien empire or whatever?
Some of us just want to help. No grand destiny or fancy powers required.
You don't have to talk to me like I'm--
Hey! Up top!
We got a problem!
4002
What's happening?
We're heading toward a drawbridge over a shipping canal!
They just lifted it to let a freighter through--and won't be able to lower it before we hit the bridge!

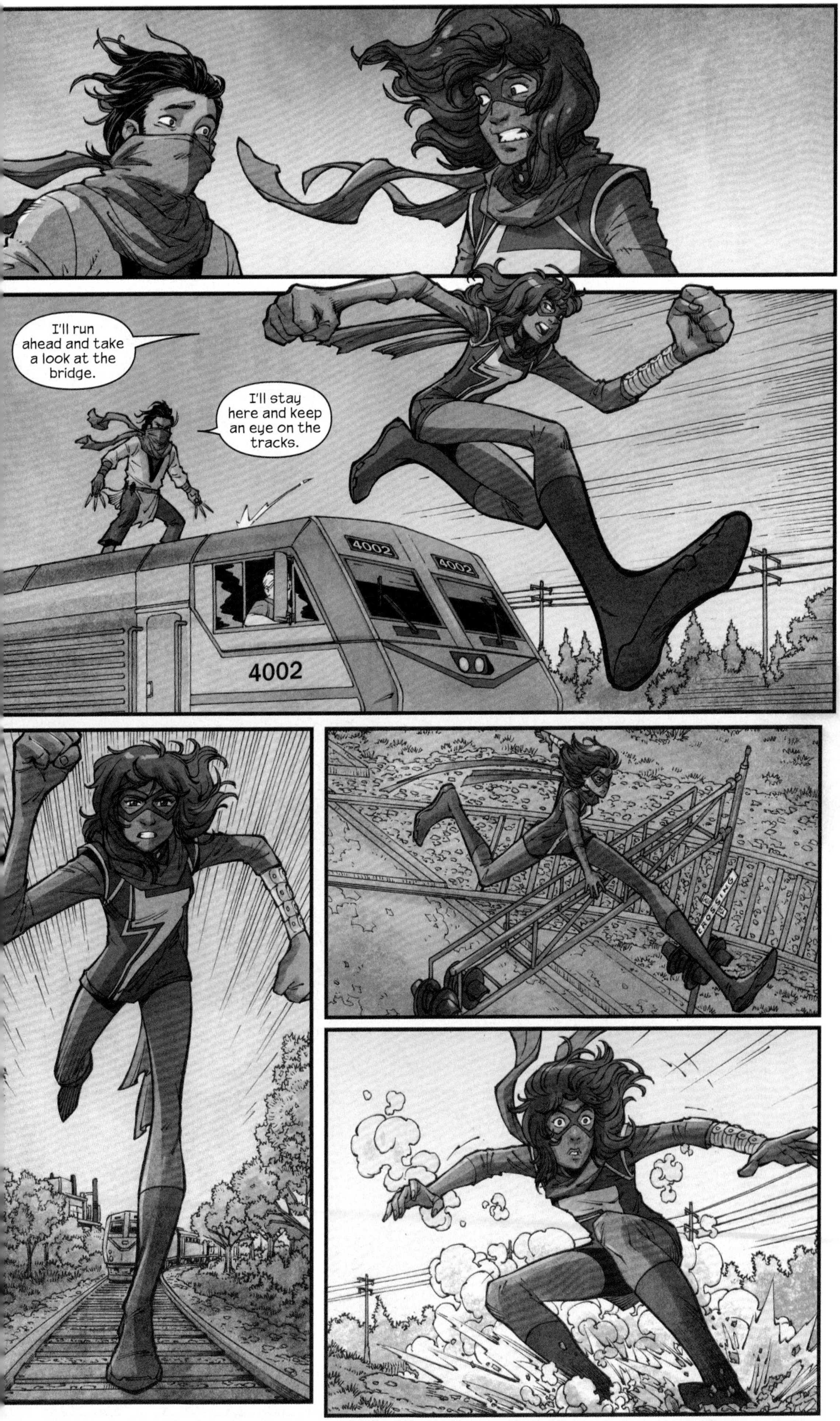
I'll run ahead and take a look at the bridge.
I'll stay here and keep an eye on the tracks.
4002
4002
4002
CROSSING

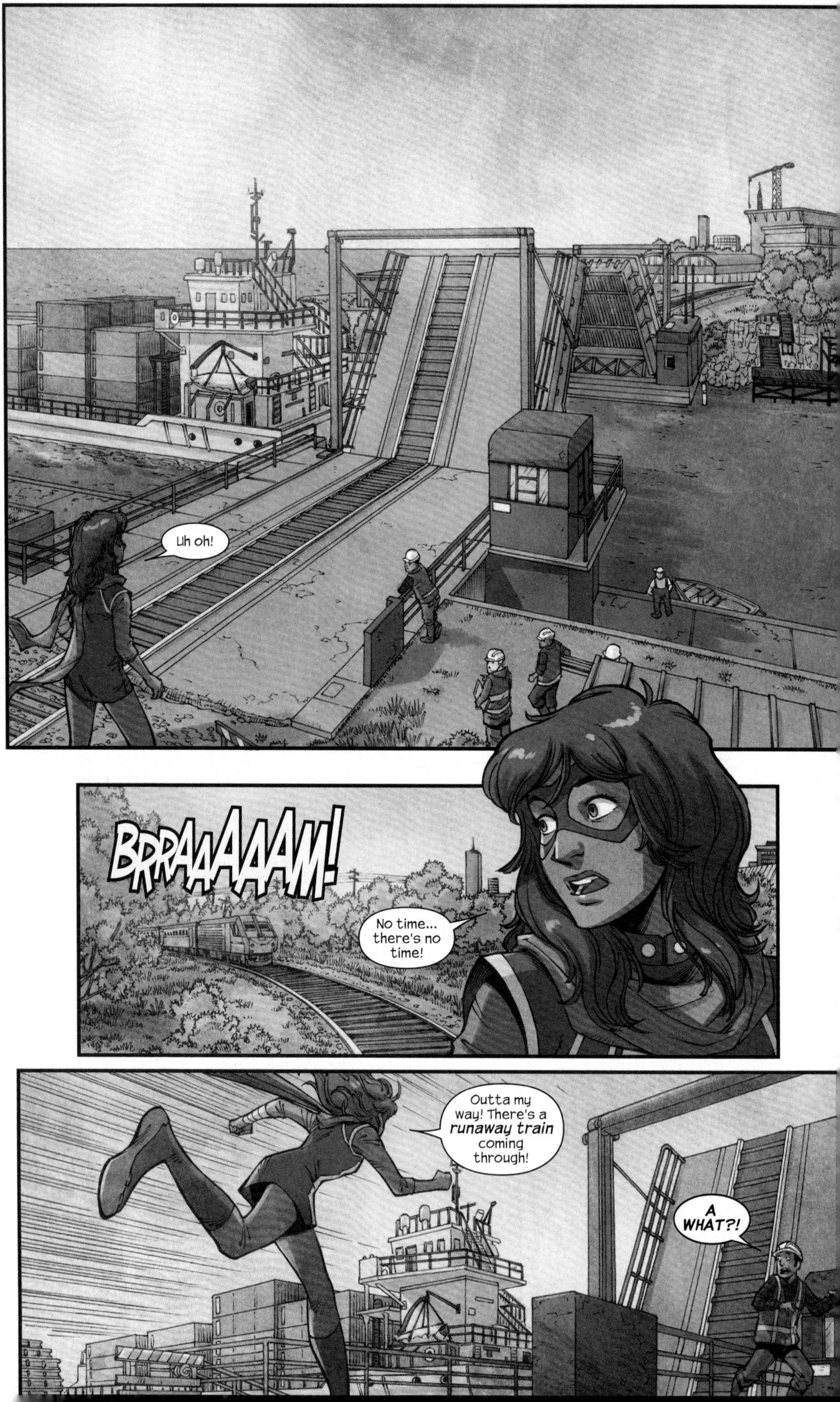
Uh oh!
BRRAAAAAM!
No time... there's no time!
Outta my way! There's a *runaway train* coming through!
A WHAT?!

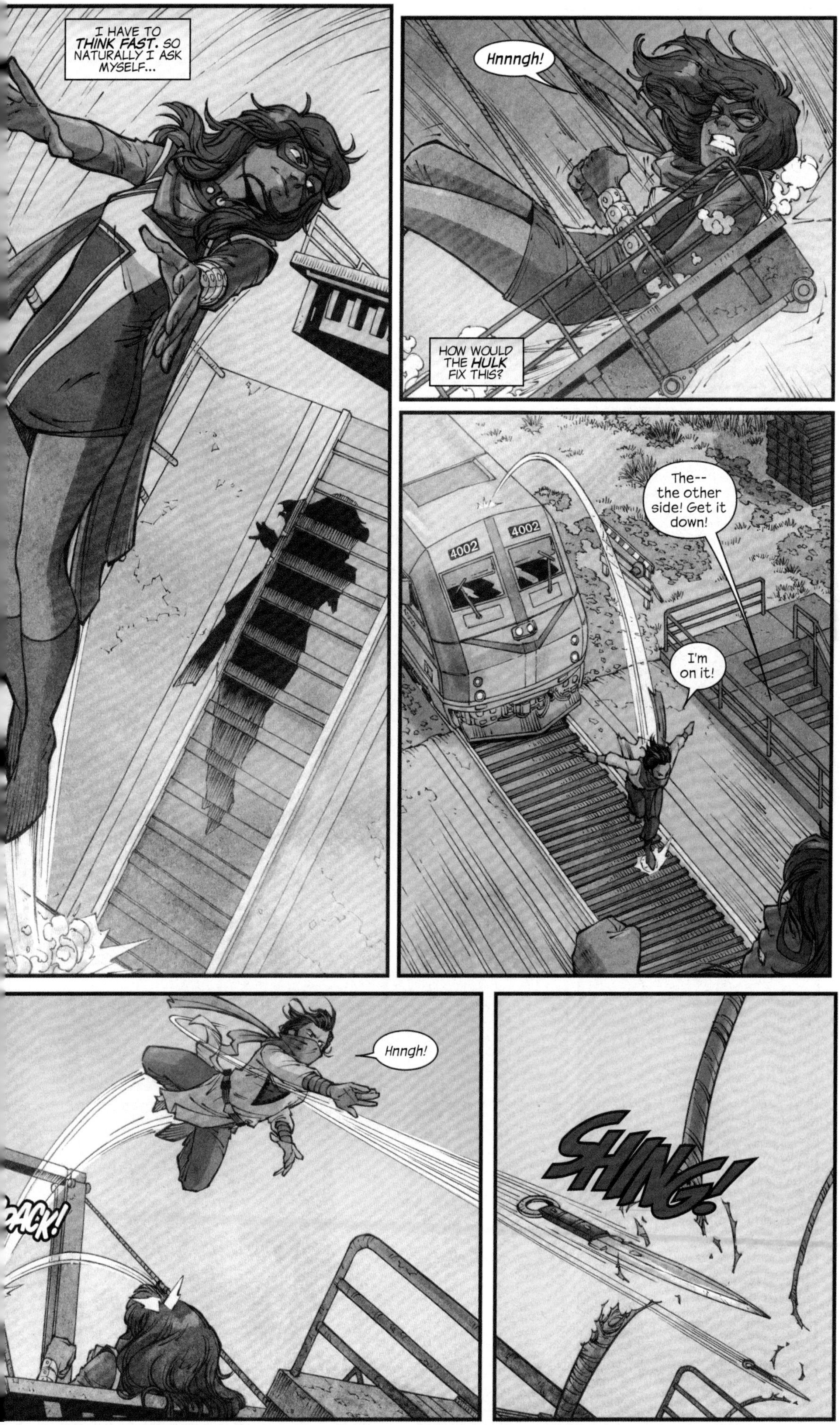
I HAVE TO THINK FAST. SO NATURALLY I ASK MYSELF...
Hnnngh!
HOW WOULD THE HULK FIX THIS?
4002
4002
The-- the other side! Get it down!
I'm on it!
Hnngh!
SHING!

CLONG

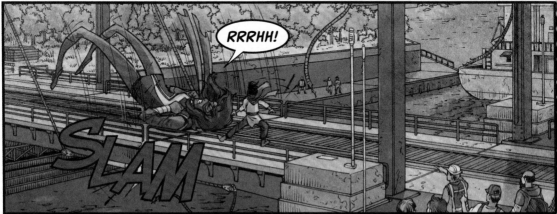

RRRHH!

SLAM

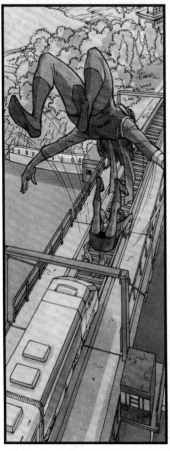

Yeah! All right!

Who is that masked man?!

That's *Ms. Marvel,* ya idiot!

No, the *other* one!

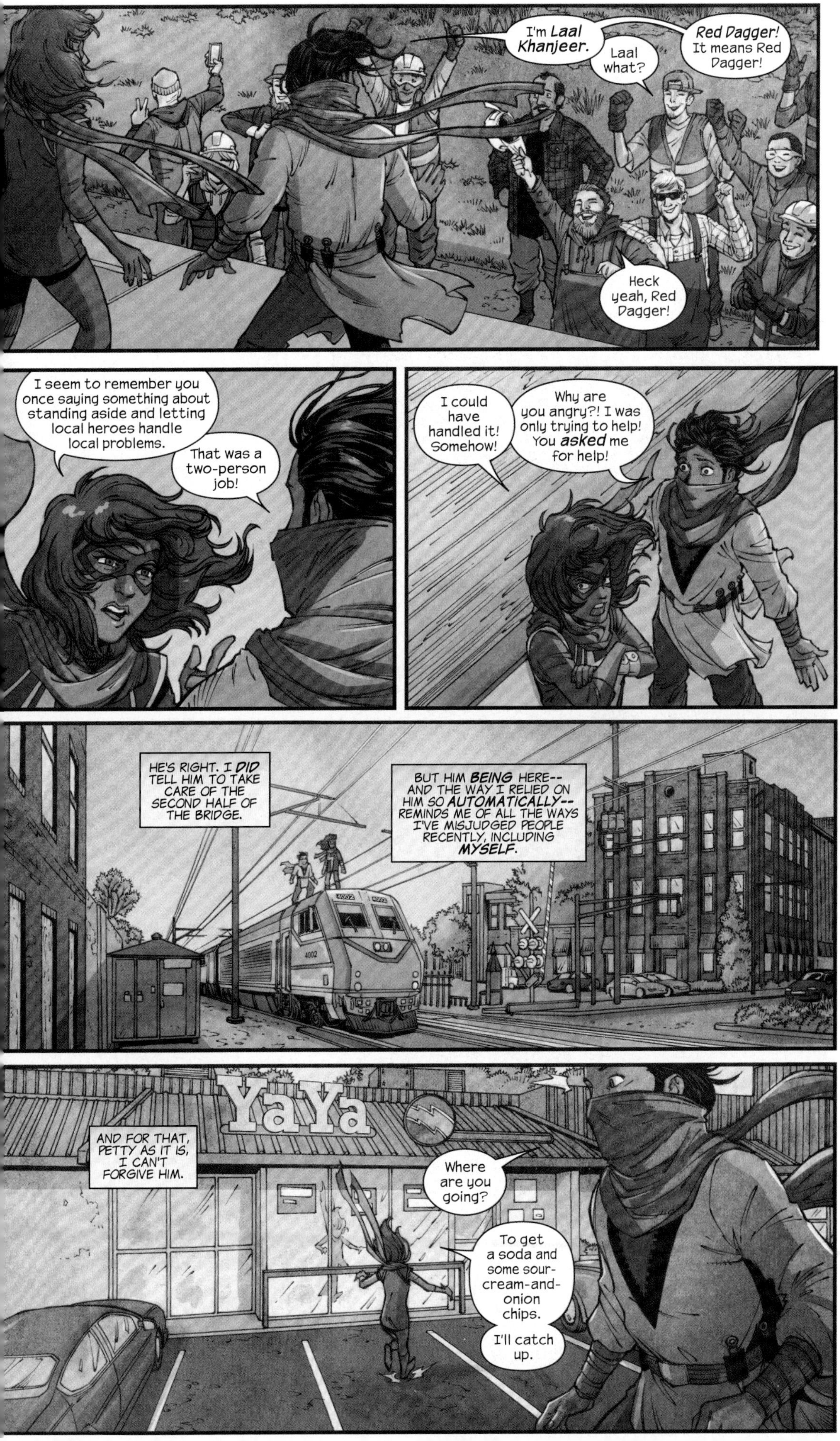

I'm Laal Khanjeer.
Laal what?
Red Dagger! It means Red Dagger!
Heck yeah, Red Dagger!
I seem to remember you once saying something about standing aside and letting local heroes handle local problems.
That was a two-person job!
I could have handled it! Somehow!
Why are you angry?! I was only trying to help! You asked me for help!
HE'S RIGHT. I DID TELL HIM TO TAKE CARE OF THE SECOND HALF OF THE BRIDGE.
BUT HIM BEING HERE--AND THE WAY I RELIED ON HIM SO AUTOMATICALLY--REMINDS ME OF ALL THE WAYS I'VE MISJUDGED PEOPLE RECENTLY, INCLUDING MYSELF.
YaYa
AND FOR THAT, PETTY AS IT IS, I CAN'T FORGIVE HIM.
Where are you going?
To get a soda and some sour-cream-and-onion chips.
I'll catch up.

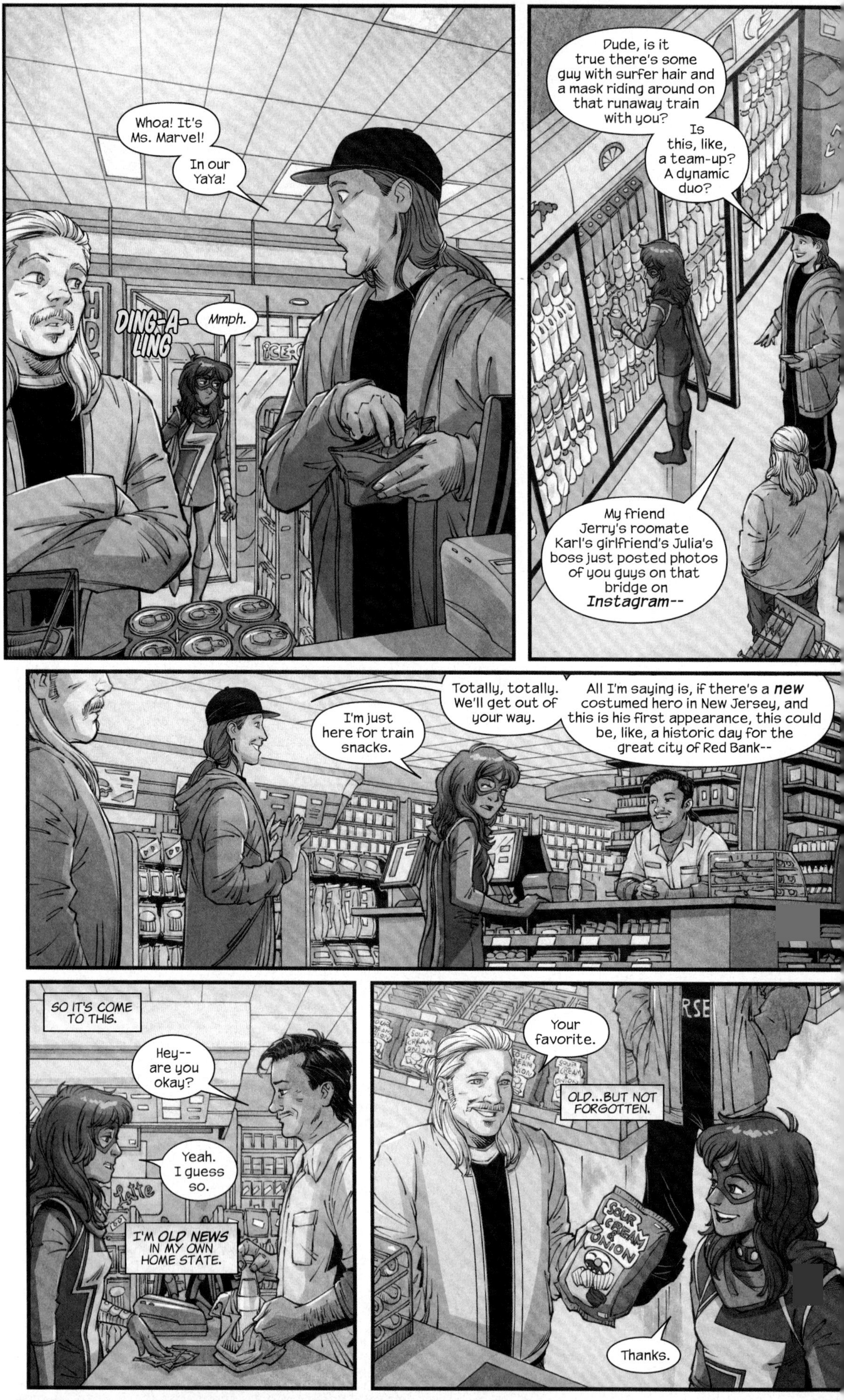

Whoa! It's Ms. Marvel!
In our YaYa!
DING-A-LING
Mmph.
Dude, is it true there's some guy with surfer hair and a mask riding around on that runaway train with you?
Is this, like, a team-up? A dynamic duo?
My friend Jerry's roomate Karl's girlfriend's Julia's boss just posted photos of you guys on that bridge on *Instagram*--
I'm just here for train snacks.
Totally, totally. We'll get out of your way.
All I'm saying is, if there's a *new* costumed hero in New Jersey, and this is his first appearance, this could be, like, a historic day for the great city of Red Bank--
SO IT'S COME TO THIS.
Hey-- are you okay?
Yeah. I guess so.
I'M *OLD NEWS* IN MY OWN HOME STATE.
Your favorite.
OLD...BUT NOT FORGOTTEN.
SOUR CREAM & ONION
Thanks.

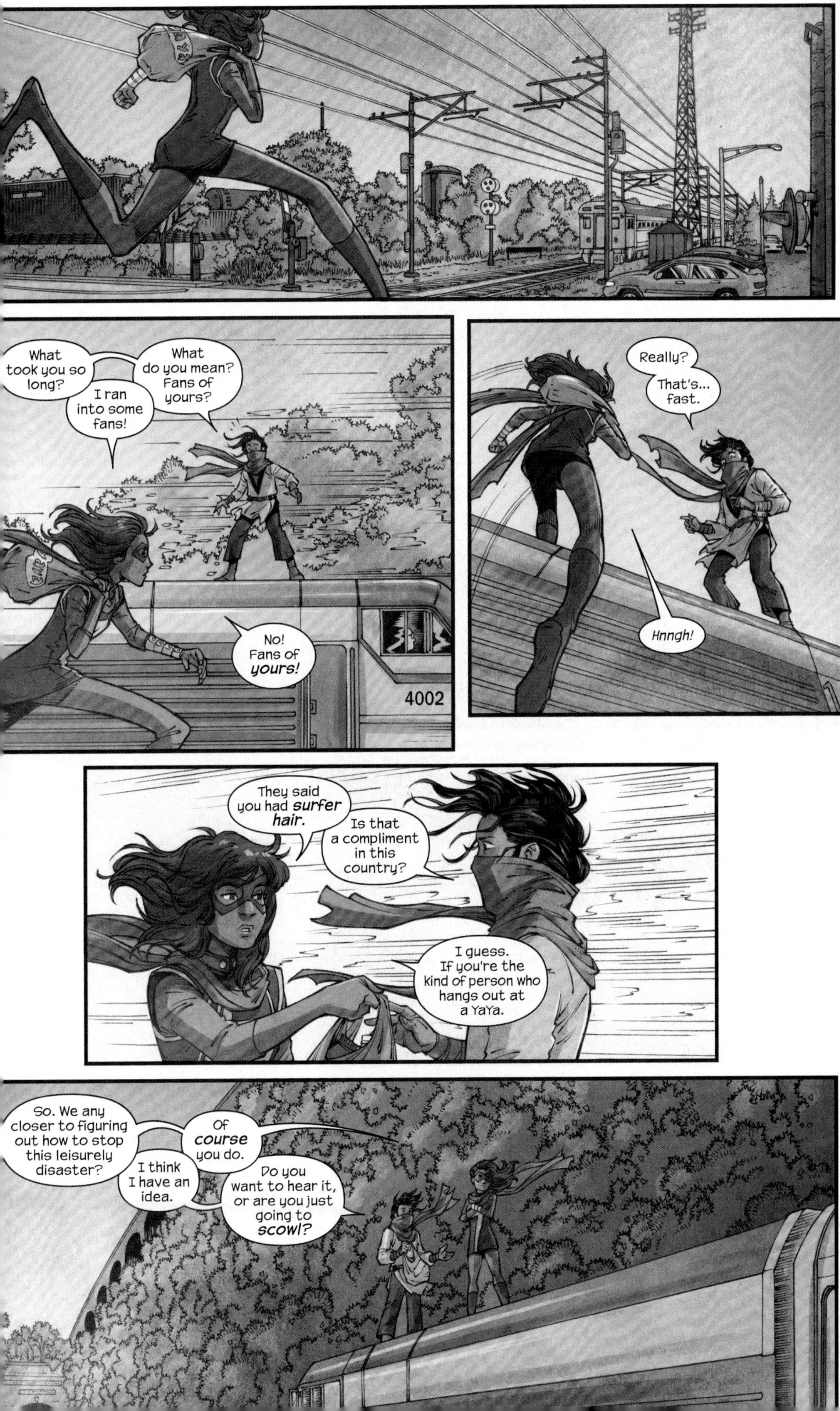

What took you so long?
I ran into some fans!
What do you mean? Fans of yours?
No! Fans of *yours!*
4002
Really?
That's... fast.
Hnngh!
They said you had ***surfer hair.***
Is that a compliment in this country?
I guess. If you're the kind of person who hangs out at a YaYa.
So. We any closer to figuring out how to stop this leisurely disaster?
I think I have an idea.
Of ***course*** you do.
Do you want to hear it, or are you just going to ***scowl?***

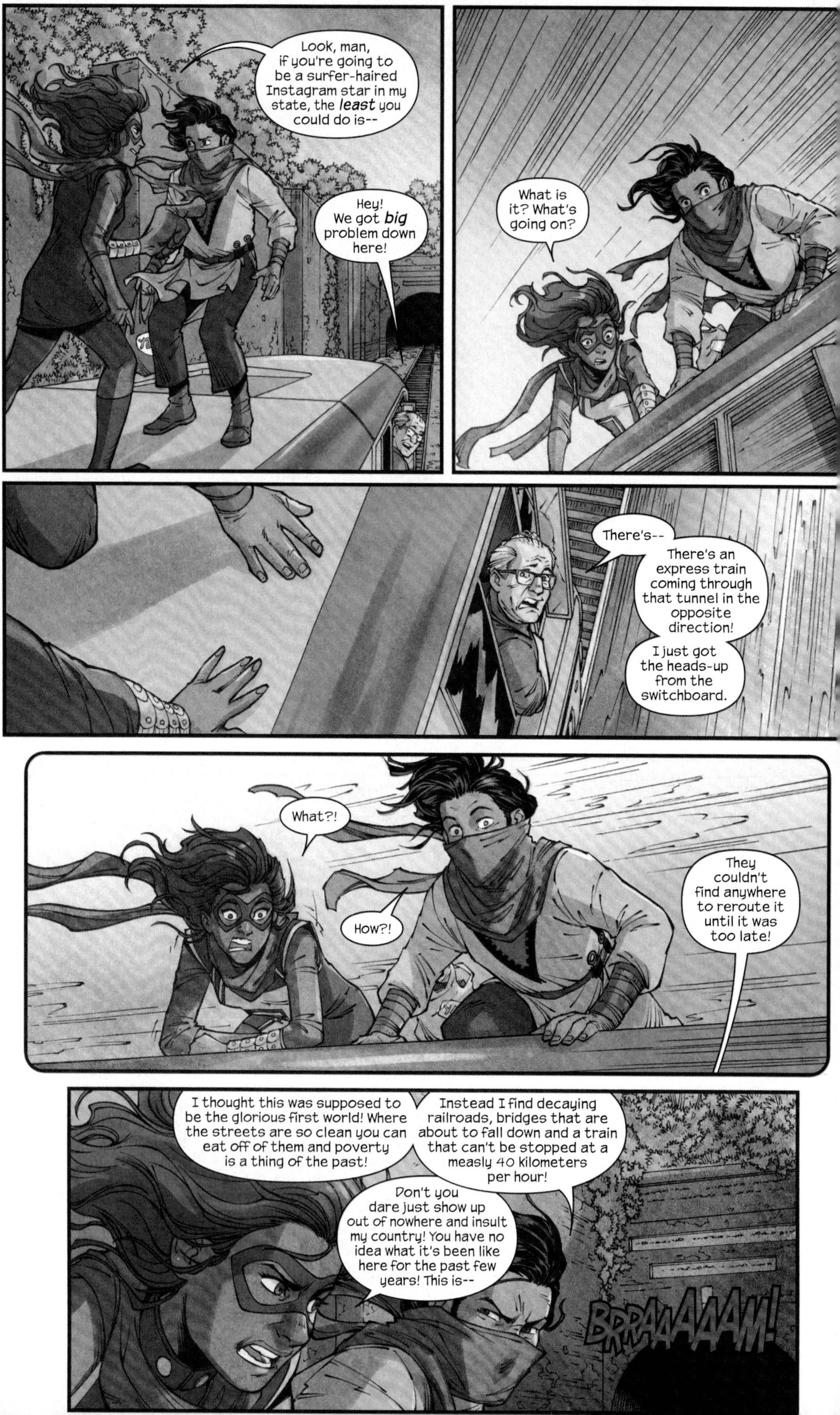
Look, man, if you're going to be a surfer-haired Instagram star in my state, the *least* you could do is--
Hey! We got *big* problem down here!
What is it? What's going on?
There's--
There's an express train coming through that tunnel in the opposite direction!
I just got the heads-up from the switchboard.
What?!
How?!
They couldn't find anywhere to reroute it until it was too late!
I thought this was supposed to be the glorious first world! Where the streets are so clean you can eat off of them and poverty is a thing of the past!
Instead I find decaying railroads, bridges that are about to fall down and a train that can't be stopped at a measly 40 kilometers per hour!
Don't you dare just show up out of nowhere and insult my country! You have no idea what it's been like here for the past few years! This is--
BRRAAAAAM!

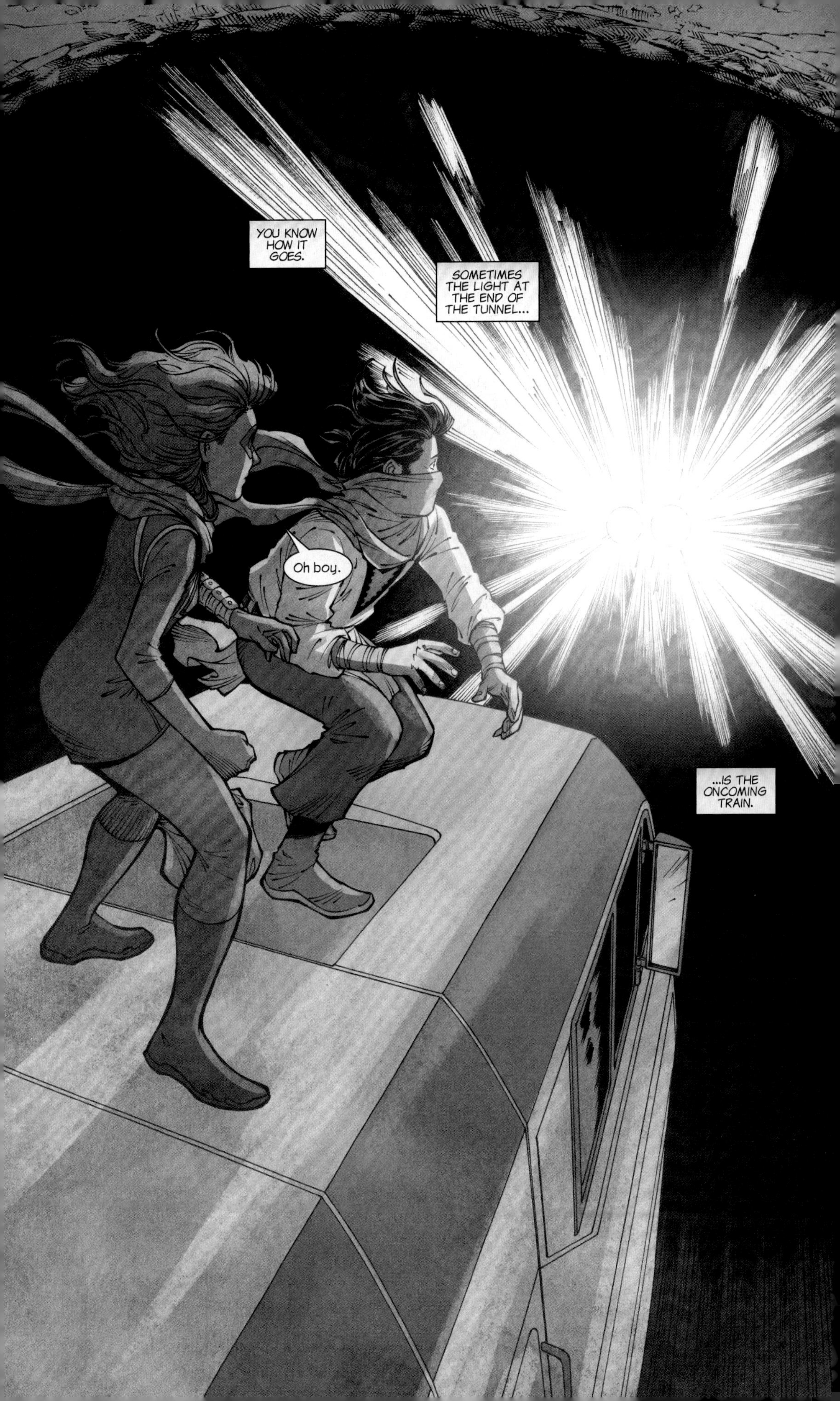
YOU KNOW HOW IT GOES.
SOMETIMES THE LIGHT AT THE END OF THE TUNNEL...
Oh boy.
...IS THE ONCOMING TRAIN.

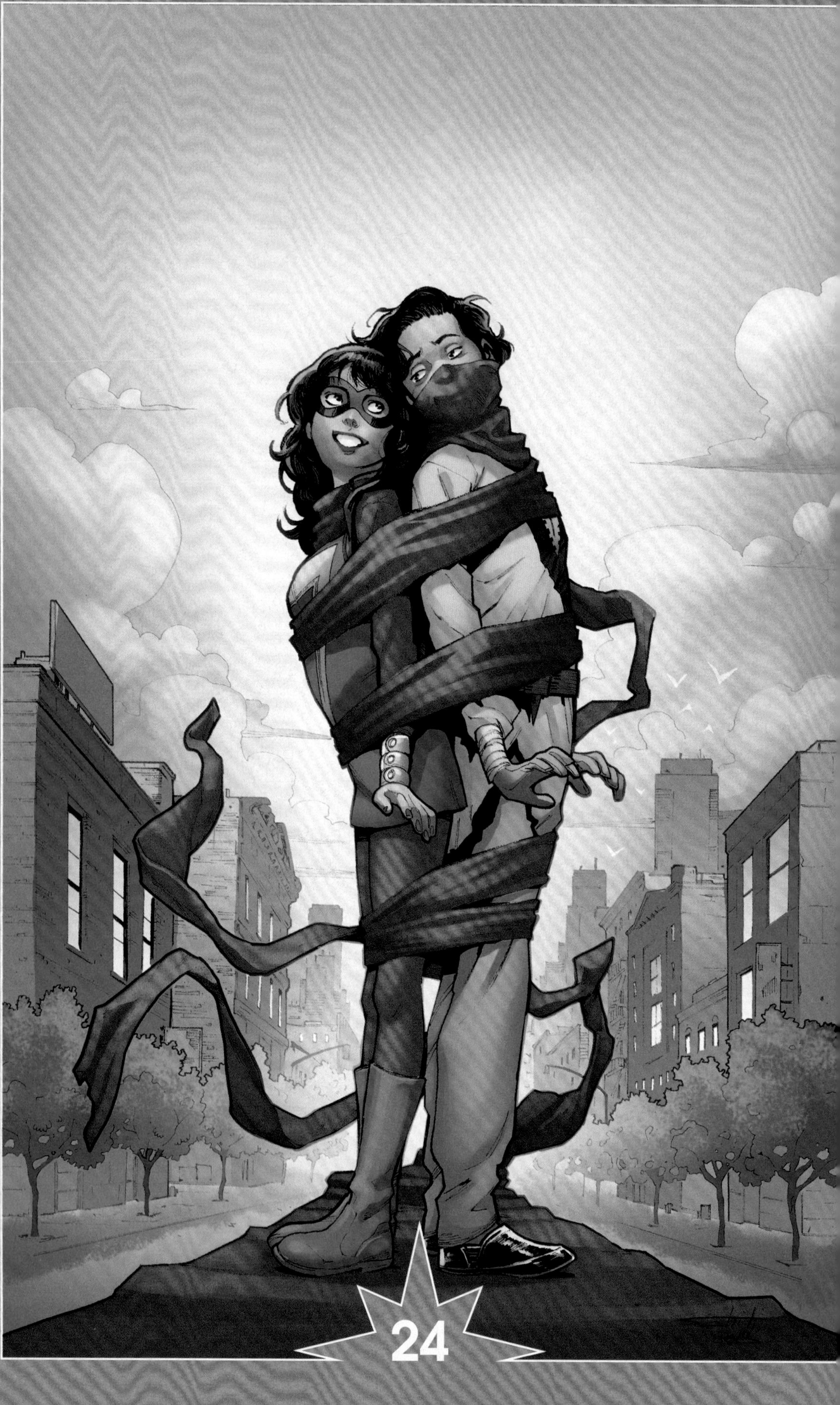
24

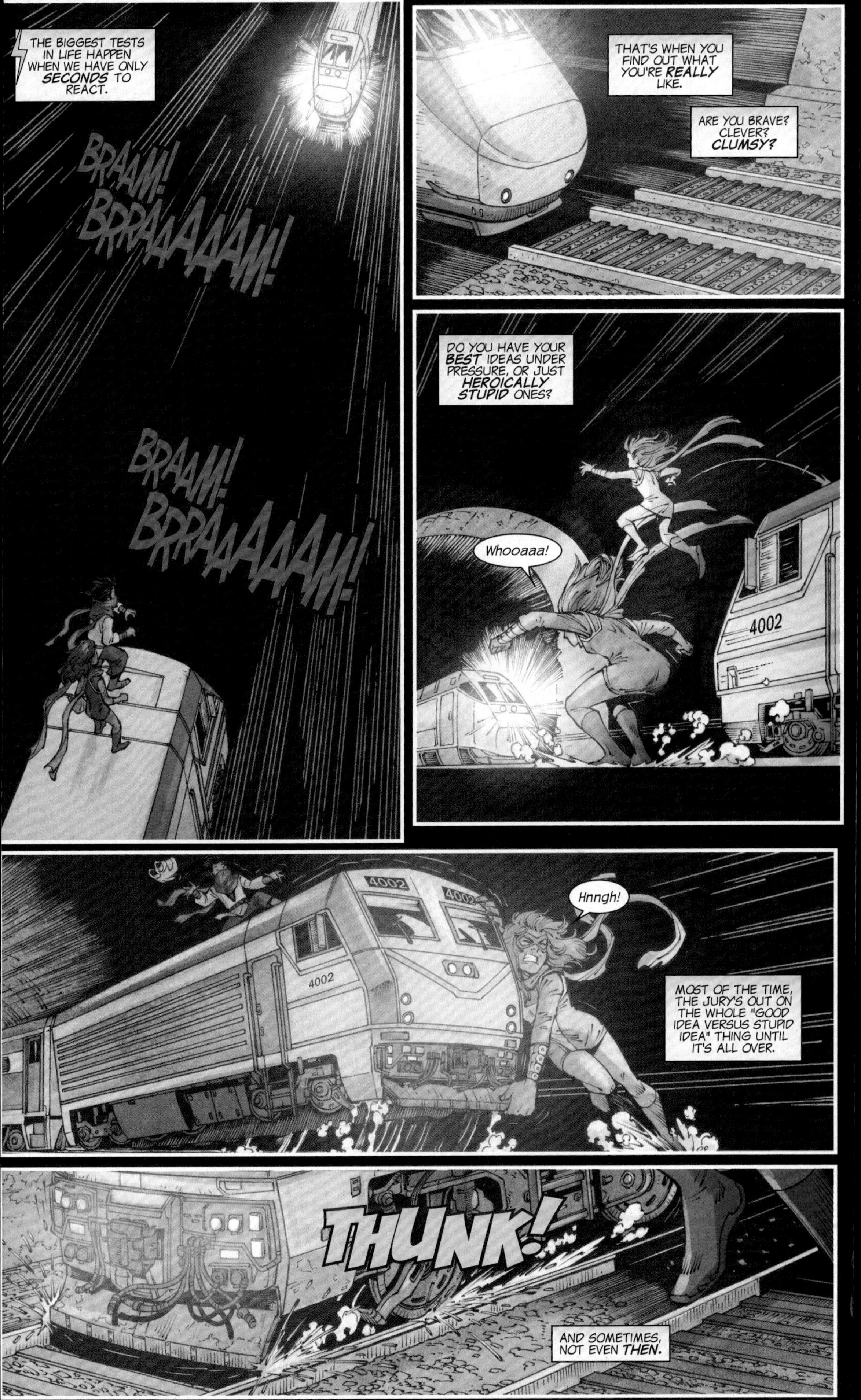

THE BIGGEST TESTS IN LIFE HAPPEN WHEN WE HAVE ONLY SECONDS TO REACT.
BRAAM! BRRAAAAAM!
BRAAM! BRRAAAAAM!
THAT'S WHEN YOU FIND OUT WHAT YOU'RE REALLY LIKE.
ARE YOU BRAVE? CLEVER? CLUMSY?
DO YOU HAVE YOUR BEST IDEAS UNDER PRESSURE, OR JUST HEROICALLY STUPID ONES?
Whooaaa!
4002
Hnngh!
MOST OF THE TIME, THE JURY'S OUT ON THE WHOLE "GOOD IDEA VERSUS STUPID IDEA" THING UNTIL IT'S ALL OVER.
THUNK!
AND SOMETIMES, NOT EVEN THEN.

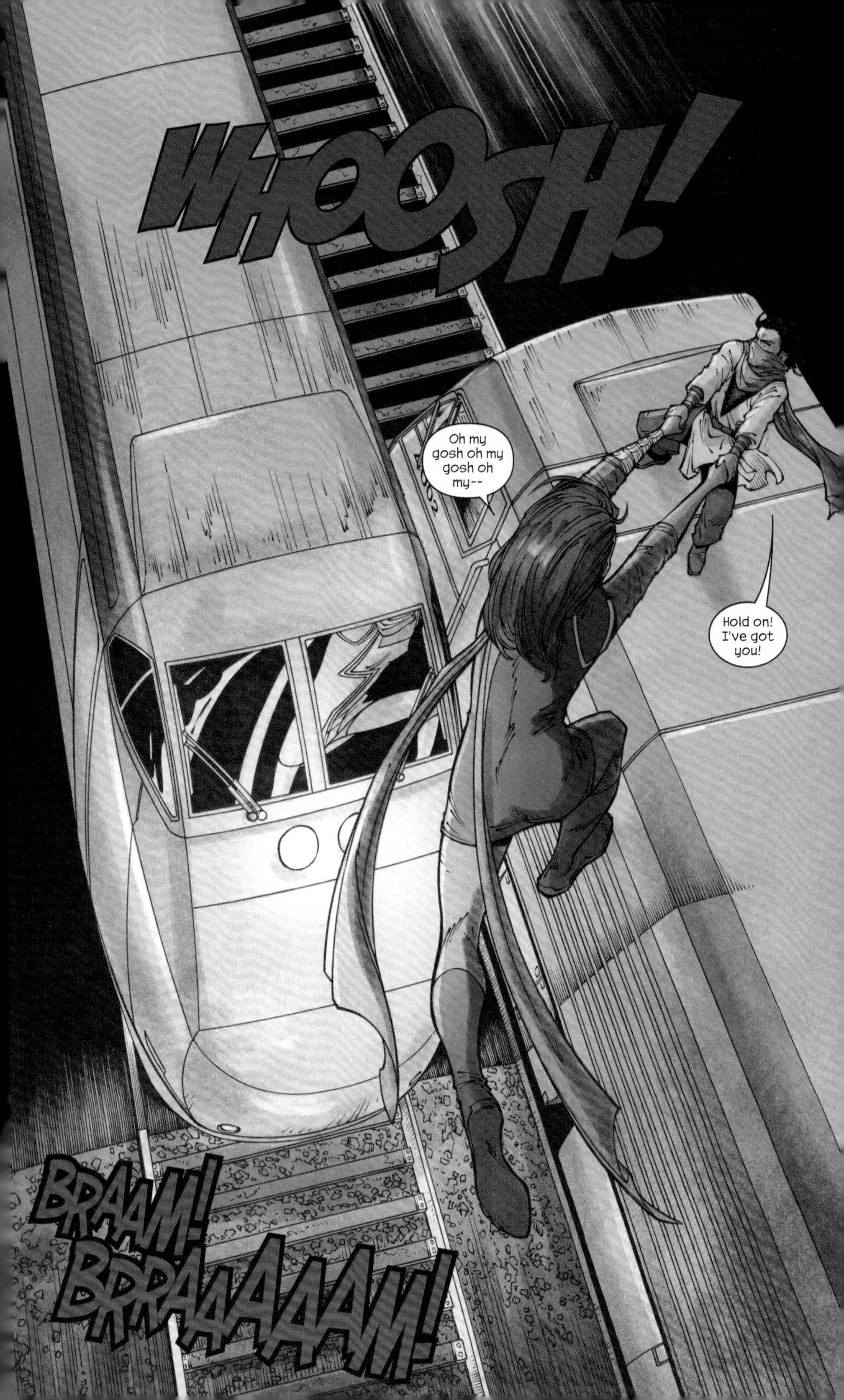
WHOOSH!
Oh my gosh oh my gosh oh my--
Hold on! I've got you!
BRAAM! BRRAAAAAM!

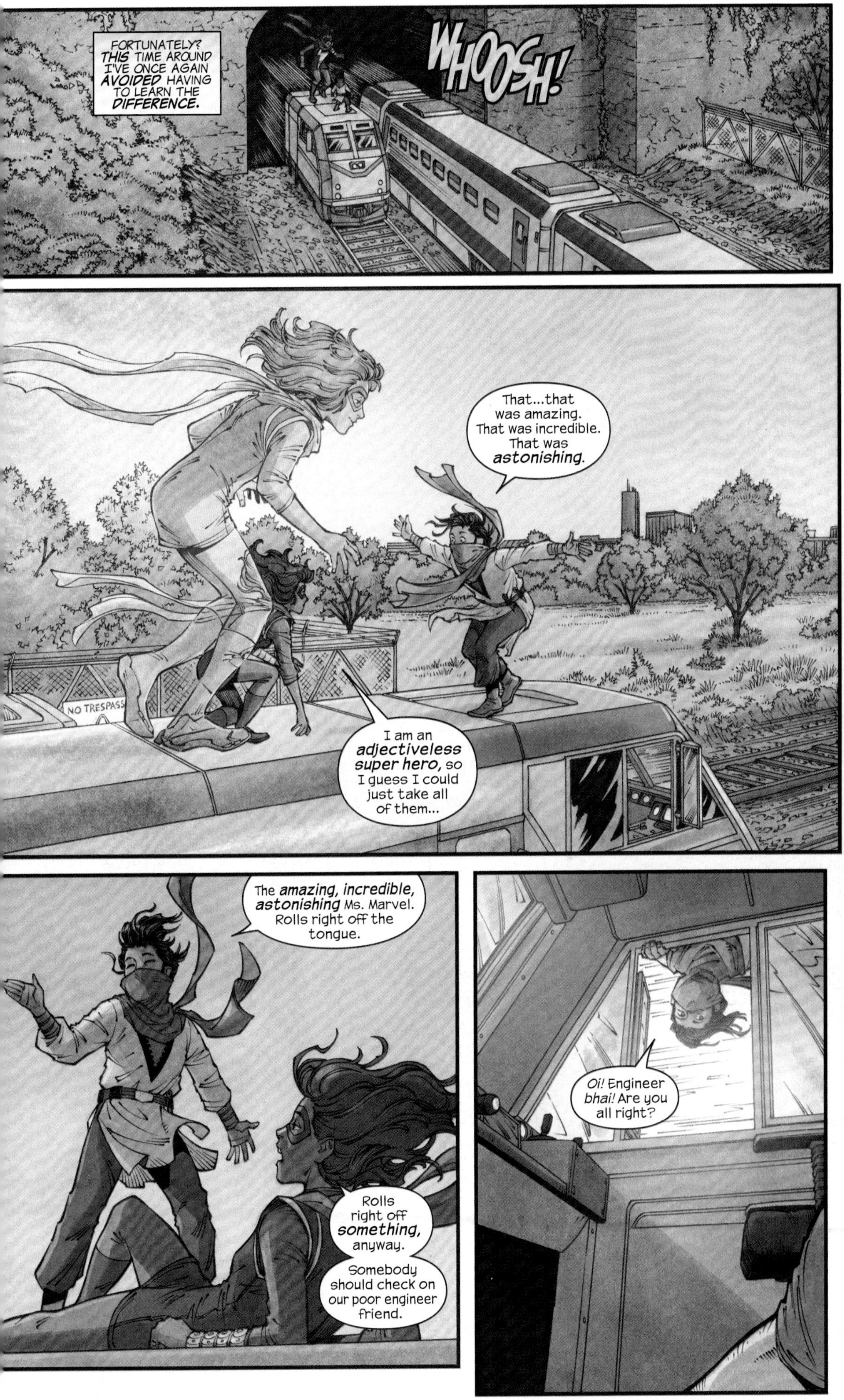
FORTUNATELY? THIS TIME AROUND I'VE ONCE AGAIN AVOIDED HAVING TO LEARN THE DIFFERENCE.
WHOOSH!
That...that was amazing. That was incredible. That was astonishing.
NO TRESPASS
I am an adjectiveless super hero, so I guess I could just take all of them...
The amazing, incredible, astonishing Ms. Marvel. Rolls right off the tongue.
Rolls right off something, anyway.
Somebody should check on our poor engineer friend.
Oi! Engineer bhai! Are you all right?

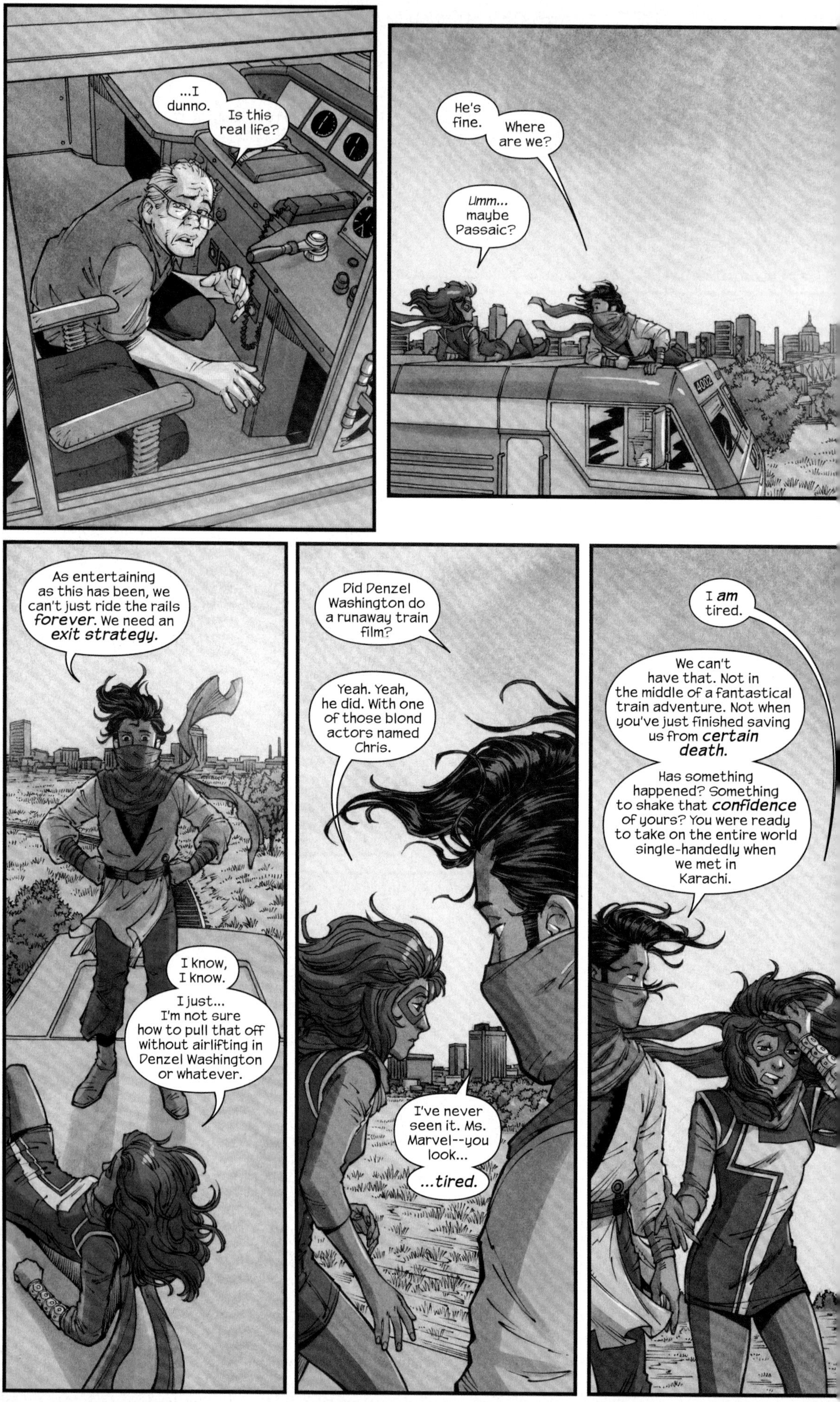
...I dunno.
Is this real life?
He's fine.
Where are we?
Umm... maybe Passaic?
As entertaining as this has been, we can't just ride the rails *forever*. We need an *exit strategy.*
I know, I know.
I just... I'm not sure how to pull that off without airlifting in Denzel Washington or whatever.
Did Denzel Washington do a runaway train film?
Yeah. Yeah, he did. With one of those blond actors named Chris.
I've never seen it. Ms. Marvel--you look...
...tired.
I *am* tired.
We can't have that. Not in the middle of a fantastical train adventure. Not when you've just finished saving us from *certain death.*
Has something happened? Something to shake that *confidence* of yours? You were ready to take on the entire world single-handedly when we met in Karachi.

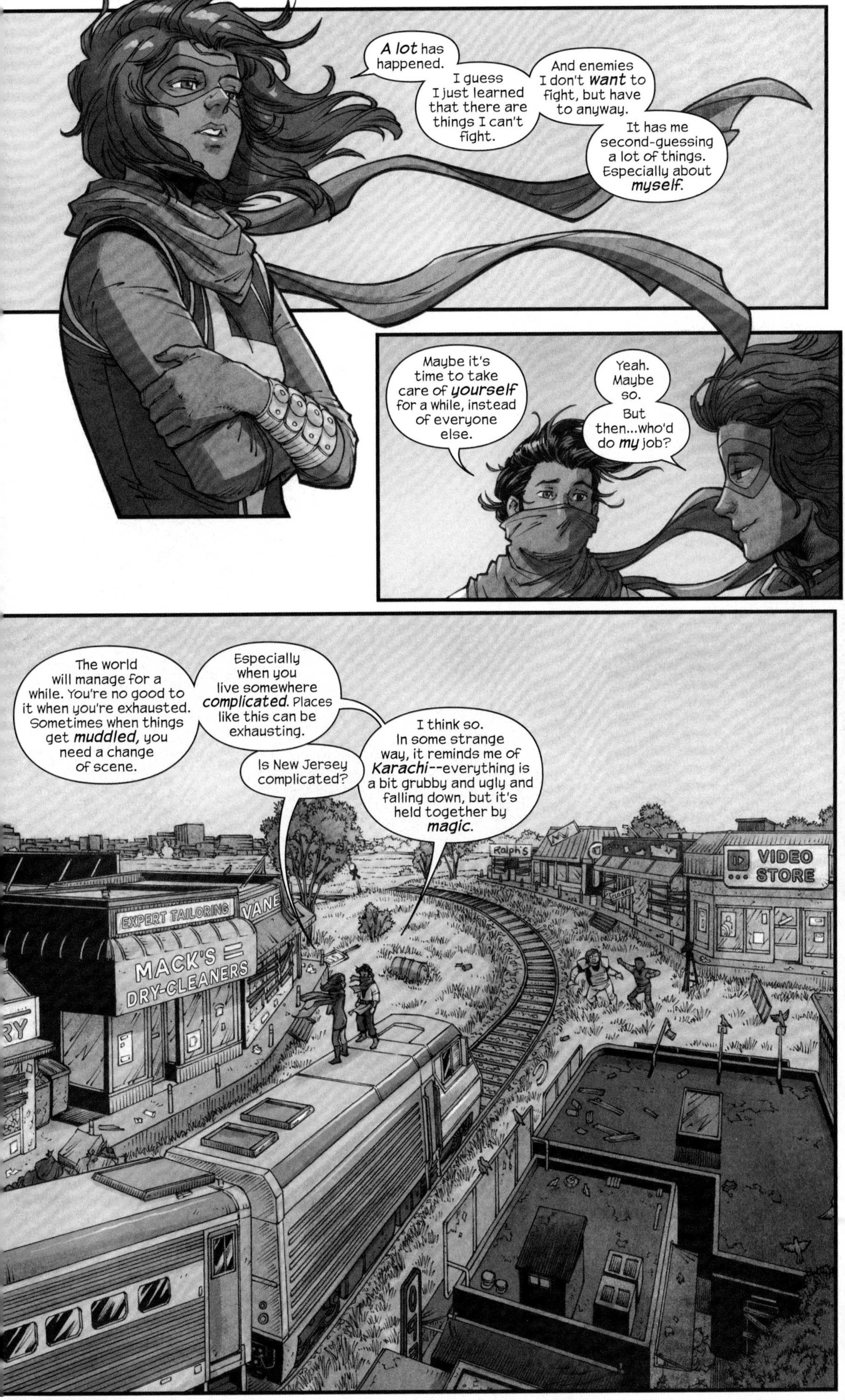
A lot has happened.
I guess I just learned that there are things I can't fight.
And enemies I don't want to fight, but have to anyway.
It has me second-guessing a lot of things. Especially about myself.
Maybe it's time to take care of yourself for a while, instead of everyone else.
Yeah. Maybe so.
But then...who'd do my job?
The world will manage for a while. You're no good to it when you're exhausted. Sometimes when things get muddled, you need a change of scene.
Especially when you live somewhere complicated. Places like this can be exhausting.
Is New Jersey complicated?
I think so. In some strange way, it reminds me of Karachi--everything is a bit grubby and ugly and falling down, but it's held together by magic.
EXPERT TAILORING
MACK'S DRY-CLEANERS
VIDEO STORE
Ralph's

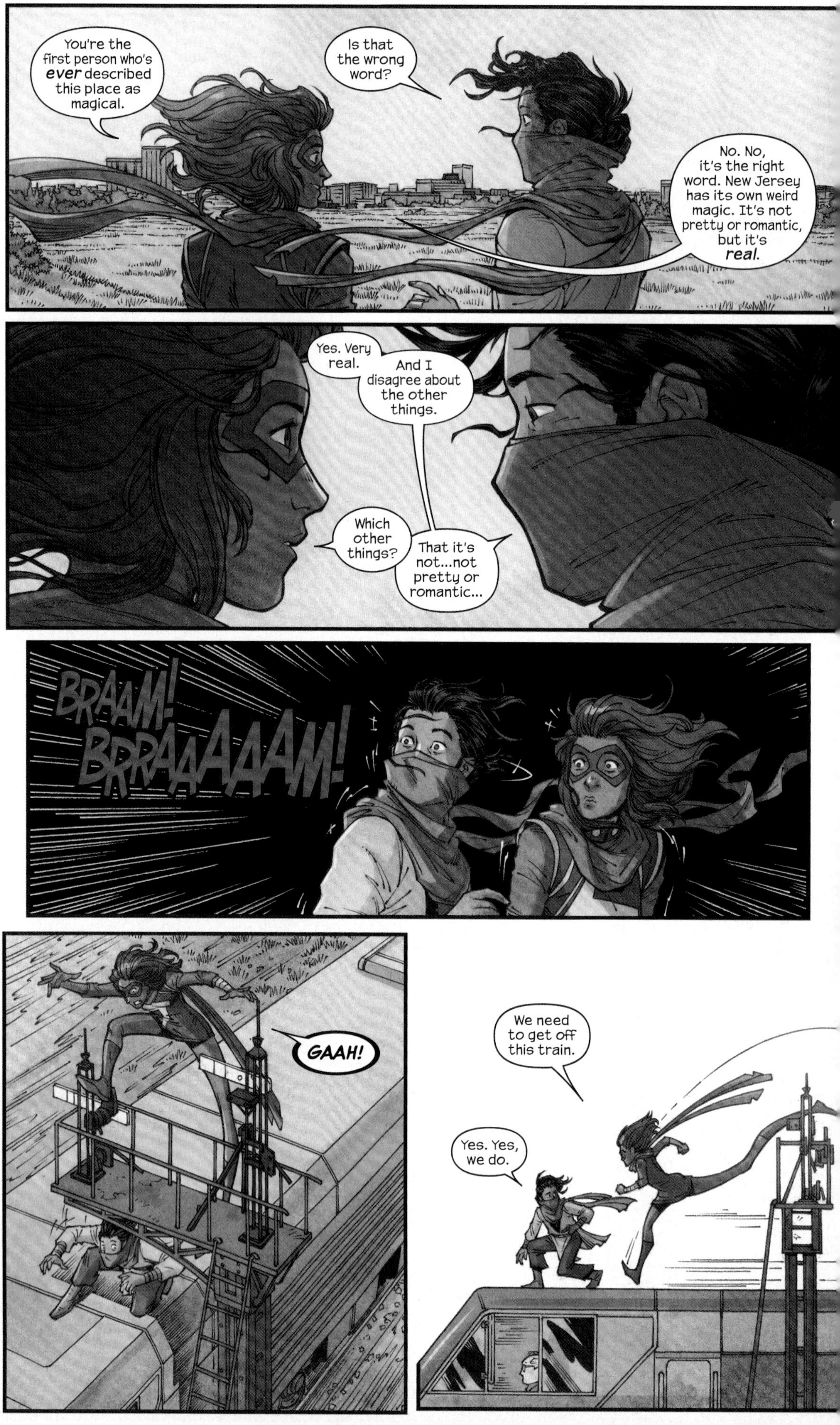

You're the first person who's *ever* described this place as magical.
Is that the wrong word?
No. No, it's the right word. New Jersey has its own weird magic. It's not pretty or romantic, but it's *real*.
Yes. Very real.
And I disagree about the other things.
Which other things?
That it's not...not pretty or romantic...
BRAAM! BRRAAAAAAM!
GAAH!
We need to get off this train.
Yes. Yes, we do.

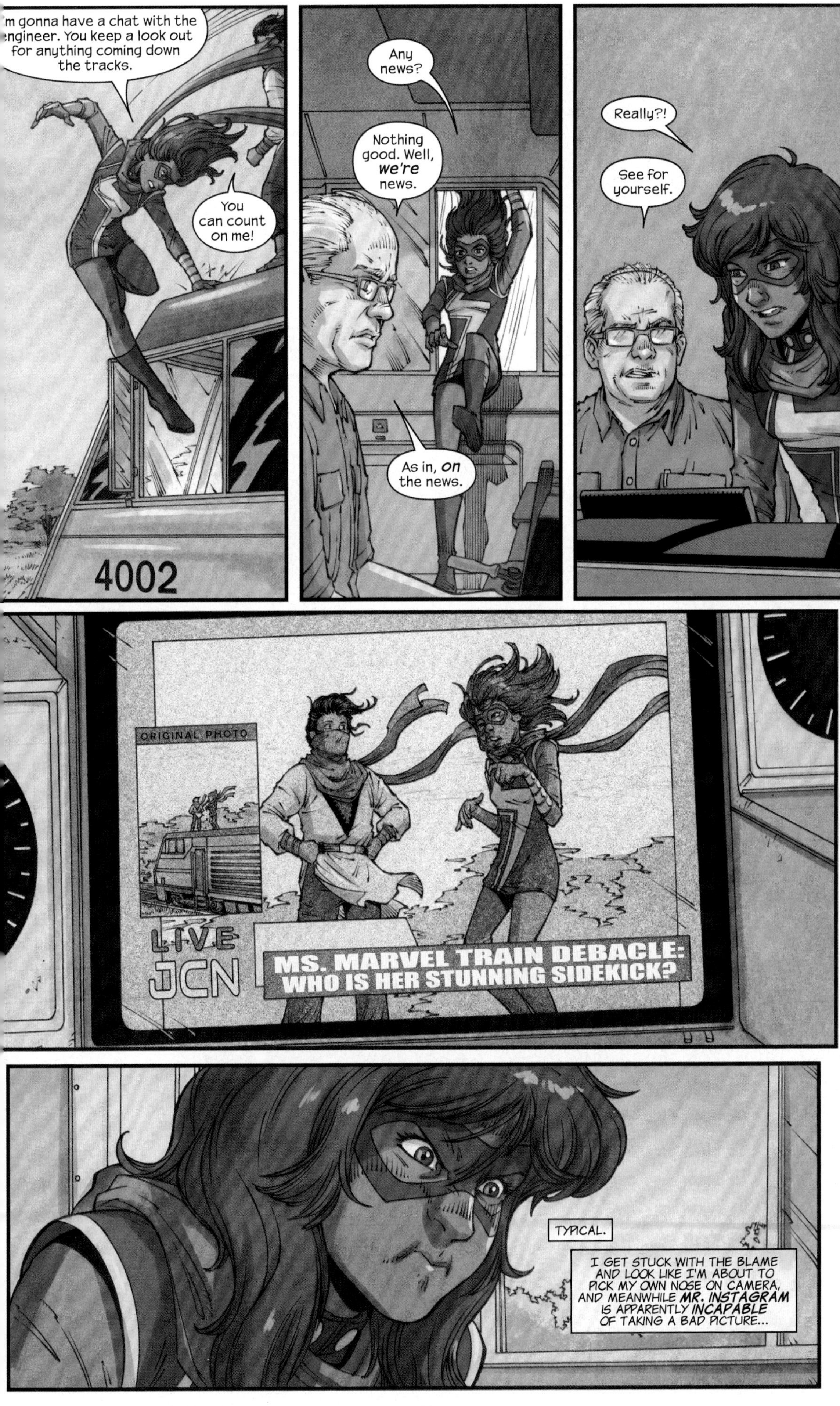

I'm gonna have a chat with the engineer. You keep a look out for anything coming down the tracks.
You can count on me!
4002
Any news?
Nothing good. Well, *we're* news.
As in, *on* the news.
Really?!
See for yourself.
ORIGINAL PHOTO
LIVE
JCN
MS. MARVEL TRAIN DEBACLE: WHO IS HER STUNNING SIDEKICK?
TYPICAL.
I GET STUCK WITH THE BLAME AND LOOK LIKE I'M ABOUT TO PICK MY OWN NOSE ON CAMERA, AND MEANWHILE ***MR. INSTAGRAM*** IS APPARENTLY ***INCAPABLE*** OF TAKING A BAD PICTURE...

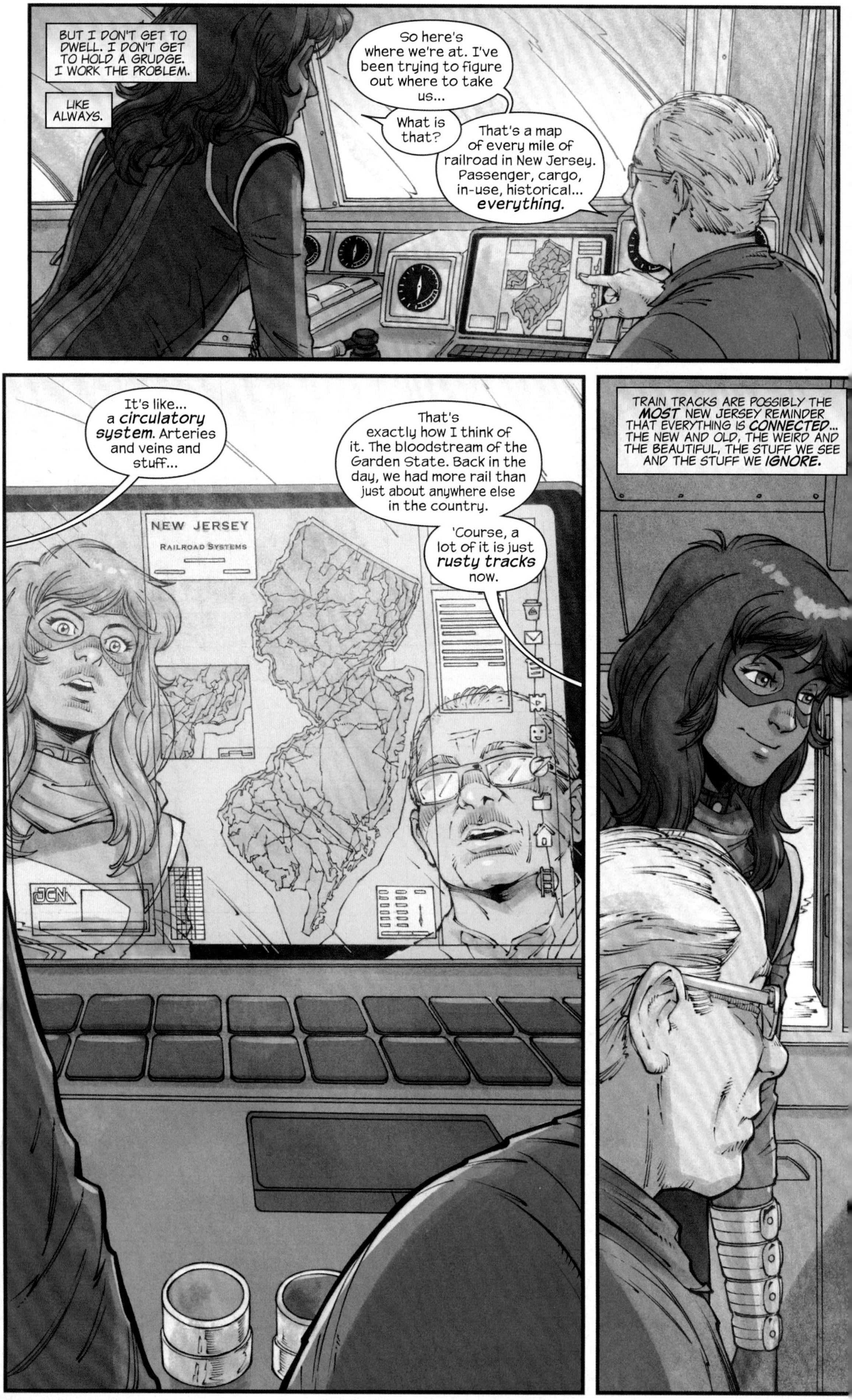

BUT I DON'T GET TO DWELL. I DON'T GET TO HOLD A GRUDGE. I WORK THE PROBLEM.
LIKE ALWAYS.
So here's where we're at. I've been trying to figure out where to take us...
What is that?
That's a map of every mile of railroad in New Jersey. Passenger, cargo, in-use, historical... *everything.*
It's like... a *circulatory system.* Arteries and veins and stuff...
That's exactly how I think of it. The bloodstream of the Garden State. Back in the day, we had more rail than just about anywhere else in the country.
'Course, a lot of it is just *rusty tracks* now.
NEW JERSEY
RAILROAD SYSTEMS
TRAIN TRACKS ARE POSSIBLY THE *MOST* NEW JERSEY REMINDER THAT EVERYTHING IS *CONNECTED*... THE NEW AND OLD, THE WEIRD AND THE BEAUTIFUL, THE STUFF WE SEE AND THE STUFF WE *IGNORE.*

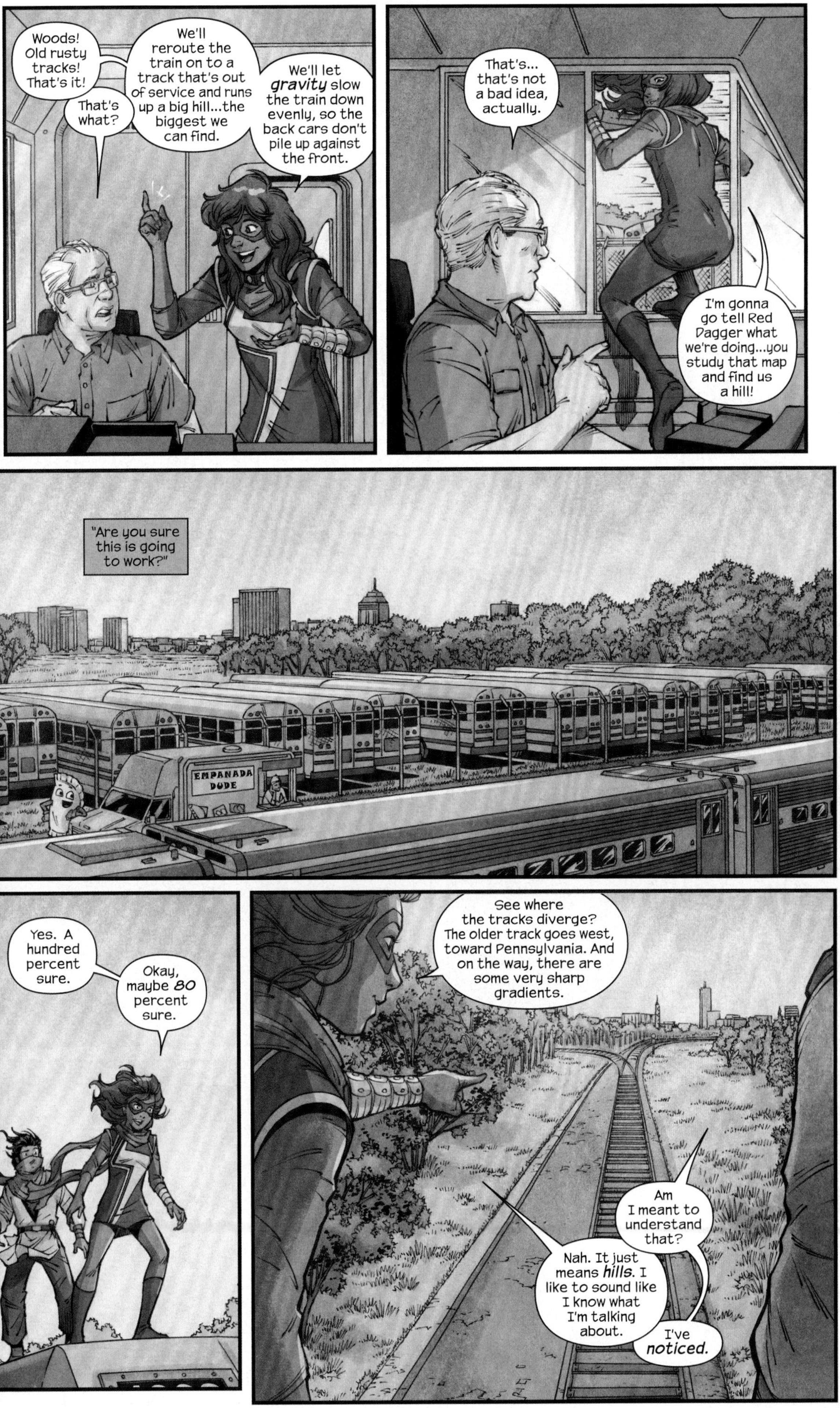
Woods! Old rusty tracks! That's it!
That's what?
We'll reroute the train on to a track that's out of service and runs up a big hill...the biggest we can find.
We'll let *gravity* slow the train down evenly, so the back cars don't pile up against the front.
That's... that's not a bad idea, actually.
I'm gonna go tell Red Dagger what we're doing...you study that map and find us a hill!
"Are you sure this is going to work?"
EMPANADA DUDE
Yes. A hundred percent sure.
Okay, maybe *80* percent sure.
See where the tracks diverge? The older track goes west, toward Pennsylvania. And on the way, there are some very sharp gradients.
Am I meant to understand that?
Nah. It just means *hills*. I like to sound like I know what I'm talking about.
I've *noticed.*

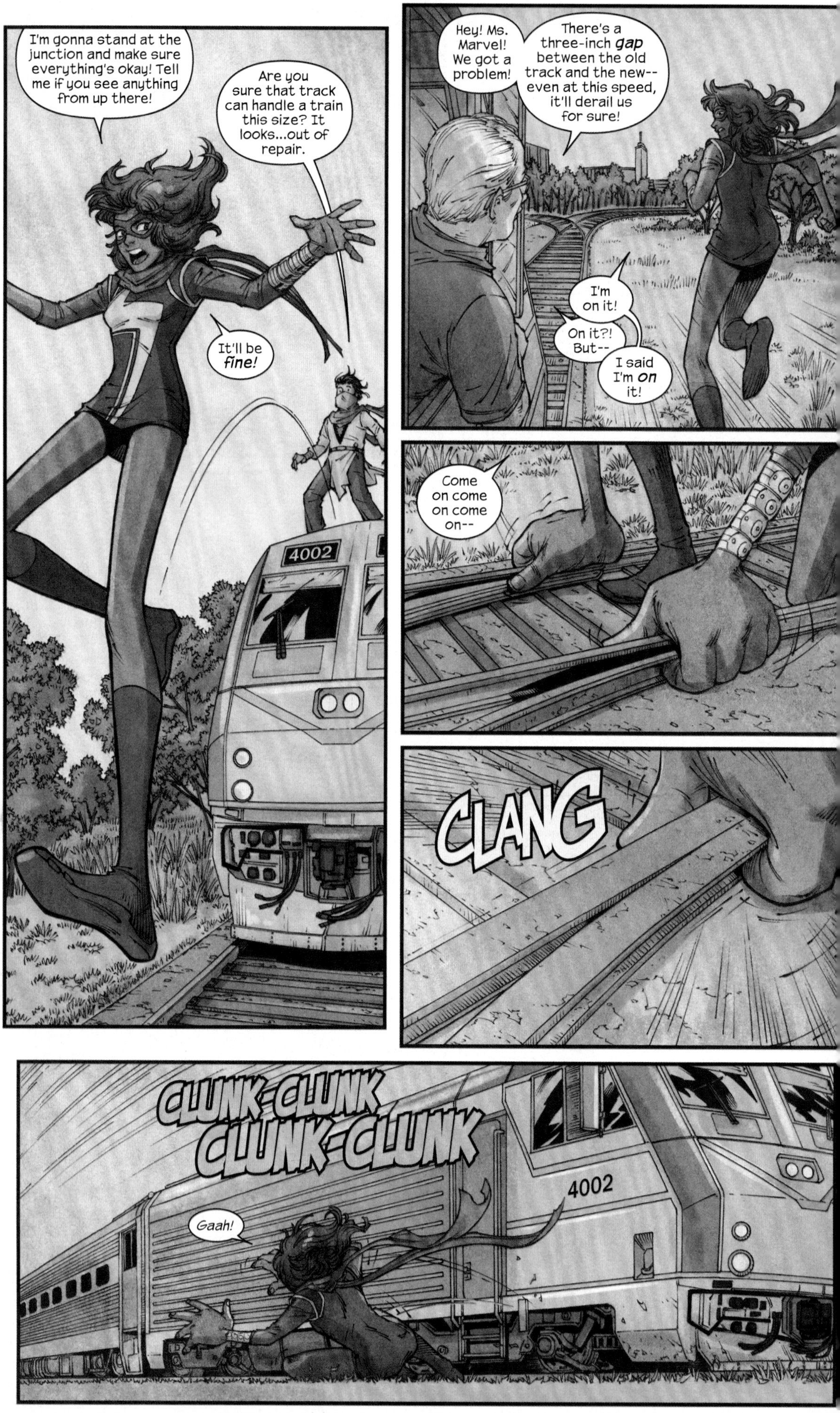
I'm gonna stand at the junction and make sure everything's okay! Tell me if you see anything from up there!
Are you sure that track can handle a train this size? It looks...out of repair.
It'll be *fine!*
4002
Hey! Ms. Marvel! We got a problem!
There's a three-inch *gap* between the old track and the new--even at this speed, it'll derail us for sure!
I'm on it!
On it?! But--
I said I'm *on* it!
Come on come on come on--
CLANG
CLUNK-CLUNK CLUNK-CLUNK
4002
Gaah!

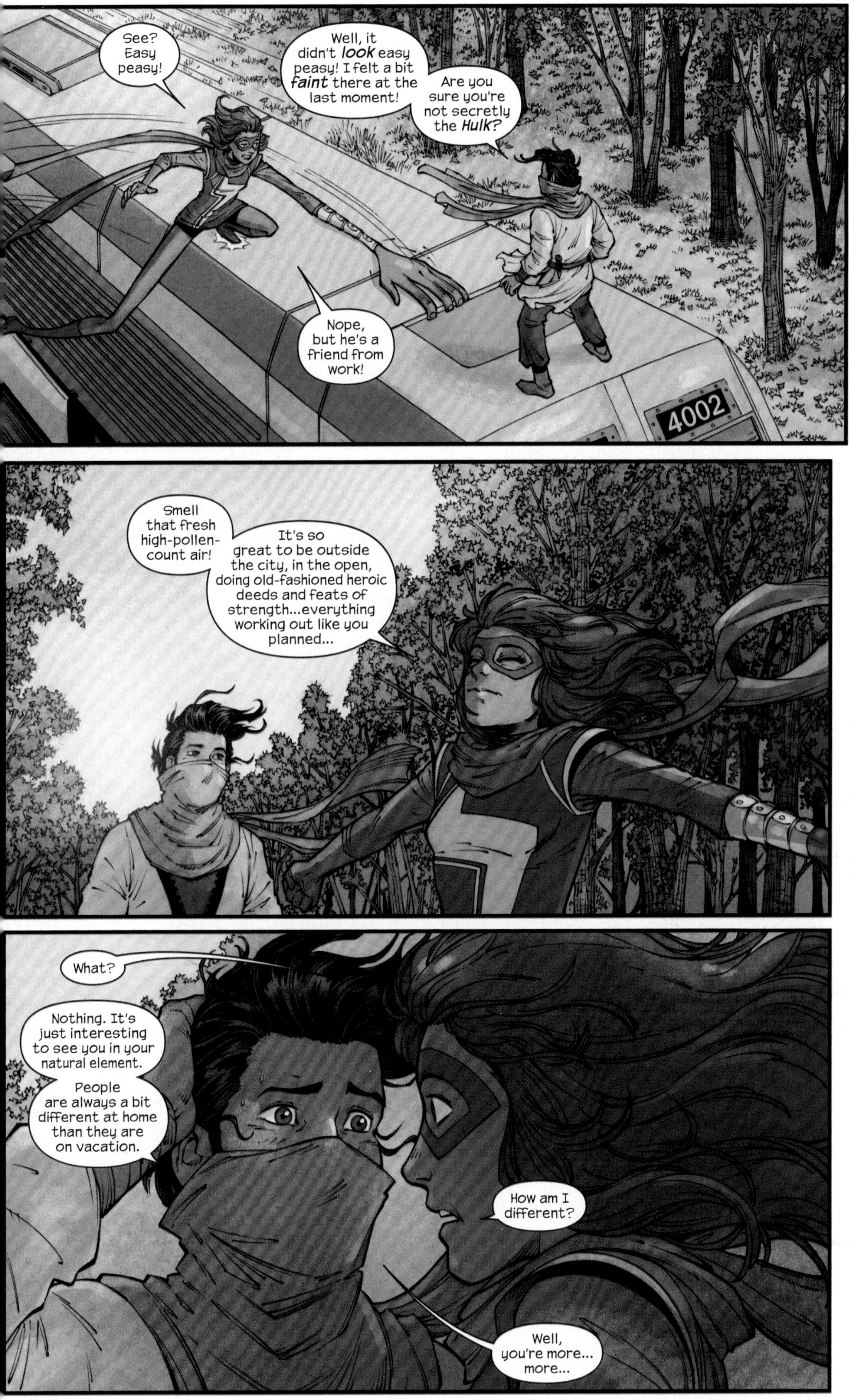
See? Easy peasy!
Well, it didn't *look* easy peasy! I felt a bit *faint* there at the last moment!
Are you sure you're not secretly the *Hulk?*
Nope, but he's a friend from work!
4002
Smell that fresh high-pollen-count air!
It's so great to be outside the city, in the open, doing old-fashioned heroic deeds and feats of strength...everything working out like you planned...
What?
Nothing. It's just interesting to see you in your natural element.
People are always a bit different at home than they are on vacation.
How am I different?
Well, you're more... more...

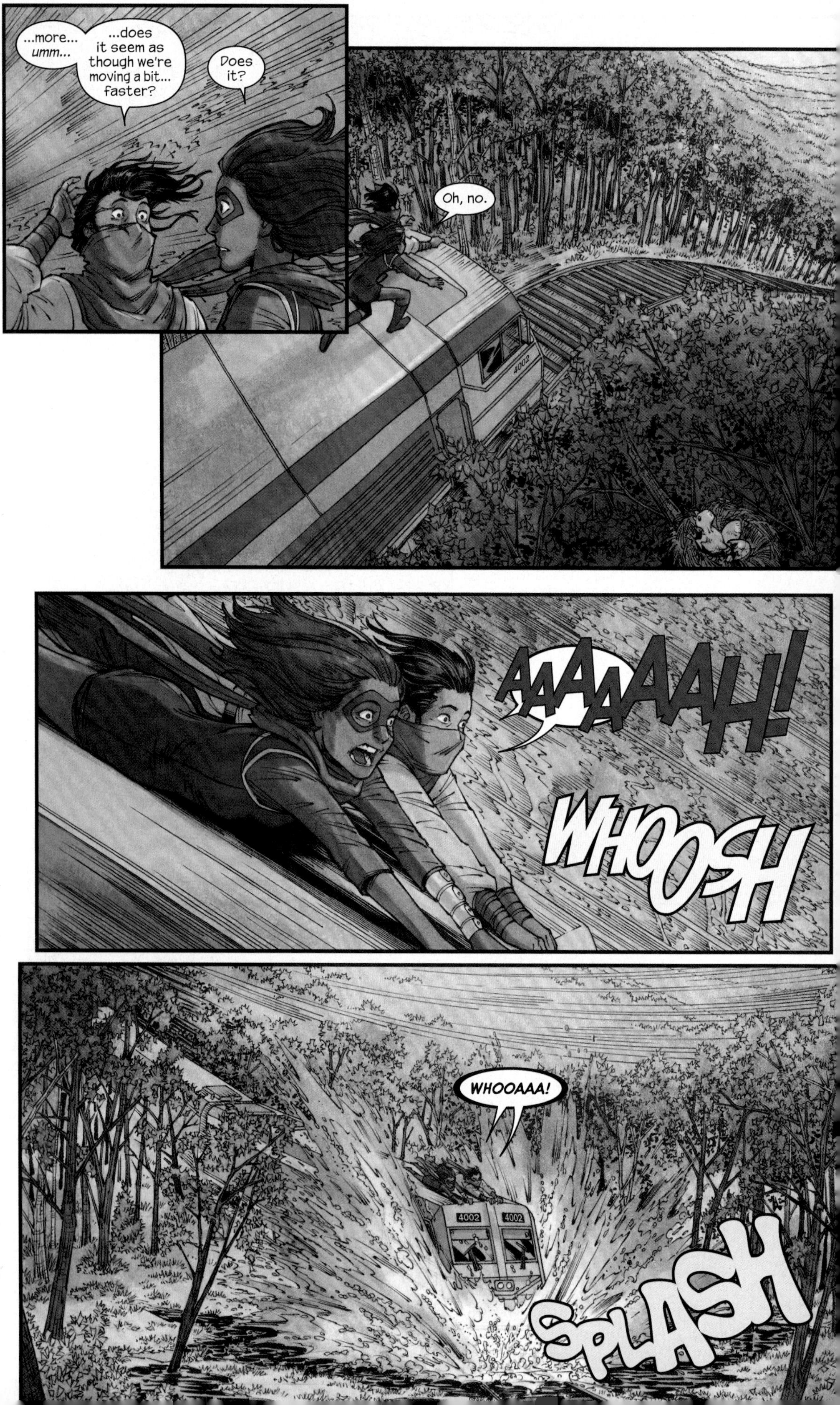
...more... umm...
...does it seem as though we're moving a bit... faster?
Does it?
Oh, no.
AAAAAAH!
WHOOSH
WHOOAAA!
SPLASH

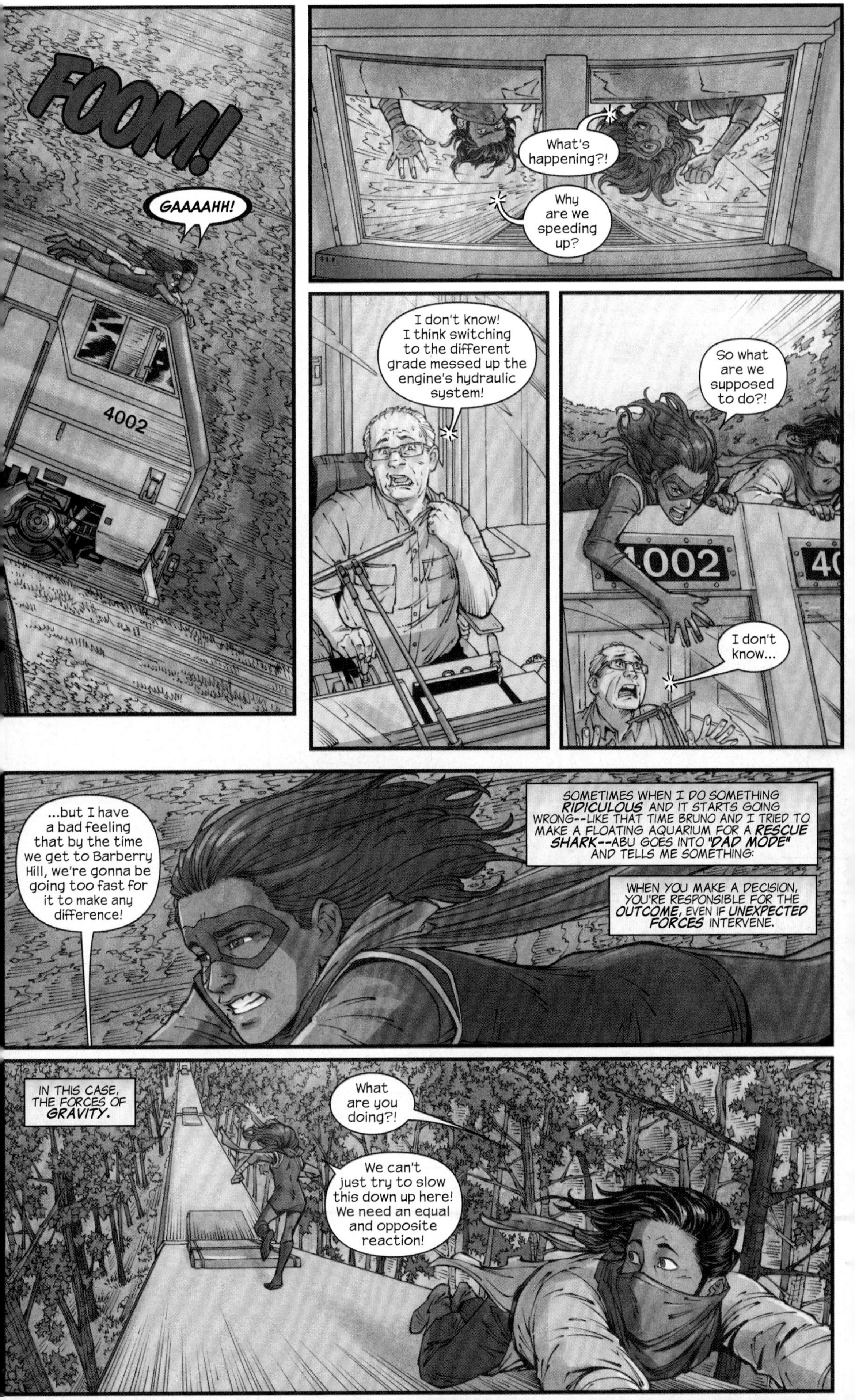
FOOM!
GAAAAHH!
4002
What's happening?!
Why are we speeding up?
I don't know! I think switching to the different grade messed up the engine's hydraulic system!
So what are we supposed to do?!
I don't know...
...but I have a bad feeling that by the time we get to Barberry Hill, we're gonna be going too fast for it to make any difference!
SOMETIMES WHEN I DO SOMETHING RIDICULOUS AND IT STARTS GOING WRONG--LIKE THAT TIME BRUNO AND I TRIED TO MAKE A FLOATING AQUARIUM FOR A RESCUE SHARK--ABU GOES INTO "DAD MODE" AND TELLS ME SOMETHING:
WHEN YOU MAKE A DECISION, YOU'RE RESPONSIBLE FOR THE OUTCOME, EVEN IF UNEXPECTED FORCES INTERVENE.
IN THIS CASE, THE FORCES OF GRAVITY.
What are you doing?!
We can't just try to slow this down up here! We need an equal and opposite reaction!

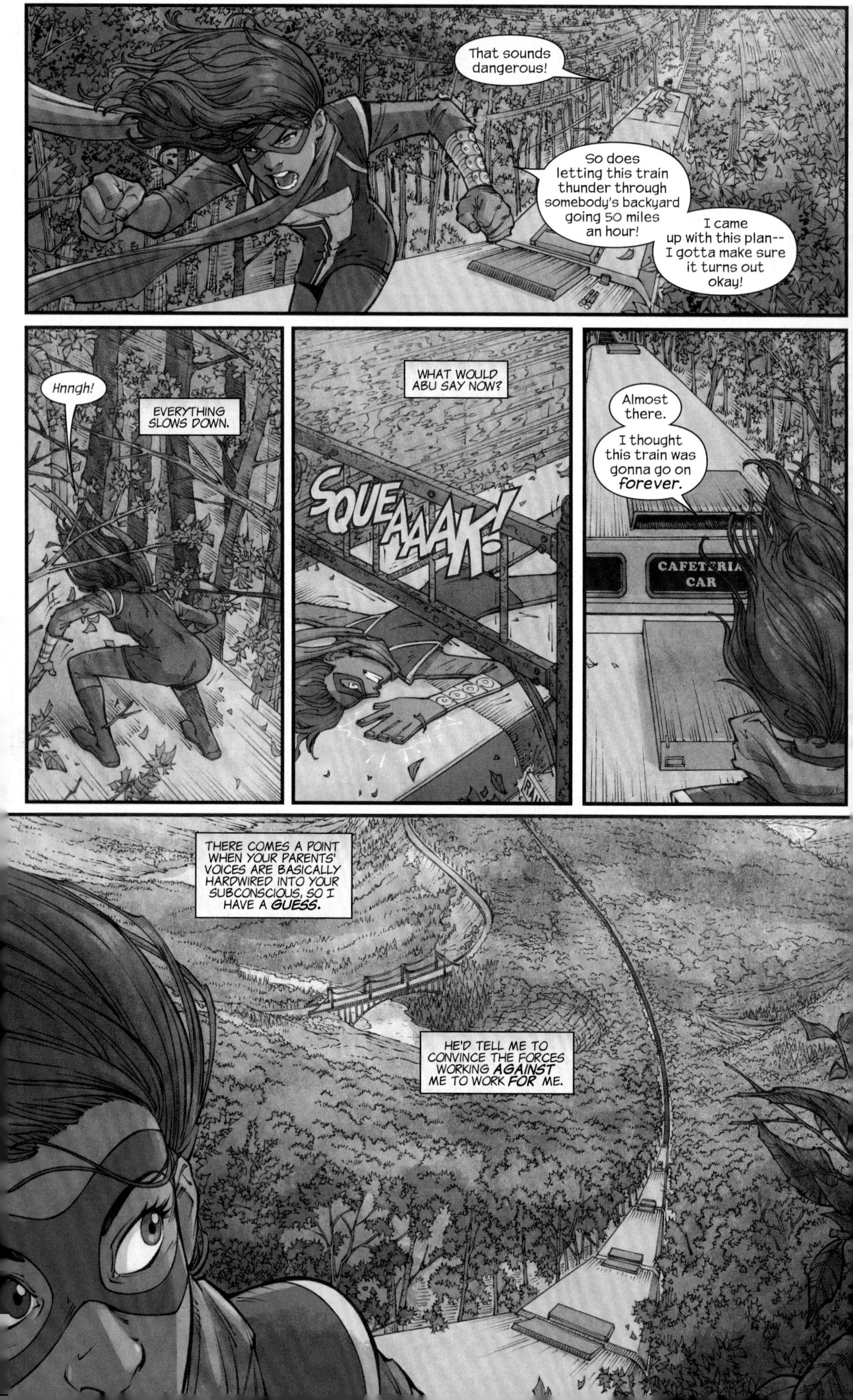
That sounds dangerous!
So does letting this train thunder through somebody's backyard going 50 miles an hour!
I came up with this plan-- I gotta make sure it turns out okay!
Hnngh!
EVERYTHING SLOWS DOWN.
WHAT WOULD ABU SAY NOW?
SQUEAAAK!
Almost there.
I thought this train was gonna go on forever.
CAFETERIA CAR
THERE COMES A POINT WHEN YOUR PARENTS' VOICES ARE BASICALLY HARDWIRED INTO YOUR SUBCONSCIOUS, SO I HAVE A GUESS.
HE'D TELL ME TO CONVINCE THE FORCES WORKING AGAINST ME TO WORK FOR ME.

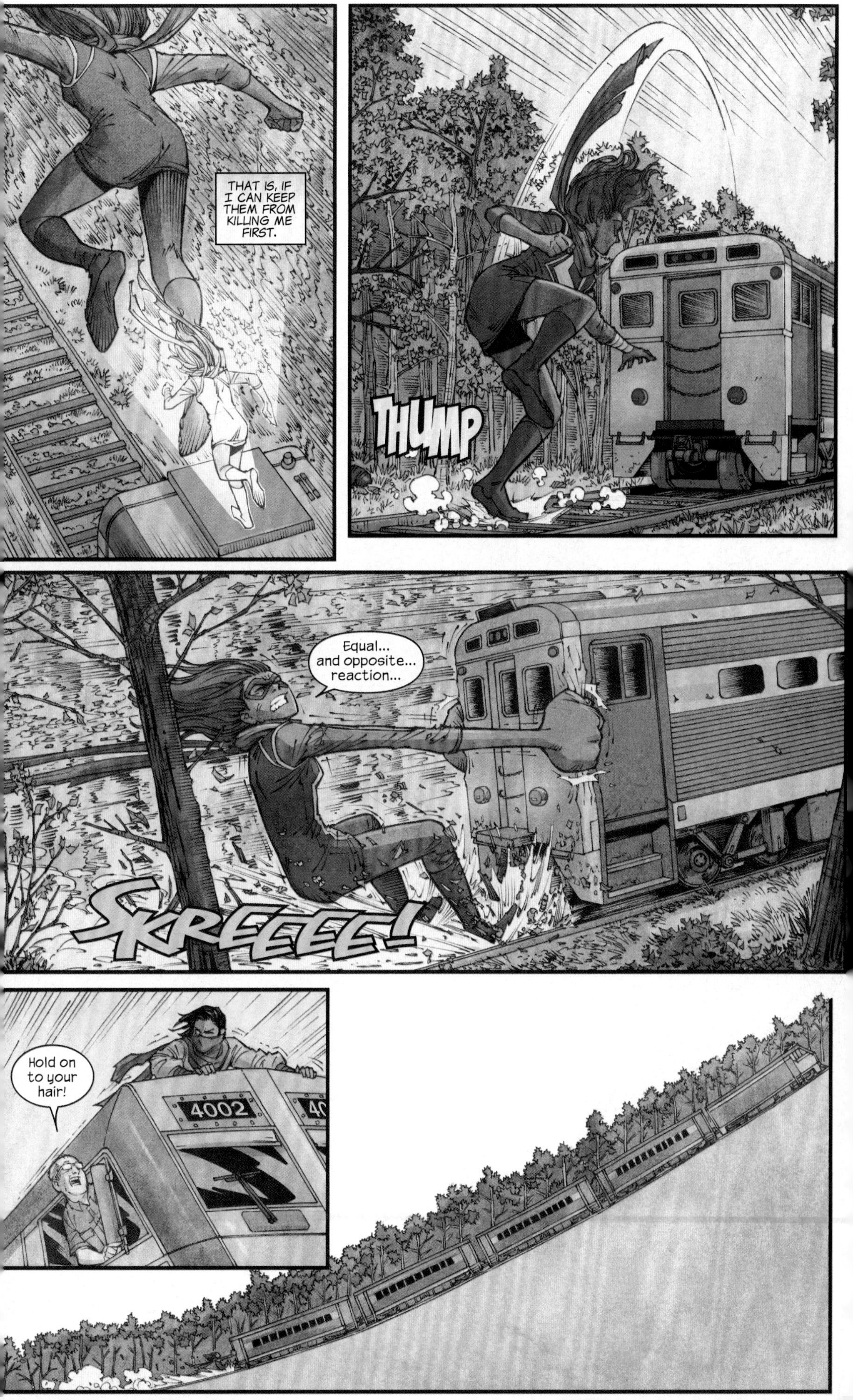
THAT IS, IF I CAN KEEP THEM FROM KILLING ME FIRST.
THUMP
Equal... and opposite... reaction...
SKREEEE!
Hold on to your hair!
4002

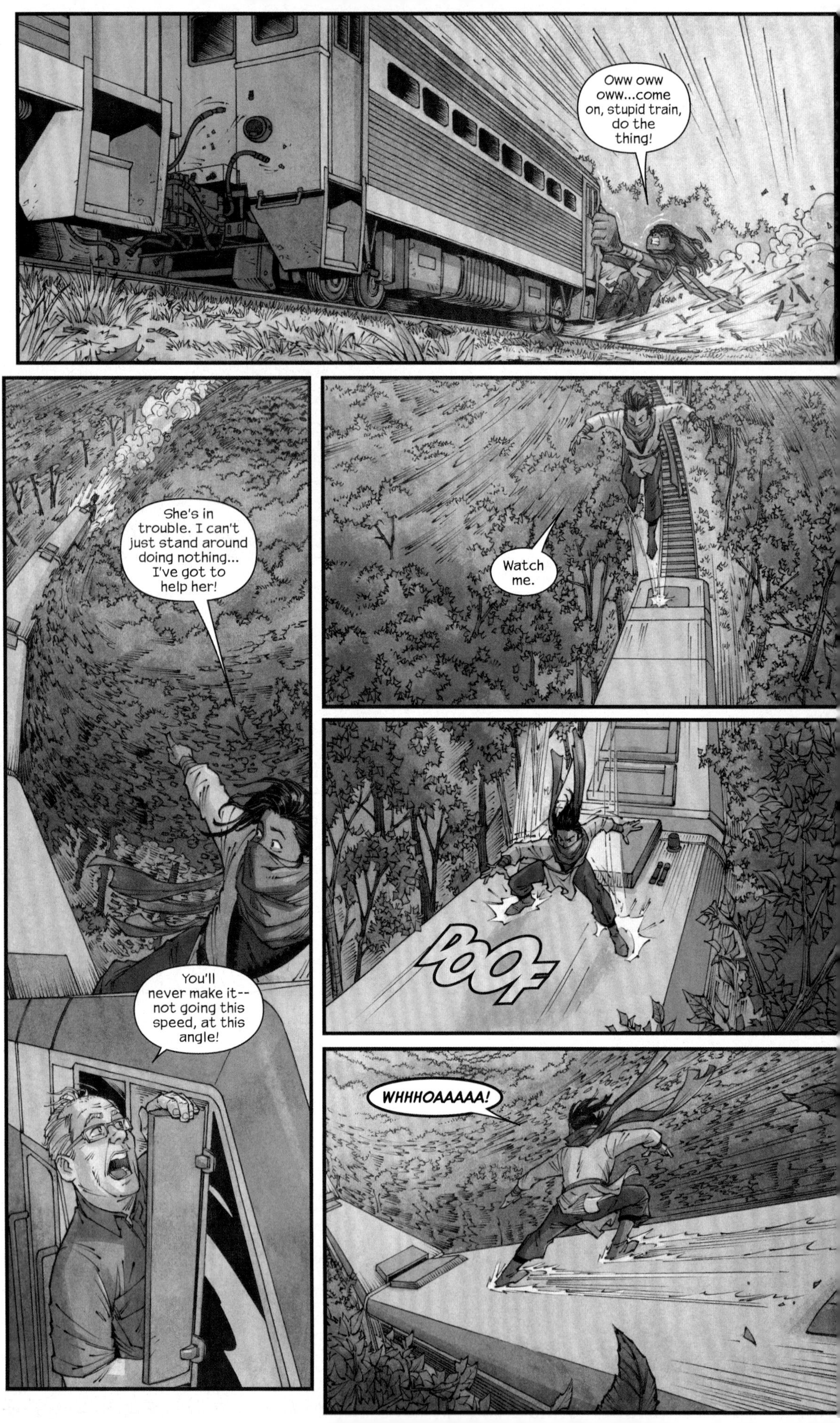
Oww oww oww...come on, stupid train, do the thing!
She's in trouble. I can't just stand around doing nothing... I've got to help her!
Watch me.
You'll never make it--not going this speed, at this angle!
POOF
WHHHOAAAAA!

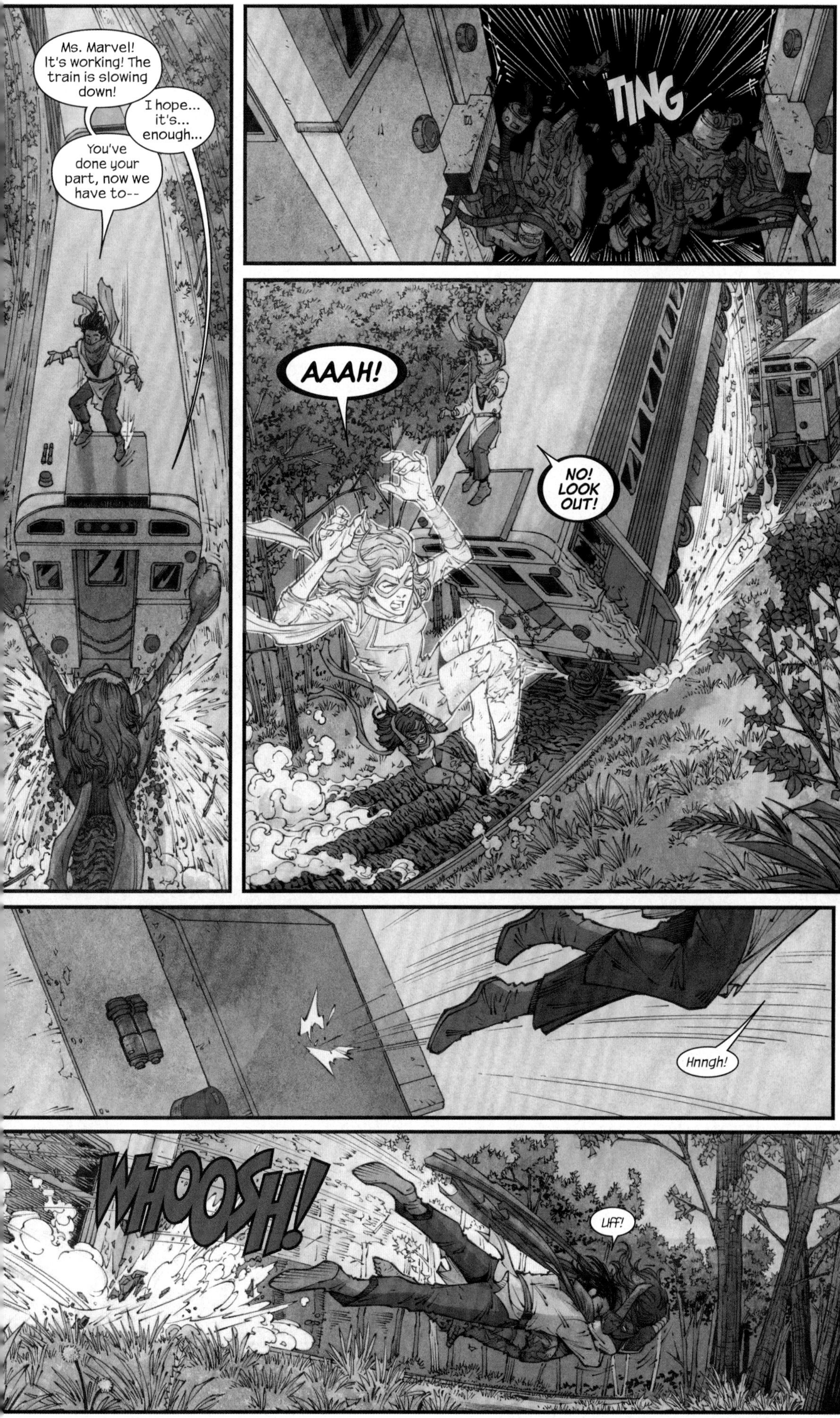
Ms. Marvel! It's working! The train is slowing down!
I hope... it's... enough...
You've done your part, now we have to--
TING
AAAH!
NO! LOOK OUT!
Hnngh!
WHOOSH!
UFF!

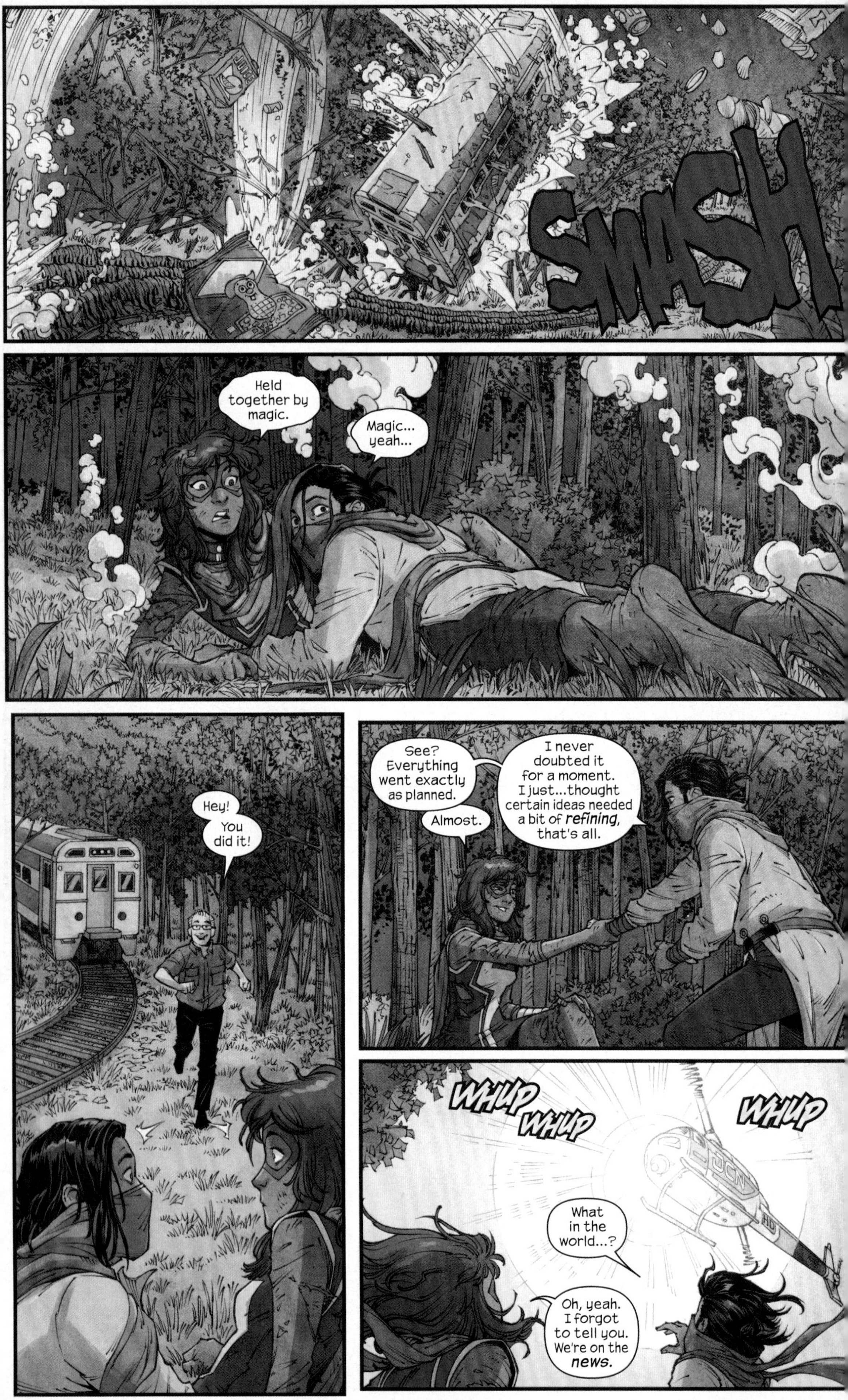
SMASH
Held together by magic.
Magic... yeah...
Hey! You did it!
See? Everything went exactly as planned.
Almost.
I never doubted it for a moment. I just...thought certain ideas needed a bit of *refining*, that's all.
WHUP WHUP
WHUP
What in the world...?
Oh, yeah. I forgot to tell you. We're on the *news*.

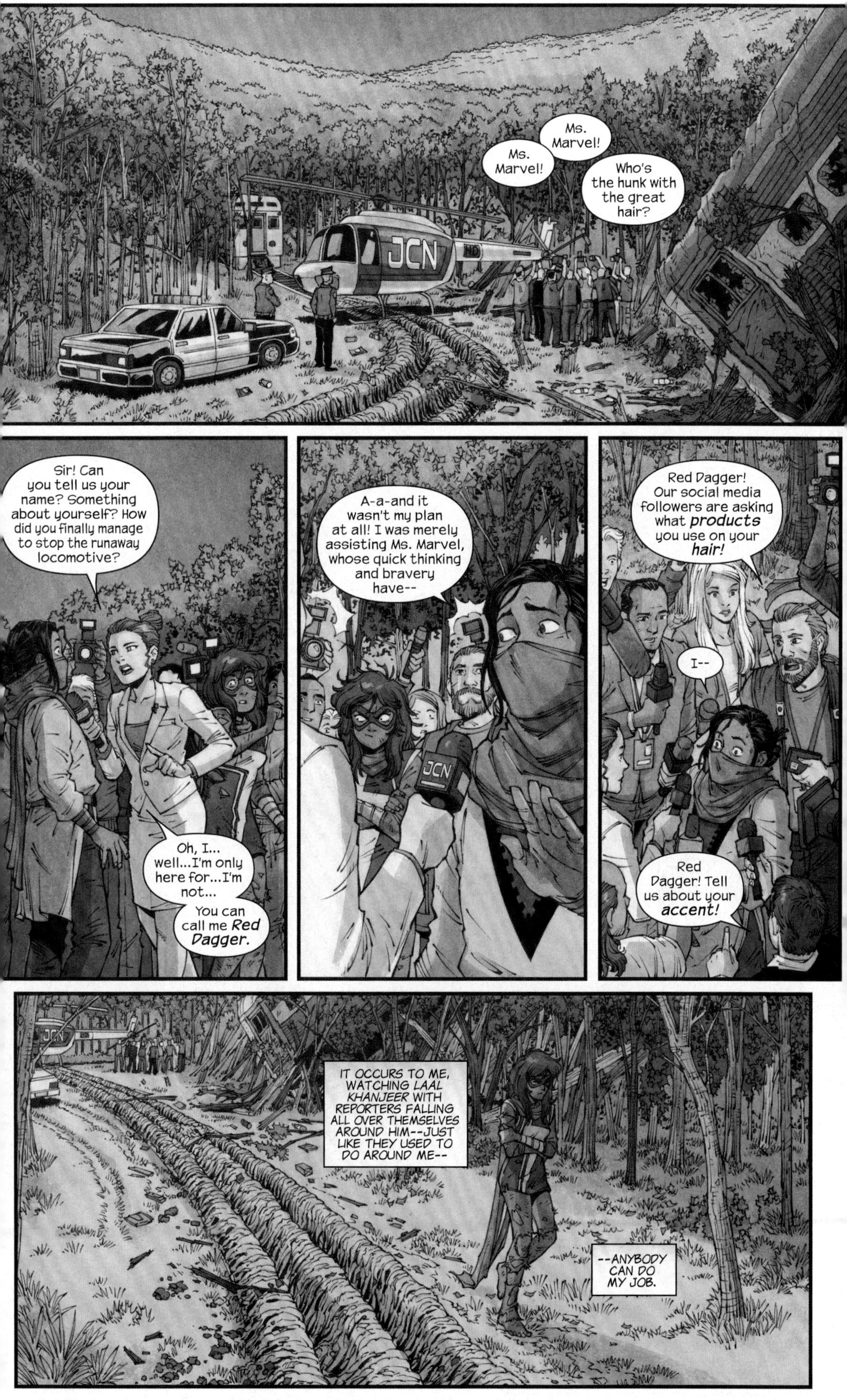
Ms. Marvel!
Ms. Marvel!
Who's the hunk with the great hair?
JCN
Sir! Can you tell us your name? Something about yourself? How did you finally manage to stop the runaway locomotive?
Oh, I... well...I'm only here for...I'm not...
You can call me Red Dagger.
A-a-and it wasn't my plan at all! I was merely assisting Ms. Marvel, whose quick thinking and bravery have--
JCN
Red Dagger! Our social media followers are asking what products you use on your hair!
I--
Red Dagger! Tell us about your accent!
IT OCCURS TO ME, WATCHING LAAL KHANJEER WITH REPORTERS FALLING ALL OVER THEMSELVES AROUND HIM--JUST LIKE THEY USED TO DO AROUND ME--
--ANYBODY CAN DO MY JOB.

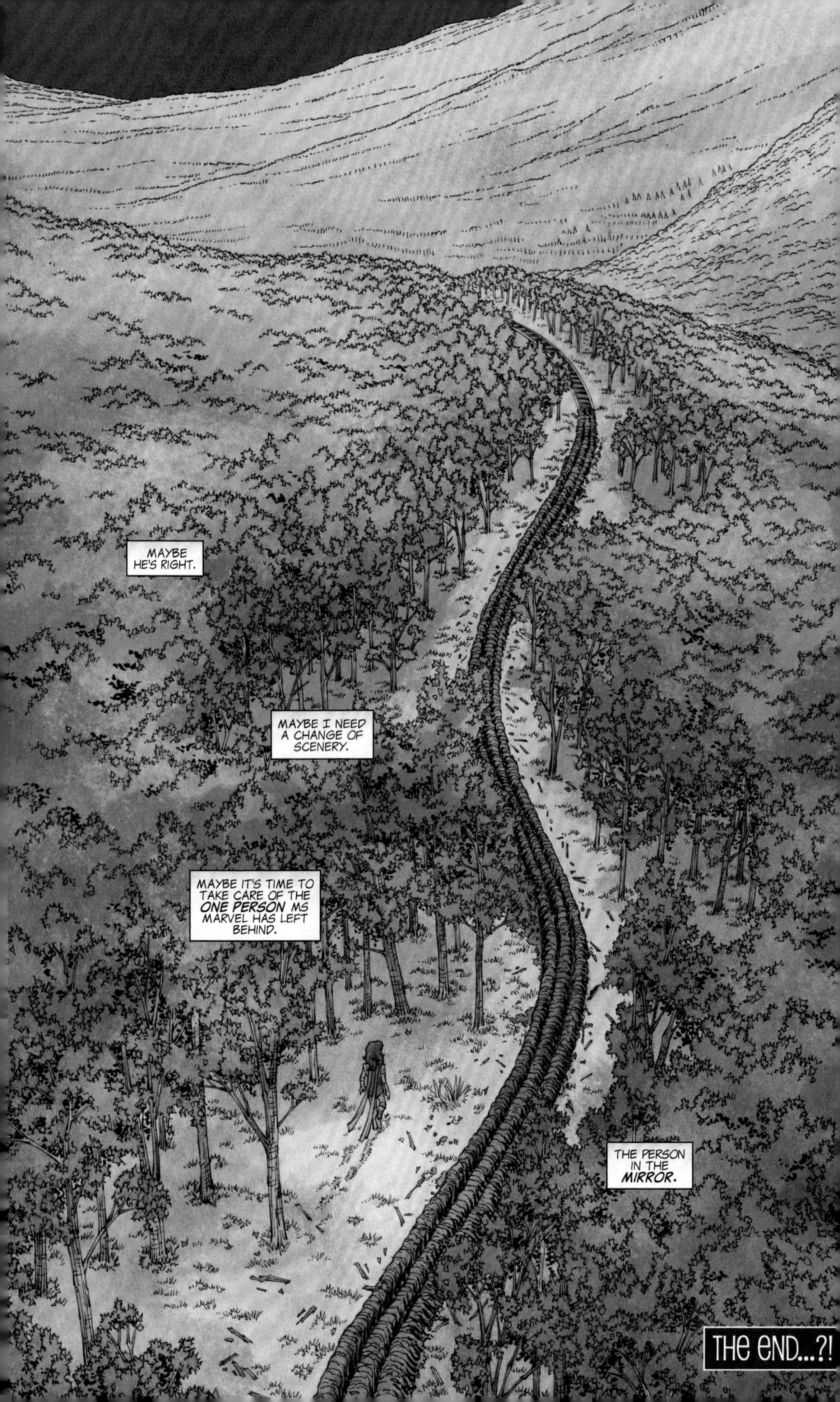

MAYBE HE'S RIGHT.
MAYBE I NEED A CHANGE OF SCENERY.
MAYBE IT'S TIME TO TAKE CARE OF THE ONE PERSON MS MARVEL HAS LEFT BEHIND.
THE PERSON IN THE MIRROR.
THE END...?!

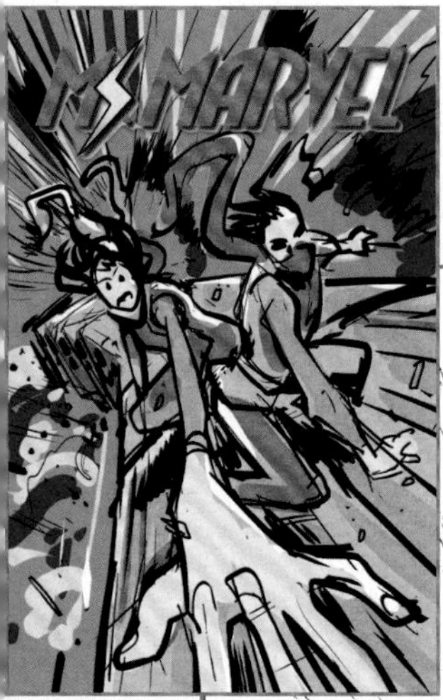
MS MARVEL

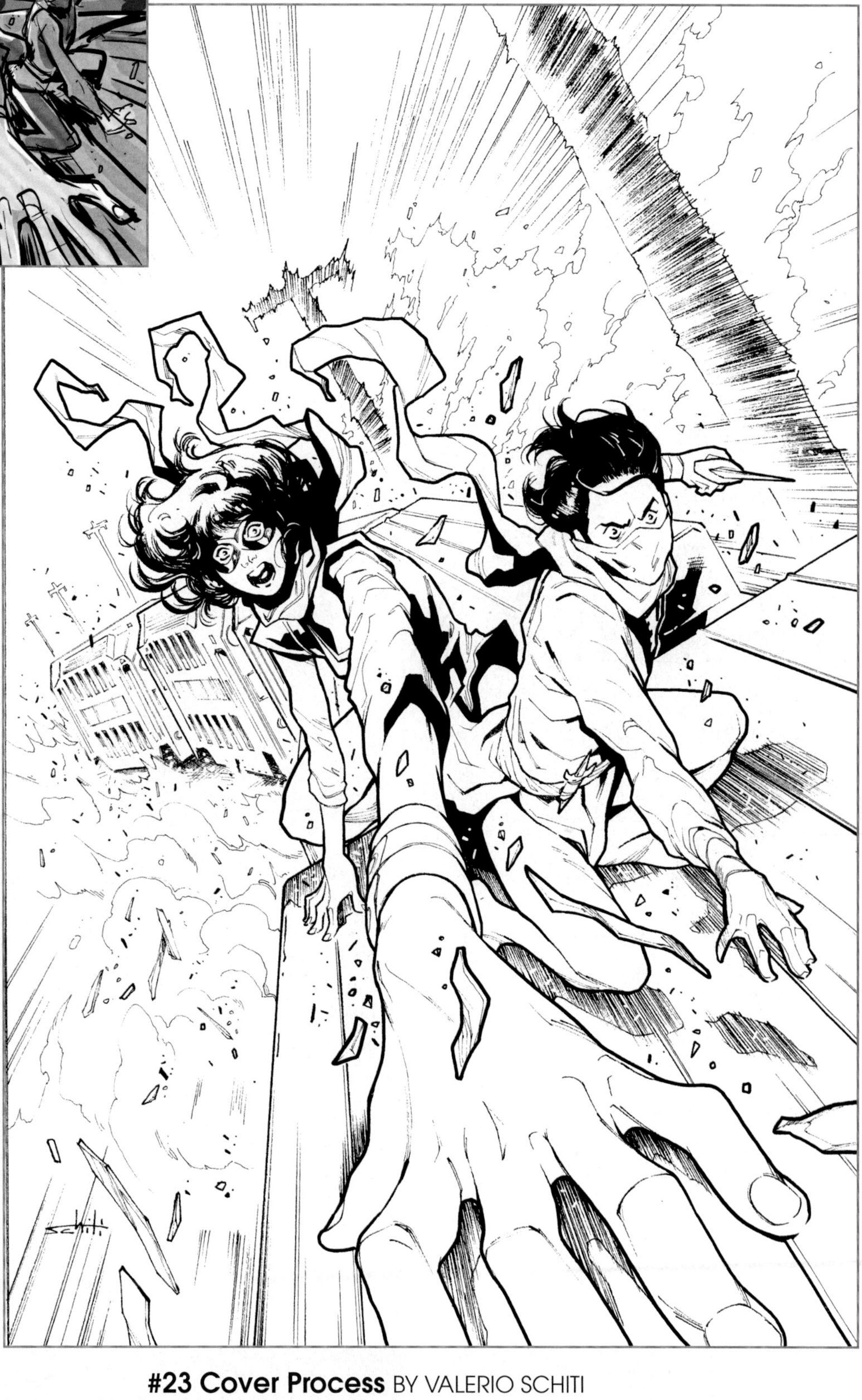

#23 Cover Process BY VALERIO SCHITI

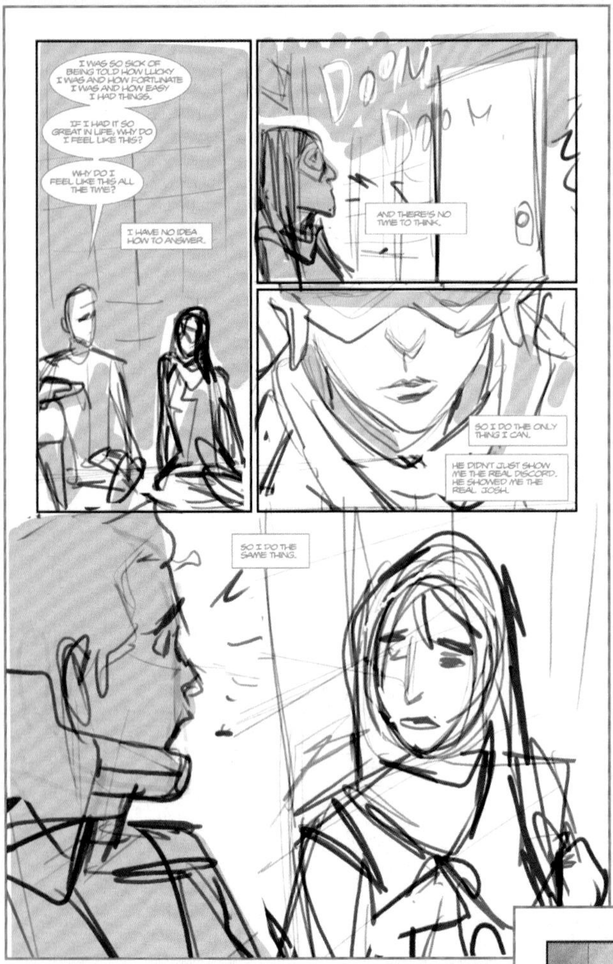
I WAS SO SICK OF BEING TOLD HOW LUCKY I WAS AND HOW FORTUNATE I WAS AND HOW EASY I HAD THINGS.
IF I HAD IT SO GREAT IN LIFE, WHY DO I FEEL LIKE THIS?
WHY DO I FEEL LIKE THIS ALL THE TIME?
I HAVE NO IDEA HOW TO ANSWER.
DOOM
DOOM
AND THERE'S NO TIME TO THINK.
SO I DO THE ONLY THING I CAN.
HE DIDN'T JUST SHOW ME THE REAL DISCORD. HE SHOWED ME THE REAL JOSH.
SO I DO THE SAME THING.

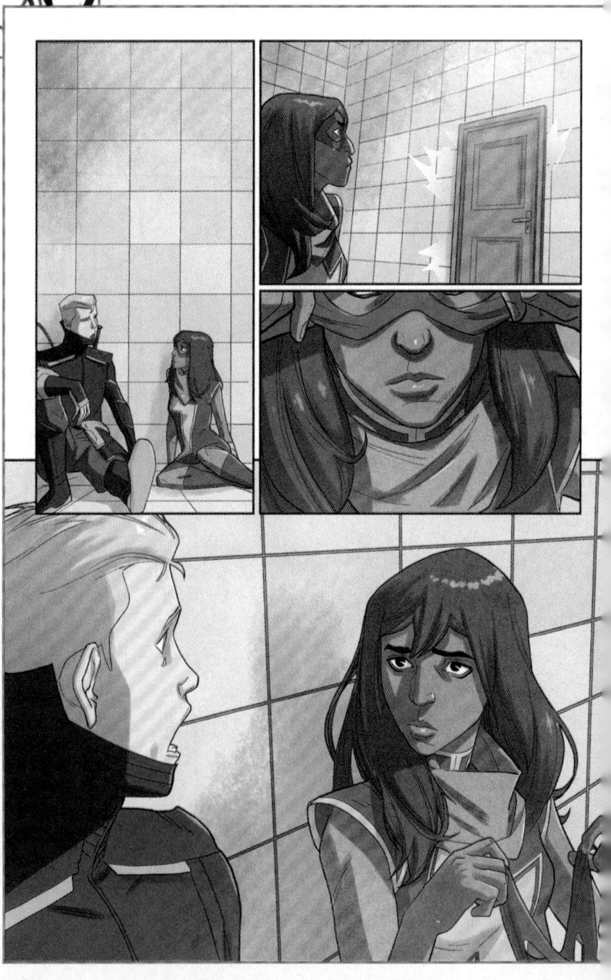

#21, p. 20 ART PROCESS
BY MARCO FAILLA
& IAN HERRING

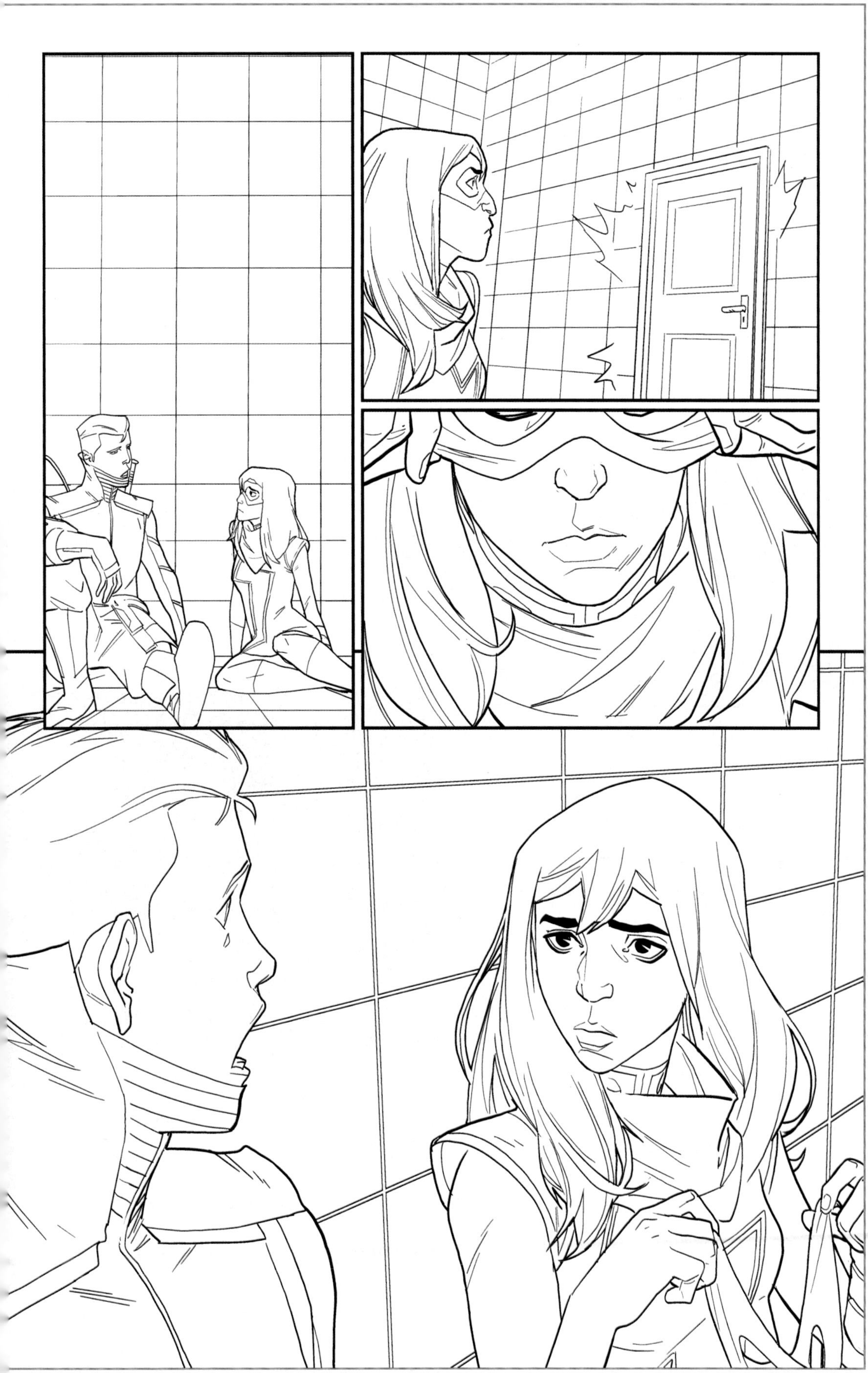

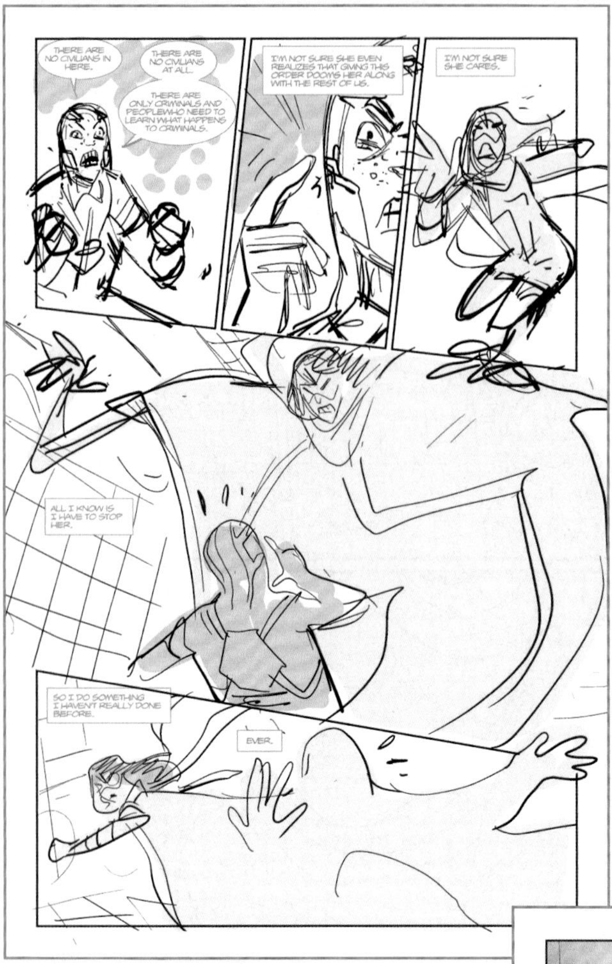

THERE ARE NO CIVILIANS IN HERE.
THERE ARE NO CIVILIANS AT ALL.
THERE ARE ONLY CRIMINALS AND PEOPLEWHO NEED TO LEARN WHAT HAPPENS TO CRIMINALS.
I'M NOT SURE SHE EVEN REALIZES THAT GIVING THIS ORDER DOOMS HER ALONG WITH THE REST OF US.
I'M NOT SURE SHE CARES.
ALL I KNOW IS I HAVE TO STOP HER.
SO I DO SOMETHING I HAVEN'T REALLY DONE BEFORE.
EVER.

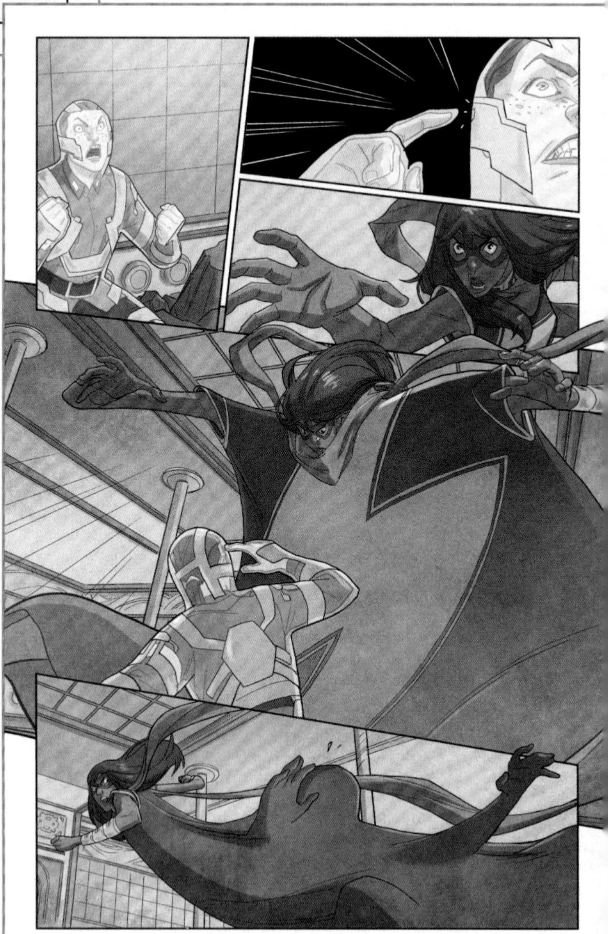

#22, p. 16 ART PROCESS
BY MARCO FAILLA
& IAN HERRING

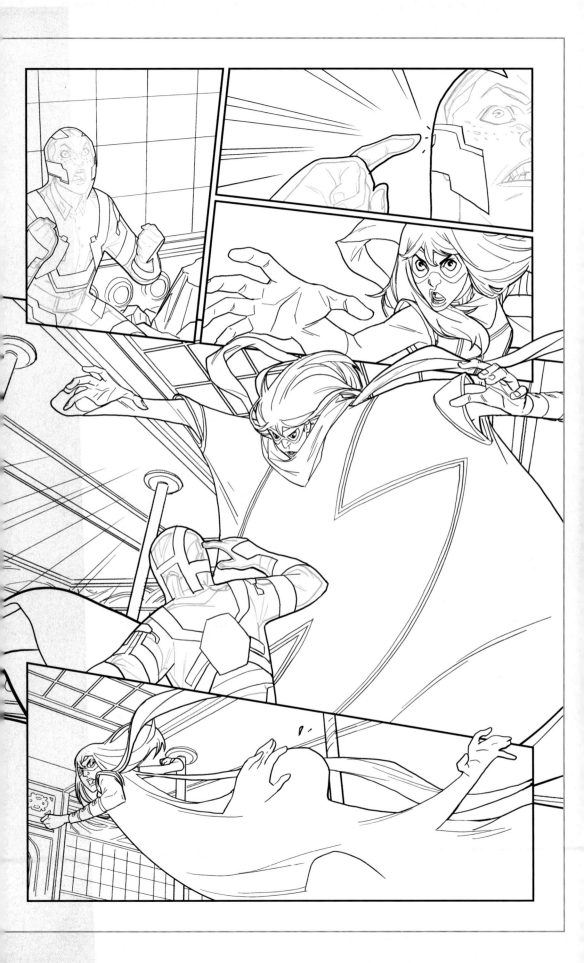

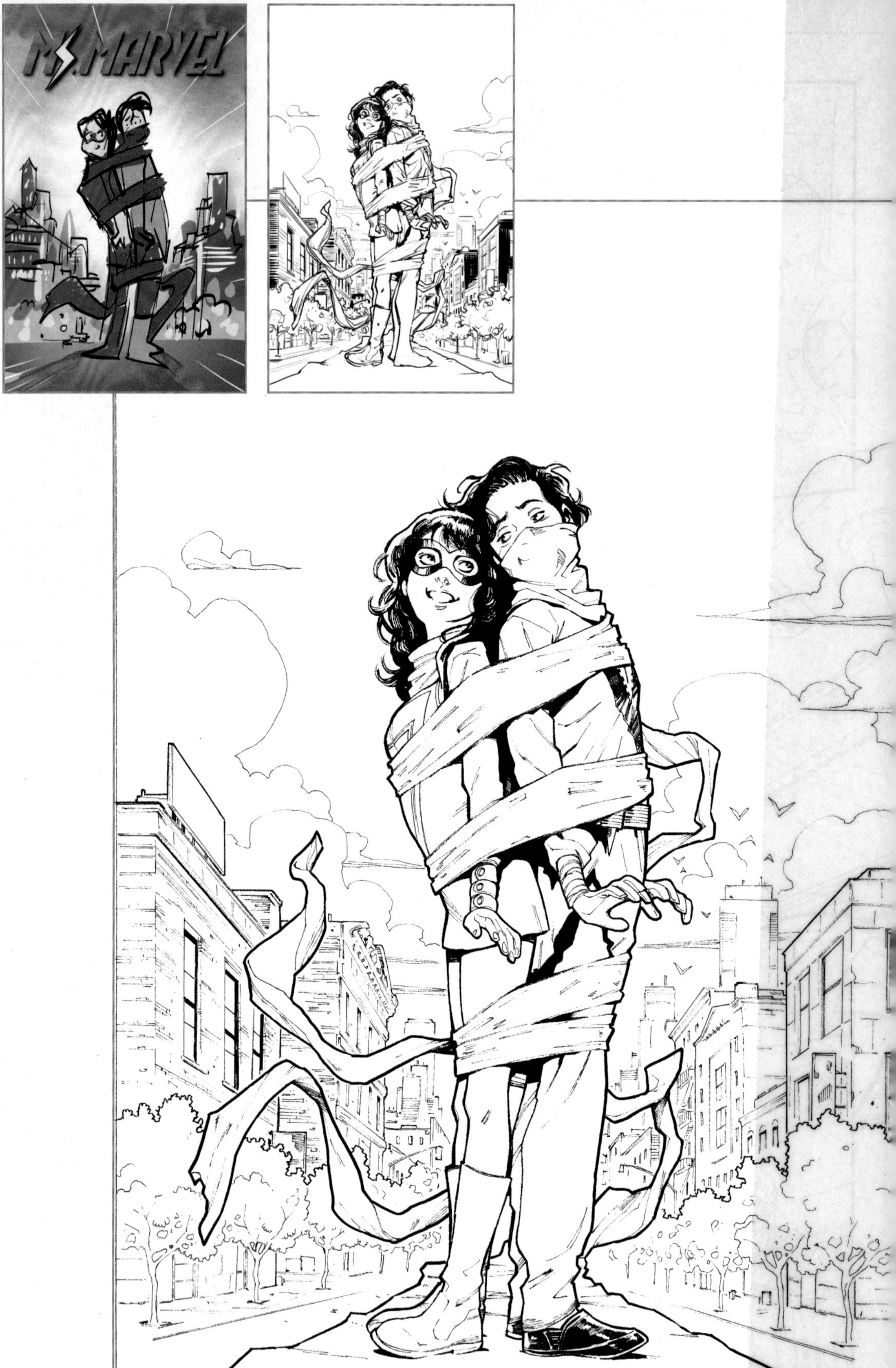
MS MARVEL
Schiti

#24 Cover Process BY VALERIO SCHITI